The New Southern University

NEW DIRECTIONS IN SOUTHERN HISTORY

Series Editors
Peter S. Carmichael, Gettysburg College
Michele Gillespie, Wake Forest University
William A. Link, University of Florida

The New Southern University

Academic Freedom and Liberalism at UNC

Charles J. Holden

THE UNIVERSITY PRESS OF KENTUCKY

Scholarly publisher for the Commonwealth,
serving Bellarmine University, Berea College, Centre College of Kentucky,
Eastern Kentucky University, The Filson Historical Society,
Georgetown College, Kentucky Historical Society, Kentucky State University,
Morehead State University, Murray State University, Northern Kentucky University,
Transylvania University, University of Kentucky,
University of Louisville, and Western Kentucky University.
All rights reserved.

Editorial and Sales Offices: The University Press of Kentucky
663 South Limestone Street, Lexington, Kentucky 40508-4008
www.kentuckypress.com

Unless otherwise noted, photographs are courtesy of the North Carolina Collection,
University of North Carolina Library at Chapel Hill.

16 15 14 13 12   5 4 3 2 1

Library of Congress Cataloging-in-Publication Data

Holden, Charles J.
The new southern university : academic freedom and liberalism at UNC /
Charles J. Holden.
p. cm. — (New directions in southern history)
Includes bibliographical references and index.
ISBN 978-0-8131-3438-3 (hardcover : alk. paper)
ISBN 978-0-8131-3439-0 (ebook)
1. University of North Carolina (1793-1962)—History—20th century.
2. Educational equalization—North Carolina. 3. Higher education
and state—North Carolina. 4. Academic freedom—North Carolina. I. Title.
LD3943.H57 2012
378.756—dc23   2011028919

This book is printed on acid-free paper meeting
the requirements of the American National Standard
for Permanence in Paper for Printed Library Materials.

♻

Manufactured in the United States of America.

Member of the Association of
American University Presses

Contents

Introduction

Anticipating a backlash against his controversial "Christmas Bombing" of North Vietnam in 1972, President Richard Nixon subjected his national security advisor, Henry Kissinger, to yet another rant against all those he was convinced were conspiring against him. After singling out the press and "the establishment," Nixon also added, "The professors are the enemy. . . . Write that on a blackboard 100 times and never forget it."[1] In 2007, an outcry arose over Columbia University's lecture invitation to Iranian president Mahmoud Ahmadinejad, a man seen by most Americans as dangerous, if not delusional. Clyde Haberman of the *New York Times* was still angry a year later as he wrote, "For reasons not universally understood, some Columbia officials have a notion that academic freedom requires them to invite this man to their . . . campus."[2] As these incidents indicate, the modern university and the college professor play roles in American society that are often controversial and misunderstood, revealing deeper social, economic, and political tensions.[3] As historian Thomas L. Haskell noted in the early 1980s: "Although we defer to experts frequently . . . we do not do so happily." Even as we acknowledge the experts' expertise, when it comes to trusting the experts *with* their expertise, Haskell adds, "We always wonder."[4]

Americans' suspicions of the modern university and college professor date back at least to the early 1900s. During the first few decades of the twentieth century, American professors defined a new mission of service for their institutions; for themselves, they defined a new identity as truth-seekers whose expertise would bring benefits to society. Establishing the new mission and new identity required the assertion of a new university standard: academic freedom. However, none of this took place without a struggle.

The university-trained intellectual's new identity likely met with the most anxiety and scrutiny in the South, a region historically resistant

1

to change. A close examination of the leading southern university—the University of North Carolina at Chapel Hill (UNC)—during the 1920s and 1930s reveals the ambitions of this new generation of college educators, the reactionary logic of their critics, and the attempts of administrators to use academic freedom to help the school navigate these difficult decades. The expertise that academic freedom made possible would, in theory, help lift the state—and, indeed, the entire South—out of its poverty and backwardness, placing it on the road to progress. UNC leaders hoped especially to apply the university's expertise to the South's two most vexing problems: race relations and labor relations.

But this commitment to academic freedom did not always keep UNC on the cutting edge of southern progress. Despite the usual association of academic freedom with liberalism, at UNC academic freedom turned out to have a conservative side, too. University leaders understood from the beginning of this era that the extent to which they could make academic freedom a reality depended in part on the public's trust. Robert Madry, the university news bureau director, explained this in the mid-1920s: "The University must be interpreted to the State in such clear and emphatic terms that there can be no doubt as to its legitimate needs."[5] Thus, the essential need to maintain public trust sometimes acted as a check against initiatives considered too risky politically. Still, the excitement surrounding the new institutional culture that embraced academic freedom at UNC was unmistakable.

But what exactly was academic freedom? Despite the concept's appeal, its precise meaning was unclear, even to university leaders. For example, UNC president Harry Woodburn Chase proclaimed in 1925: "What the university . . . believes with all its heart, is that a teacher has a right to state the honest conviction to which he has come through his work, that he has the right of freedom of speech in teaching just as any other citizen has that right under the constitution. The university believes that if teaching is to be intellectually honest it must be free."[6] Here Chase introduced two possible meanings of academic freedom. In one part of his remarks, Chase linked the university's academic freedom to its expertise. Faculty had to have the freedom to publish and teach the fruits of their work as experts, work that their "honest conviction" as academics had produced. Elsewhere in the same sentence, however, Chase made passing reference to academic freedom as a matter of free speech, a right held by "any other citizen under the constitution" and therefore not just the special instrument of academics.

Harry Woodburn Chase, president of UNC from 1919 to 1930.

Harry Chase appeared to be following the confusing lead established by the American Association of University Professors (AAUP), who first attempted to set the parameters for academic freedom. The AAUP's 1915 Declaration of Principles also argued for academic freedom as both a necessary component of faculty expertise and as a matter of free speech. The declaration's authors called for "freedom of inquiry and research; freedom of teaching within the university or college" as well as "freedom of extra-mural utterance and action."[7] Legal scholars such as William Van Alstyne and David M. Rabban have traced the constitutional implications of this confusion.[8] Drawing from a series of court cases involving academic freedom, R. George Wright concludes that the concept was "largely unanalyzed, undefined, and unguided by principled application, leading to its inconsistent and skeptical or questioned invocation."[9] Dahlia Lithwick and Richard Schragger have pointed out that even today the courts have "never pinned down exactly what academic freedom means." As a result, they argue, "the assertion of 'academic freedom' raises more questions than it resolves."[10]

UNC's Harry Chase indulged in some wishful thinking when he invoked academic freedom as a part of a broadly defined right to freedom of speech. Courts at that time still interpreted the free speech implications of the First Amendment narrowly. William Van Alstyne observes that in the early 1900s, the First Amendment was "prehistory as far as academic freedom is concerned." In fact, he continues, "The First Amendment had no real immediate significance for free speech in general."[11] The "American judiciary's extremely cramped view of the amendment's scope" therefore meant that many jurists would have disagreed with Chase's contention that UNC professors, like "any other citizen," had a right to free speech.[12]

Freedom of speech had even less First Amendment support when it came to the rights of public employees, which would have included UNC professors and administrators. Oliver Wendell Holmes Jr.'s oft-quoted 1892 opinion in *McAuliffe v. Mayor of New Bedford* summed up the expectation that a public employee could not count on the First Amendment to protect his or her right to freedom of speech: "The petitioner [a policeman fired for comments critical of the department] may have a constitutional right to talk politics, but he has no constitutional right to be a policeman."[13] Although Holmes did eventually change his mind, this view was still widely accepted in the 1920s.[14]

Lacking a solid constitutional basis as a First Amendment right, what academic freedom needed in its early career was, as Van Alstyne notes, "some compelling justification, at least as a strongly defensible professional imperative in higher education," because "there was no immediate prospect of finding support in hard law."[15] University leaders needed to drive home the social value of the academic freedom of university experts. Much of the history of UNC during the 1920s and 1930s was defined by the university's struggle to get watchful southerners to accept its academic freedom as a "defensible professional imperative" that was ultimately beneficial to all.

UNC's embrace of academic freedom was in keeping with the "university revolution" of the early 1900s, when the American university focused less on "conserving the truth rather than searching for it."[16] As one UNC student writer explained in 1922: "Here men are taught to think, not to accept theories and creeds simply because our ancestors handed them down to us, but to think things out for themselves."[17] Another UNC student writer described the university's commitment to progress in 1931 as a pledge to aid "the further advancement of civilization in this commonwealth. . . . Long now has education been satisfied to rest in conservatism," this student writer continued, "restrained by tradition, when it should be the intellectual beacon guiding men onward into the unknown but knowable."[18]

The idea of academic freedom as a necessity in the search for truth began to emerge at the turn of the century thanks to the writings of John Dewey and in response to a few well-publicized attacks on the autonomy of college professors.[19] The University of Wisconsin made the most eloquent defense of academic freedom during this time, when in 1894 it supported embattled economist Richard T. Ely, who was accused of labor organizing and promoting socialism in the classroom. The committee investigating the charges issued a proclamation defending the professor and establishing an important benchmark in the early history of academic freedom: "We believe the great state University of Wisconsin should ever encourage that continual and fearless sifting and winnowing by which alone the truth can be found."[20]

In a 1902 essay, "Academic Freedom," John Dewey briefly but brilliantly surveyed the emergence of the modern university, the state of academic freedom, and the challenges to both. The modern university had to have the freedom to "investigate truth; critically to verify fact; to reach conclusions by means of the best methods at command, untrammeled by external fear or favor; to communicate this truth to the student; to interpret to him its bearing on the questions he will have to face in life—this is precisely the aim and object of the university. To aim a blow at any one of these operations is to deal a vital wound to the university itself."[21]

However, John Dewey also understood that the purpose of both the modern university and academic freedom caused confusion outside of the academy. Some of this confusion was simply unavoidable, Dewey admitted. In an era of newer disciplines such as sociology, psychology, and economics, the public remained dubious as to their "scientific" qualities. There was, he conceded, "no gainsaying the fact that some of the studies taught in the university are inherently in a much more scientific condition than others."[22] Indeed, he added, these newer disciplines were still trying to improve the "scientific" aspects of their specific methodologies. And the reality of their relative infancy posed a problem when these newer disciplines "dare[d] to emerge from a remote and technical sphere, and pass authoritative judgment upon affairs of daily life." There they faced "little but skepticism or hostility or, what is worse, sensational exploitation."[23]

The example Dewey used to demonstrate the challenges facing this new expertise—a hypothetical examination of the social impact of capitalism—would be demonstrated in actuality at UNC throughout the 1920s and 1930s. In Dewey's scenario, a member of the academy might adhere strictly to his discipline's methodology, conduct his research fully in the spirit of objectivity and thoroughness, and conclude that "many and grave evils and injustices are incident" to capitalism. But outside the academy, "views at the bottom exactly the same can be stated in such a way as to rasp the feelings of everyone exercising the capitalistic function."[24] Dewey's point here was that another writer without academic credentials, such as a radical labor organizer, could also weigh in on the ills of capitalism. How was the public supposed to know the qualitative difference if each writer arrived at the same conclusion? Dewey answered by pointing again to the need for academic freedom: these newer disciplines needed the freedom to develop their methods enough that the public would recognize and accept their conclusions as unquestionably "scientific" and therefore more valid and potentially useful.

John Dewey played an instrumental role in the creation of the AAUP in 1915 and the effort to define a public need for academic freedom. Following his precedent, the leaders of the AAUP applauded their own professionalization and the commitment of trained specialists, such as sociologists, historians, and biologists, to protecting disciplinary autonomy and professional integrity.[25] Dewey asserted that "the consciousness of being a member of an organized society of truth-seekers" would "solidify and reinforce otherwise scattered and casual efforts." Dewey clearly understood the challenges of getting the public to accept that intellectuals needed academic freedom, but he also saw the moment as one of great opportunity. There was, he believed, "never . . . a time in the history of the world when the community so recognized its need of expert guidance as today."[26] Scholarly work would produce useful, beneficial knowledge that would enhance the lives of those outside the academy— knowledge that would help "get the world's work done," as Daniel Singal puts it.[27] Moreover, if in the modern perspective the "truth" was constantly shifting, then intellectuals needed to have freedom of thought, expression, and research in order to constantly rediscover it and reapply it for the betterment of society.[28] The leaders of the AAUP, therefore, offered a "functional defense of academic freedom" that was "utilitarian in temper and conviction." The AAUP unapologetically made special claims for expertise, arguing, as Walter Metzger explains, that "by virtue of their special gifts and learning," academics "possess the ability . . . that the laymen who appoint them lack." But, Metzger continues, they also believed earnestly that it was "for society's sake, not for their own sakes, that professors must be academically free."[29]

In this dynamic intellectual context, UNC leaders' invocations of academic freedom in the 1920s and 1930s as a social good, an institutional necessity, and the very key to southern progress generated headlines and created a campus environment that buzzed with a new spirit of inquiry and possibility. Former UNC president William C. Friday, who came to the university as a law student shortly after World War II, still recalls the energy on campus, despite having arrived in what he calls the "sunset of that era": "I don't think the university at Chapel Hill ever experienced an age like that interval of time," Friday remarked.[30] During one stretch of newsworthy activity in 1926, famed UNC sociologist Howard Odum wrote, "matters relating to the State University have maintained constantly first-page interest in all the dalies [sic]. . . . I think this may be taken as fair evidence that the state is interested in its University."[31]

UNC's influence and reputation was not confined to North Carolina, however. UNC news bureau director Robert Madry was not bragging when he wrote that "the University is a unique institution in the South, and that fact should be explained continuously."[32] UNC's emergence as a regional leader caught the attention of many southerners, influential and unknown alike. In the tiny Arkansas town of Marked Tree, local attorney C. T. Carpenter surprised *Raleigh News & Observer* editor Jonathan Daniels in the 1930s by asking, "Do you know Odum?" "Yes," Daniels replied. Carpenter then gestured proudly to a shelf full of books from UNC Press: "I've got 'em all. That's a great University at

Chapel Hill."[33] Many southerners shared Carpenter's admiration for UNC and pointed to its "freedom" as the explanation for the university's newfound prominence. Moreover, UNC's efforts to promote academic freedom, and the degree to which it was successful, stood out in a region where attacks on ideas were common and usually effective. In addition to the well-documented assaults on academic freedom at Trinity College (now Duke University) and Emory College in the early 1900s, the flagship universities in Virginia, Georgia, Texas, and Mississippi all faced fierce challenges to their autonomy and academic freedom in the 1930s and 1940s.[34]

Still, worries arose as UNC took on the more scientific, research- and service-driven mission of the modern university. UNC's role in North Carolina's fierce debate over the teaching of evolution offers an excellent example of the opposition confronting the university over matters related to academic freedom. Famed revivalists William Jennings Bryan and Mordecai Ham toured the state in 1923 and 1924, placing their attacks on evolution at the heart of their rousing speeches. In April 1923, Bryan made a "smashing attack" on evolution, while in November 1923 and February 1924, Ham blasted evolution as being "as much fact as Santa Claus."[35] Ham especially linked the teaching of evolution to purported godlessness and radicalism in the universities. "You today are listening to false prophets," he warned, "and seeing the prophets of God slapped in the face and are doing nothing. You put men in your colleges who are known to believe the Christ was an illegitimate child. . . . You wonder why Russia is swept by bolshevism, why England and even your own country are swept by disruption. The day is not far distant when you will be in the grip of the Red Terror and your children will be taught free love by that damnable theory of evolution."[36]

Roughly two weeks before legislation was introduced in Tennessee that led to the famous Scopes trial, David Scott Poole of Raeford introduced for consideration by the state house the resolution that "it is injurious to the welfare of the people of the State of North Carolina for any official or teacher in the State, paid wholly or in part by taxation, to teach or permit to be taught, as a fact either Darwinism or any other evolutionary hypothesis that links man in blood relationship with any lower form of life." Poole, a Presbyterian and a part-time teacher, printer, and newspaper editor, had read *On the Origin of Species* and concluded that it directly contradicted his religious faith. On the other hand, Poole believed "every word of the Bible."[37]

Because the bill struck directly at state-supported schools, UNC played a pivotal role in the controversy surrounding it.[38] Noting the high number of UNC-trained lawyers in state government, historian Willard B. Gatewood Jr. goes as far as to claim that "the outcome of the antievolution legislation depended to a large extent upon the ultimate stand adopted by the 'University lawyers' in the General Assembly."[39] But UNC leadership also waged an all-important battle in the press. UNC's Harry W. Chase faced this enormous challenge by asserting the university's academic freedom in one of his finest hours as president.

The Poole Bill ended up in the House Committee on Education, chaired at that time by Henry Groves Connor Jr. The UNC connections were already coming in handy: not only had Connor attended the university, he also had a brother, Robert D. W. Connor, who was a history professor at Chapel Hill. In early February 1925, Henry sent an insightful message to his brother, the professor: "I don't think that it should be assumed that the Poole Bill may be taken lightly. I am quite sure our academic friends do not realize the fact that there is throughout North Carolina a very strong undercurrent of feeling that the doctrine of Darwinism or Evolution, or whatever it is called, is an invention of the Devil."[40] Henry was correct; most of the UNC leadership had not fully measured the depth of feeling statewide on this issue. Robert Connor must have passed this message on within the university, because shortly thereafter Harry Chase took on a very public role arguing against the Poole Bill.

Chase could not have been pleased when Poole himself explained, at the outset of the Committee on Education hearings, that "the religion of the Lord Jesus is on trial."[41] Thus alerted, Chase agreed to testify at the hearings.[42] In his testimony, Chase countered that the real debate was not over the survival of Christianity or even evolution; rather, the issue was academic freedom. He said that he was testifying "on behalf of an institution which has the reputation of intellectual honesty." Chase continued that the "constitution of the United States guarantees freedom of speech and freedom of the press and declares that it shall not be abridged. Shall we write into that article 'except to school teachers'?"[43] When reminded in a thinly veiled threat that next year's university appropriations were still up for budgetary consideration, Chase retorted: "If this University doesn't stand for anything but appropriations, I, for one, don't care to be connected with it."[44]

Chase returned to the theme a few days later, this time playing for the home crowd at UNC. Speaking to a packed Memorial Hall, Chase reported the university's efforts against the Poole Bill. This, he insisted, was a matter of principle, and the struggle being waged in Raleigh at that moment was "entirely removed from the realm of expediency. I realize that it might injure the university's support, that it might alienate some of its friends," he continued, "but the real university is more than buildings, is more than the present generation of its faculty and students. The lasting thing about the university is its ideal, a spiritual goal. It is a perpetuation of that ideal with which we must be most concerned."[45]

UNC, he pointed out, "is not interested in cramming evolution or any other scientific theory down anybody's throat. It is not the university's business whether you accept evolution or not. . . . It holds that a student has the right, if he wants to, to put himself in touch with the facts, theories, conclusions in biology or any other branch of learning. . . . No man can be called an educated man who has not been taught to find facts, to weigh evidence and to reach conclusions."[46] The *Greensboro Daily News,* a supporter of UNC, reported the next day that Chase's position was "getting the hearty indorsement [sic] of faculty members and students." With the decision on the university's appropriation request still looming, "few men . . . would have thrown political expediency to the winds while facing such a situation even for the sake of preserving an ideal. But in doing so President Chase apparently has stepped into a greater leadership."[47]

Chase organized his own campaign to defend the university. He wrote to Bertram Wells, a well-regarded botany professor at North Carolina State, that they should be prepared to "turn loose on the Senate" should the bill pass the House.[48] In the meantime, he wrote to state representative Walter Murphy, a UNC alumnus, and supplied him with a "talking point" that Murphy could use in defense of the university. Murphy, Chase suggested, could observe that passage of the Poole Bill would drive off "many of its [UNC's] best men who feel that their self-respect is impaired if they have to work under such restrictions."[49] (He had a point; when the bill was reintroduced in 1927, one of its defenders stated that he did not care about its passage so much as the effect the campaign had on university professors.)[50] Chase also wrote to Edgar Pharr, the Speaker of the House, that the Poole Bill would "virtually set up a tribunal before which every teacher of science and related subjects could be badgered, worried, and disgraced. Good men will simply not teach in an environment of that sort." The bill put "genuine and earnest men, devoted to truth, in the position of criminals in the eyes of the State any-time that an utterance of one of these men may appear questionable un-der the act to any hearer. This is an intolerable position for men to find themselves in."[51]

Chase was describing what in today's parlance would be called the "chilling effect" of the Poole Bill. He understood correctly that the fun-damentalists' aim was not only to protect good, Christian students from godless Darwinism; as he wrote to Pharr, "the question is not whether people are teaching evolution as a fact."[52] The question was, who would control the university mission? Those trained and hired to do univer-sity work, or the fundamentalists who had taken their crusade against academic freedom and the modern university into the political realm?

On the eve of the vote for the Poole Bill, the *Presbyterian Standard*, a weekly published in Charlotte, challenged Chase by employing Wil-liam Jennings Bryan's tactic of invoking the power of the majority in a democracy to determine the shape "freedom" took. In "Freedom of Speech," the *Presbyterian Standard* started off dramatically by refer-encing France's Reign of Terror in 1793–1794: "In reading the frequent pleas, by those who seek to teach views contrary to what the majority of the people of the state believe, that they have a right to freedom of speech, one is forcibly reminded of that oft-quoted saying of Madame Roland—'O Liberty! Liberty! how many crimes are committed in thy name!' There is nothing more ambiguous than the expression 'freedom of speech,' or more misleading in the ears of the average hearer."[53] This introduction constituted the high point of the *Standard*'s rebuttal. For the rest of the article, its logic grew more muddled with nearly every sentence: "Every man has the right to claim freedom of speech, if he means, the right to talk," the editorial continued; "that is a power giv-en him by his Maker." But "every man in talking has no right to express views that would destroy the very foundations of morality as well as re-ligion, as the majority of people of a state believe." In other words, every man had the right to claim freedom of speech, but not the right to actu-ally speak freely if it offended the majority.

On February 18, 1925, members of the House of Representatives gathered to vote on the Poole Bill. Both sides brought out many of the same arguments. One high point for those defending the university came when Sam Ervin Jr., a young representative from Burke County who would later go on to fame in the Watergate hearings, argued that the Poole Bill "served no good purpose." He called it a "weak-kneed" resolution that, far from defending Christianity, insulted it instead. If Christianity needed such a resolution for its protection and survival, Ervin continued, "then that religion cannot claim to be powerful enough to save men's souls."[54]

On the next day, February 19, Walter Murphy, a local legend from his days as UNC's star quarterback, administered the final blow against the bill's proponents. The chamber fell into a hush when Murphy rose to speak. Murphy said he worried that the Poole Bill would cause more problems than it would solve. But more importantly, he insisted, a man's religion was private: "strictly a matter between him and his God." Murphy hit the right note for many when he said, "I am not so much interested in what I am evolved from as in whither I am going. That which shall come to me in the future as far as good is concerned will come through the atoning blood of Jesus Christ."[55] When the votes were tallied, the Poole Bill was defeated by a healthy margin.

UNC's relatively brief battle against the antievolutionists was the least complicated and most successfully resolved of the university's controversies during the 1920s. UNC's commitment to academic freedom involved the university in labor and race issues, sparking long-running controversies that drive the narrative of this book. As the evolution controversy demonstrated, critics accused UNC experts of being everything from meddling intellectuals to an enemy presence. Even friends of the university weighed in with their concerns that there might be too much freedom on campus. William C. Dowd Jr., president and manager of the *Charlotte News*, made a refreshingly candid confession when he wrote to UNC president Frank Graham in 1940: "I dislike some of the things that are going on at Chapel Hill. I think academic freedom carries an obligation with it, although I realize that this might be just another way of saying that I approve of academic freedom only so long as it is extended to those of whom I approve."[56] W. M. Cartwright of Wilmington made the same point in 1928. Disturbed that UNC students were going to invite political leaders from both major parties, Cartwright complained that "North Carolina has always been a Democrat state and the University is a state supported school. This means your school gets its money from a Democrat legislature." Republicans, on the other hand, "have been trying hard for a long time to break in this state and destroy the Democrat government." Cartwright insisted that he believed "in fair play," but when it came to state-supported political debate under the banner of academic freedom, "this is a different matter."[57]

Dowd's and Cartwright's criticisms were not unusual during the 1920s and 1930s, reflecting widespread uneasiness among southerners over how far to apply—and how much to tolerate—academic freedom at UNC. The university's leaders had to learn how to maintain public trust while living with the inherent tension caused by trying to make academic freedom a reality in a context where one person's "fair play" was another's fear that the enemy had been loosed in their midst. As David Cohn wrote of UNC in 1941: "No one in North Carolina (or elsewhere) denies that it is the business of a university to uphold the standard of freedom, truth, and justice. But the university president who actually does it not infrequently finds himself in trouble."[58]

UNC did not really begin to resemble the "Wisconsin Idea"—the model of the public-supported, research-oriented, modern university—until the 1920s, as the state experienced a burst of government-led reform following two decades of economic transformation.[59] "The need for industrialization was almost a civic religion" in North Carolina in the early 1900s, writes Rob Christensen.[60] David Carlton argues that by the beginning of the new century, North Carolina had risen to regional leadership in tobacco and furniture production.[61] Jacquelyn Hall and her team of coauthors note that between 1890 and 1908, there was a sixfold explosion in the number of southern cotton spindles—many of them in the North Carolina Piedmont—giving a clear sign that the textile industry was emerging as a critical component of the state's industrialization.[62]

Following World War I, the need for adjustment and reform was apparent. George B. Tindall notes that among southern states, North Carolina stood "at the forefront . . . more in the 1920s than in the pre-war progressive era." Reform costs money, and North Carolina's taxes, starting from a low level that was typical among southern states, rose 554 percent between 1913 and 1930; state expenditures increased 847 percent between 1915 and 1925.[63] Nonetheless, progressive leaders in the state, both before and after World War I, pushed hard for reforms in health, sanitation, and education, to continue the progress and pace of industrialization. As William A. Link explains, "better schools and better health would reshape public attitudes in such a way as to replace backwardness and poverty with a fresh determination to achieve regional modernization."[64] To those in the forefront of promoting change, these were heady times in which UNC figured to play an important part.

In the first two decades of the 1900s, UNC expanded campus

Liberty, Uncle Sam, and Plenty at a campus July 4 festival, ca. 1916.

facilities and added significantly to its social science curriculum. George Brown Tindall, Louis Round Wilson, and William D. Snider all credit Francis Preston Venable with what Tindall describes as "certain beginnings" of the modern UNC. Venable, UNC's president from 1900 to 1913 and a former chemistry professor trained in the German method of research, brought a new empirical emphasis to North Carolina. As a result, the university began to develop its libraries and laboratories. Edward Kidder Graham succeeded Venable in the president's office, and he, too, added an important element to what became the modern UNC: the commitment to serve the needs of the state. During Graham's tenure, the university established its Extension Bureau and developed departmental lines in sociology, rural education, business administration, and drama.[65]

During the Edward Kidder Graham years, plans for the Kenan Professorships began. Lily Kenan Bingham came from a prominent eastern North Carolina family. Her father and two uncles graduated from UNC, thus establishing close family ties to the university. Through family inheritance and two marriages, Bingham accumulated an estate worth $70,000,000. At the time of her death in late 1916, university officials received word that she had established an annual gift of $75,000 to pay "the salaries of from twenty to twenty-five professors per year." The *Asheville Times* reported that "it is difficult to fully realize the full significance of this splendid gift to the University. . . . The University is now undoubtedly on firm ground and will grow in usefulness, greater than ever before."[66] Former UNC president William C. Friday concurs: the Kenan Professorships marked a "turning point" in the university's history. There was, he said, "no doubt in my mind" that they gave UNC the chance to "move from being a regional university" to national and international recognition.[67]

When the influenza epidemic claimed both Edward Kidder Graham and his successor, Marvin H. Stacy, following World War I, the university turned to Harry Woodburn Chase as president in 1919. Chase was a northerner—or, as journalist Gerald W. Johnson playfully wrote, "a Damyankee, a genuine blown-in-the-bottle Massachusetts Bluebelly."[68] He had come to the university in 1910 and had worked his way up through the ranks as a professor, first of education and then of psychology, and later as chairman of the faculty. Chase was an enthusiastic supporter of Edward Kidder Graham's Extension Bureau, through which he became widely known and admired throughout the state, despite his northern roots. Chase's April 1920 inaugural address stressed the university's commitment to progress and offered "a call to broaden the vision of Edward Kidder Graham, who had said that the walls of the university extend to the boundaries of the state." Signaling to all that UNC should play an even greater role in the lives of all southerners, Chase "called upon the university to extend its horizons . . . to the region at large."[69]

Harry Chase's presidency coincided with the election of Cameron Morrison as governor, and the university benefited from the burst of reform already mentioned. Morrison embarked on an aggressive program of building highways and public schools.[70] The campus went through an impressive phase of new dormitories, classroom buildings, and office buildings. The massive university library was finished in 1929. Under Chase, UNC added still more departments: journalism, psychology, business, and library science all got started during this time. The newly hired Howard Odum not only headed up the new sociology department; he also ran the School of Public Welfare and started both the Institute for Research in Social Science and the *Journal of Social Forces*. In 1922, the University of North Carolina Press—the first of its kind in the South—was founded, and the university received membership in the prestigious Association of American Universities (AAU), the first southern university to be so acknowledged.[71]

In 1931, looking back over the previous decade, the *Daily Tar Heel* announced that the expansion of the university had been "astounding."[72] In his widely heralded book, *The Advancing South*, Edwin Mims announced: "All in all, the University of North Carolina has now a larger and better academic faculty and a better graduate school than any other institution in the South."[73] Even H. L. Mencken, a caustic critic of most things southern, was quoted as saying: "I know of no American state with a more vigorous and praiseworthy university than that of North Carolina."[74] In 1926, Robert Madry explicitly linked the university's expansion with the state's progress: "Today one finds in Chapel Hill a real university in the modern sense of the word, with the manifold and complex tasks of a modern university." All of its research and expansion, he continued, had been "shot through with one primary purpose . . . the advancement of the state of North Carolina."[75] Praise for UNC's efforts even came from the University of Wisconsin itself, when political science professor F. A. Ogg said in 1928 that "by common agreement the leadership in the new research movement in the South is traceable to the University of North Carolina."[76]

The 1930s presented UNC with grave financial challenges but also with new, buoyant presidential leadership provided by Frank Porter Graham. Despite the onset of the Great Depression, a time when university budgets were slashed and enrollments were threatened nationwide, UNC managed to maintain its student body size of between 2,600 and 3,000. Through the school's connections with the new Democratic administration in Washington, DC, UNC continued new building projects and extension programs. More dormitories, a medical building, and a new gymnasium all went up at UNC thanks to New Deal federal dollars. But it was Frank Graham's influence and his well-publicized defense of academic freedom and liberalism that highlighted the decade for the university. It is, therefore, in the 1930s that both advocates and critics began to link academic freedom and liberalism to the point where the two became, for some, interchangeable.

I have selected what I judge to be the most critical controversies UNC faced during the 1920s and the 1930s—the university's response to labor unrest and the growing challenge to segregation—which were also the two areas that UNC leaders identified as being most in need of their expertise. I have divided the book into two parts: part I concentrates on the 1920s, while part II examines the 1930s. Chapter 1 shows how UNC leaders and professors used their expertise and academic freedom to publicly condemn the rise of the Ku Klux Klan and to work more closely with African American leaders. Through participation in organizations such as the Committee on Interracial Cooperation (CIC), UNC leaders—especially sociologists, considered experts in race relations—created new and important contacts with the black community. Increased awareness of racial issues led to a dramatic expansion in the study of race relations at UNC in the 1920s. These efforts resulted in UNC leaders calling on white southerners to concern themselves more with issues such as poverty and poor health among the black population and to acknowledge the contributions of talented African American artists of the Harlem Renaissance.

Chapter 2 explores how the state's textile mill ownership, and in particular editor David Clark of the *Southern Textile Bulletin*, began taking a dim view of university activities in the 1920s, especially those coming from the new Institute of Research in Social Science. Identifying the deplorable working and living conditions of mill hands as a "problem," university researchers hoped to find solutions. Clark, however, speaking on behalf of the textile leadership, rejected the university's freedom to conduct research as "meddling" and raised provocative questions about UNC's trustworthiness. For people like David Clark, the university's modern mission was nothing more than an invitation for radicalism to infiltrate the South. Clark attacked UNC relentlessly, using conspiracy theories and hyperbole. UNC leaders, especially Harry Chase and Howard Odum, were stung by Clark's ferocity. They compromised with the textile industry by defending their freedom to investigate living conditions among textile workers, but they promised quietly not to ask the really hard questions. Nonetheless, by the end of the 1920s the Chase presidency had successfully established academic freedom as a core value of the institution and had generated broad support for UNC's pursuit of its modern mission.

Part II and the 1930s begin in chapter 3, which presents a brief introduction to Frank Porter Graham's presidency. Graham's stirring 1931 inaugural address reasserted the university's aspirations to be a beacon of academic freedom for the state and the South. His speech also revealed Graham's keen insights into the challenges facing the university and academic freedom itself. Delivered on November 11, on the anniversary of the armistice ending World War I, Graham saw a world still troubled by violence, hunger, and prejudice. The world, as he saw it, needed the fruits of academic freedom more than ever. A well-known liberal, his presidency also signaled a new day for southern progressives. But the decade also reveals white southern liberalism's limitations and academic freedom's overlooked conservative side.

Chapter 4 discusses how UNC continued to try to open up new avenues of interracial cooperation and gain a more realistic look at African American life through the research of its faculty and graduate students. However, a new wave of African American assertiveness created a different kind of challenge for UNC. Black leaders, reeling from the crisis of the Great Depression and increasingly encouraged by the Franklin Roosevelt administration, issued new demands for racial justice. When UNC leaders and scholars were urged to join forces with those in the black community calling for even bolder action against the injustice of Jim Crow, they responded with their "expert" view that gradual change through education was the surest, safest route to "progress." For UNC to push too hard for a sudden change in the South's racial order, they explained, would provoke a violent response and jeopardize the state's trust that the university would use its academic freedom responsibly. As George Streator described in the December 1933 issue of the NAACP monthly *The Crisis*: "Having formed the habit of dictating the program of Negro education and welfare, these men . . . [were] reluctant to listen to the very people to whose training they have contributed."[77]

Chapter 5 illustrates how the university's response to the economic collapse of the 1930s brought more accusations that radicalism—and not just unwanted liberalism—was a by-product of academic freedom. As North Carolina experienced waves of labor unrest, some UNC faculty and students took up labor's cause, revealing along the way signs of campus support for Marxist-inspired changes to capitalism. Evidence of Marxist sympathies at UNC, along with unfounded rumors to that effect, sent critics into a fury. The labor controversies of the 1930s also brought different dimensions of academic freedom to light, because many of the UNC professors supporting labor's aggressiveness were from the English Department and were therefore not advocating from a position of scholarly expertise on industrial capitalism. Why, critics asked, should antilabor southerners care what a UNC English professor said about labor unrest? In a state rife with anticommunist beliefs, could UNC be trusted if it employed Marxists in its English Department? Not surprisingly, the critics urged the university to remove the "radical" professors from its ranks.

UNC leaders like Graham could not defend the proposition that their English professors were experts on industrial capitalism, so they defended the professors' right to free speech as private citizens. From there, Graham then invoked a different aspect of academic freedom: if these radical professors, despite their off-campus activism, did the job they were hired to do and obeyed the laws of the state, on what grounds could he fire them? Striking a more cautious tone, UNC leaders also argued that the campus had few, if any, genuine radicals, and those who were would be watched carefully. Therefore, the university could still be trusted. This approach did not satisfy the critics, of course; but at least UNC did not experience the same kind of conservative purge that other southern universities did during the 1930s and 1940s.

This study addresses three different areas of historiography. First, an examination of UNC during these critical years leading up to World War II pushes the study of academic freedom in a different direction. This book examines UNC as a living institution, as a political, cultural, and economic force in the South. As Edwin Mims wrote in 1926 of UNC, "the events of the life and thought of the world flow there."[78] UNC was both a product and a shaper of its surrounding context. My approach therefore places itself within what Melissa Kean has called the "new university history," wherein "historians have begun to produce more critical examinations of institutions of higher education set in the context of their times."[79]

Historians have yet to look at academic freedom on the ground, so to speak, down in the day-to-day messiness of campus and community life. As discussed earlier, those who have studied the history of academic freedom tend to focus on the philosophical innovations that accompanied its emergence as a concept, its embattled legal status as a subset of First Amendment law, or those specific moments and episodes when the commitment to academic freedom failed or succeeded.[80] This book tries to go beyond the narrower philosophical and legal analyses and the single-episode approach by studying the long-term relationship between a university committed to academic freedom and the world outside of the academy. It examines how academic freedom worked over time in the hands of flawed, idealistic advocates dealing with critics, and it reveals the gaps between the goals of academic freedom and what was really possible for academic freedom to achieve.

Second, a number of historians have contributed to our understanding of the complexities and conflicts gripping white southern liberalism after World War I. In these accounts, the struggle for power usually includes reactionary segregationists, an increasingly assertive (and often younger) African American leadership, a handful of white radicals daring to introduce leftist ideas to the region, and, caught somewhere in the uneasy middle, white southern liberals. The scholarship on white southern liberalism, as such liberalism existed before the landmark *Brown v. Board of Education* ruling of 1954, sits on either side of a fault line between that productive span of the 1970s and 1980s and the work of the past decade or so. In the 1970s and 1980s, historians such as John Kneebone, Morton Sosna, Charles Eagles, and Daniel J. Singal all produced important books attributing white southern liberals' downfall in the 1940s to their unwillingness to push for an end to segregation. More recently, however, Glenda Gilmore, Patricia Sullivan, John Egerton, Jonathan W. Bell, and Tony Badger have all found strong evidence of white southern liberal persistence on issues such as workers' rights and an activist state government, despite their uneasiness on race issues.[81]

Notwithstanding their disagreements over emphases and influences, these historians largely agree on the positions that marked a white southerner as liberal in the 1930s and 1940s. White southern liberals shared a commitment to improving the quality of life for working-class southerners through unionism; improving race relations by, among other things, openly condemning white-on-black violence; pushing for more public funds for black schools; and greater interaction between the leaders of the black and white communities. They also called for greater federal involvement to help facilitate the wrenching changes the South so desperately needed. Both conservatives and liberals of this era frequently lumped academic freedom in with these other liberal values. This book argues that while many of UNC's most passionate defenders of academic freedom self-identified as "liberal," the relationship between academic freedom and liberalism was more complicated than one leading naturally to the other. Moreover, it shows that many conservatives at UNC accepted the importance of academic freedom even as they opposed the liberal views of their colleagues.

Third, historians have done very little work on the history of trust in American society. Yet UNC leaders fretted constantly about maintaining trust as they introduced and then defended the school's academic freedom.[82] Trust was (and is) critical to making academic freedom real on campus and acceptable off campus. Trust held all interested parties together in the same endeavor. UNC professors had to trust their administrators to defend their academic freedom to do their research and teach their classes unimpeded by hostile external political forces. Administrators had to trust their faculty and students to use their academic freedom responsibly. The public had to trust that the fruits of academic freedom would be of social value and would, someday and somehow, make their lives richer and more fulfilling. Moreover, trust is always contingent, a fact that ought to make its examination an inviting target for historians.

Luckily, historians need not feel they are wandering into a wilderness as they begin to consider the historical construction of trust. Sociologists and especially political theorists have examined the critical role trust plays in functioning democratic societies. For instance, scholars (such as James Coleman and Robert Putnam) who study social capital—defined by Putnam as "the networks, norms, and social trust that facilitate coordination and cooperation for mutual benefit"—have established lines of analysis that can be helpful to historians wanting to study trust.[83] The extensive literature in these disciplines on the relationship between trust and social capital has informed my effort to examine the ways UNC leaders worked to bring trust and academic freedom together. Other scholars have looked more generally at the role trust plays in a democracy. Gerald M. Mara, for example, in his readings of Thucydides and Plato, offers a succinct overview of how political theorists have studied the importance of interactions among social institutions, as well as interactions between institutions and citizens, in producing and maintaining trust in successful democracies.[84] Mara's work therefore provided me with a useful way of thinking about UNC's academic freedom as a factor in a larger network of social interactions. University leaders had to navigate their way through the desires of other "actors" and in relationship with other institutions to make academic freedom real while maintaining public trust.

What I conclude is that despite the excitement of the interwar years, pervasive beliefs in white superiority and the power wielded by the state's textile leadership imposed clear limits on what UNC could achieve through its efforts to establish academic freedom. Progress on race and labor reform still seemed a long way off in North Carolina as the 1930s ended. Segregation remained firmly in place, even though the *Missouri ex rel. Gaines v. Canada* decision in December 1938 caused some worry among the more prescient segregationists. When the FBI took an interest in UNC student Marxism in the late 1930s, UNC officials turned student records over to investigators.[85] Having survived a wave of labor unrest and activism, O. Max Gardner wrote to the chairman of the Coca-Cola Company that "our forces are in complete control," after the defeat of a pro-union candidate for governor in 1936.[86]

Still, the story here should be seen as one of partial success in the establishment of an institutional value—UNC's academic freedom, not just its liberalism—that continues to shape its identity as a top-flight university today. Academic freedom did not make UNC "liberal" in the 1920s and 1930s; it made some liberalism possible on an otherwise conservative campus in a conservative state. For all their trials, university leaders such as Harry W. Chase and Frank P. Graham succeeded in making academic freedom a "defensible professional imperative," even if people could not agree on how exactly it should work. Additionally, by invoking academic freedom as a necessary function of the modern intellectual's expertise, some at UNC took and defended extremely unpopular positions against segregation and industrial exploitation of workers.

In the next few decades that are beyond the scope of this book, defending workers and decrying racism were not unpopular positions, even in the South. But in the 1920s and 1930s, UNC was well ahead of other southern universities in grappling with the most important developments of the twentieth century, even with all the limitations it operated under (both from within and from without). As David Cohn wrote of UNC in 1941, the "intangible achievements of the University are perhaps greater" than the building and programmatic accomplishments of the interwar years. "They lie," he continued, "in an unremitting and successful struggle for academic freedom in an area where the weight of lethargy, as well as the dynamics of industrial opposition and inherited prejudices, operates against academic freedom. They consist in teaching students the truth about the South even when the truth hurts."[87]

Part I

The 1920s

1

"Race Was
a Delicate Matter"

The Academic Study of Race Relations

In January 1921, the Ku Klux Klan came to Chapel Hill. They burned no crosses and administered no beatings. The UNC student newspaper, the *Tar Heel*, reported that a "Mr. Smith" had arrived in town with the purpose of starting up a Klan chapter in Chapel Hill, having recently launched one in Durham. The "mysterious" Smith spoke to a meeting of "students and the town people" at the local schoolhouse, introduced by Jesse Harper Erwin Jr. of Durham. But, the story continued, "very little enthusiasm" greeted the Klan leader. Skeptics in the audience included the local chief of police, the principal of the local high school, and UNC drama professor Frederick Koch. Smith explained that the Klan's purpose was "to assist, not to take the place of law and order." Without elaboration, he singled out for special mention "the malicious activities of certain Catholics and Japanese among the negroes." At one point Smith reached into his handbag for reading material, "disclosing as he did the mystical red-crossed white robe and helmet which are the insignia of the Order." After finishing his address, Smith then asked those interested in forming a Chapel Hill klavern to stand. When, as the *Tar Heel* reported, there were "very many remaining seated," the Klansman "became rather warm under the collar." Revealingly, however, the student paper then contrasted the lackluster interest in this new Klan with the "glorious history of the old Ku Klux Klan" that "did so much to restore

25

peace and prosperity to the South in the troubled times of the 'carpet-bag' government."[1]

Elsewhere the *Tar Heel* reported at least some campus support for the Klan. The university's Philanthropic Assembly debated the recently failed attempt by the state legislature to pass an "anti-mask" law meant to discourage Klan activity.[2] According to the student paper, the Phi Assembly included a handful of staunch defenders of the Klan, members "especially favorable toward the robed fraternal order's stand in regard to Jews, Catholics, and colored peoples." But at the end of the meeting, the group voted overwhelmingly in favor of the bill that the state legislators had rejected.[3] The next week, another debating society, the Dialectic Society, emerged from a lively debate to go on record as being opposed to the Klan.[4]

The resurgence of the Ku Klux Klan in the early 1920s gave the university a timely opportunity to demonstrate the importance of the university mission of academic freedom and expert leadership to the South. To people like Harry Chase, Howard Odum, and sociologist Guy B. Johnson, the rise of the Klan represented just the opposite of UNC's self-image. The Klan's popularity rested on emotion rather than the intellect; it represented a case of bad, thoughtless leadership instead of the calm, informed direction UNC offered. The Klan's efforts would make life in the South worse by inflaming hatreds and suspicions, while UNC dedicated its own efforts to promulgating wisdom and light, to make life better for all southerners.

The university's ability to treat southern race relations as an academic issue with real-life implications allowed UNC scholars to invoke their expertise and kept them relatively free to look more closely into the reality of segregation. The analyses coming from UNC leaders and students during the decade increasingly reflected modern ideas on "race" emerging from the academy, with an emphasis on environmental factors determining behavior, health, and intelligence. Research by university faculty such as Guy Johnson criticized the Klan at a time when the organization was reaching its peak nationwide. UNC faculty members subjected the Klan to tests of scholarly investigation to uncover the true "facts" behind the organization's frantic claims. Also, as a result of new levels of interaction with the black community, some university officials and students embraced the work of African American leaders and writers. Exposure to the work of the artists of the Harlem Renaissance encouraged some to question the assumptions upon which segregation was based. By the end of the decade, UNC's willingness to examine race issues as a legitimate category of academic inquiry had produced a much more critical stance on segregation.

As an institution, however, UNC was still far from disavowing segregation any time soon. As Guy Johnson reflected years later, "Race was a delicate matter. . . . If you began [to] talk about social problems, or the rights of black people, then you began to get into trouble."[5] The practical, daily reality remained that UNC could not afford to get too far ahead of the views of most white southerners on segregation. To do so, university leaders feared, would jeopardize the trust UNC depended on. As Daniel Singal notes, "the one issue that was to prove most difficult for Modernist intellectuals in the South" was "whether or not to maintain racial segregation. . . . The safest and most comfortable course by far, almost everyone concluded, was to agree that the matter of segregation was closed."[6] Sympathetic white writers could lament persistent poverty and poor health in the black community, but caution remained the byword of the day: "There could be no openly acknowledged 'race problems' in the South, only a 'task' of 'adjustment' that could be readily met through the 'cooperation' of leaders of both races."[7]

One finds plenty of examples of the thoughts and words of UNC officials, faculty, and students fitting Singal's assessment. Most of those at UNC who championed better treatment of black southerners did so as a means to preserve segregation and white supremacy. They in fact invoked the responsibilities of the more "advanced" race to secure a better quality of life for black southerners. Locally, as John Chapman points out, the rise of Jim Crow in Chapel Hill in the early twentieth century "limited and denied the hopes of African Americans and their material well being, diverting privileges and resources to white people and to white institutions. White workers gained even greater preferential employment opportunities, while men and women of the elite hired servants at low wages, thereby granting greater time to devote to leisure and their careers. . . . Rigid segregation, unknown in Chapel Hill before 1900, was not simply a reflection of racial bigotry: it was part of a new mechanism of social control."[8]

But UNC's handling of race reveals one of the benefits of examining academic freedom over time and at a single institution. While Chapman's assessment of Chapel Hill in the early 1900s is certainly accurate, the establishment of academic freedom at UNC created an environment in which modern research increasingly brought segregation's inequities and cruelties to light. Already in the 1920s, especially among a handful of student writers, one can find members of the UNC community openly questioning whether segregation could ever be made right—since, they now learned, it had never been "right" to begin with.

Many southerners, white and black, sensed that World War I had altered the racial landscape in important ways. The combination of the closing off of European immigration, northern wartime industrial employment opportunities, and temporarily high cotton prices that put money in the pockets of black sharecroppers for once sparked the massive relocation of millions of black southerners to the north. Military service in the cause of making the world safe for democracy added to a new sense of possibility within the black community. As W. E. B. Du-Bois famously wrote at the end of World War I: "We return. We return from fighting. We return fighting."[9] White Americans responded with a mixture of fear and resentment. White-on-black violence erupted in the first postwar years in Arkansas, South Carolina, Oklahoma, Texas, Illinois, Nebraska, and Washington, DC, among other places.[10] Some white southerners, pointing to the persistent threat of violence and the fact that cheap black labor was leaving in droves, concluded that a crisis existed in local race relations.

Local black leaders astutely pushed the daily injustices they lived with before the still-opening eyes of white leaders and challenged them with claims to democracy newly justified by the black contribution to the war. The new interest in race relations did establish some important precedents. In North Carolina, a new constitutional amendment in 1918 expanded educational opportunities for black students. NAACP chapters were started in Durham, Raleigh, and Greensboro in 1917.[11] Thus, fear of economic and social disorder combined with the Progressive Era confidence that problems could be solved with "facts" and research to give rise to an altered approach to race relations among educated white southerners like those at UNC.

Newfound white southern interest in better race relations after World War I did not mean that segregation was about to be challenged seriously. New interracialist organizations such as the Committee on Interracial Cooperation (CIC) still took segregation as a given—at least its white members did. But the new interracialist approach questioned two core values of prewar segregation: that white paternalism was humane and that the races were fundamentally different. Although its approach appears cautious to us now, the CIC broke new ground by seeking to "find out what blacks want."[12] Black CIC members confronted their white associates with stories revealing that white paternalism was all too often a lie.[13] As a result of such interactions, along with new scholarly work questioning the very notion of race itself, white interracialists began to back away from the hard-and-fast conviction that there existed innate, immutable racial differences.[14]

The CIC explicitly focused on gaining the attention of sympathetic white southern college students, reflecting the more modern view of young minds being shaped and not just taught in school.[15] UNC sociologists Howard Odum, Arthur Raper, and Eugene Branson, all active supporters of the CIC during these years, incorporated courses on race relations into the sociology curriculum.[16] Joining the CIC was a bold move for a white southerner in the 1920s. Odum held out until 1927, when he joined reluctantly, with the prodding of the NAACP's James Weldon Johnson. Still, as Daniel Singal observes, Odum's experience in the CIC revealed "southern racial problems in all their unlovely particulars" and put him "in touch for the first time with the region's sizable black elite."[17] Learning about segregation's "unlovely particulars" through face-to-face contact with the CIC's black members was, in essence, research—research that then made its way into UNC classrooms.

Prior to the 1920s, UNC's YMCA chapter served as the locus for campus interest in race relations. As early as 1913, the university Y—under Frank Graham's leadership as secretary—modeled itself after programs established by W. D. Weatherford, the leader of the YMCA movement in the South, and began working with the African American community in Chapel Hill.[18] In 1913 the campus Y conducted a "housing and sanitation" survey of Chapel Hill's blacks; the survey's results, as characterized by Charles Maddry Freeman, "ran the gamut of offenses against sanitation." Home ownership, size, location, and capacity all featured in the survey, as did questions about water supply, bathrooms, and health conditions generally. According to the survey, the black community in Chapel Hill fared better than the average "for Negro communities in the South" but still "exhibited room for improvement."[19]

After completing the survey, the Y then recruited UNC faculty members to conduct a lecture series in local African American churches on proper sanitation. The Y also worked with the Community Club to spearhead a weeklong cleanup effort in black neighborhoods, inviting African Americans to bring their trash out to the street for pickup.

The city still did not have garbage collection designated for black neighborhoods yet.[20]

The Graham-led Y also reached out to the local black community through educational programs. First, however, the university students themselves needed to be educated. Using Weatherford's *Negro Life in the South* as its text, the Y conducted a lecture series to coincide with their regular dormitory prayer meetings. The first lecture, delivered by UNC dean M. H. Stacy, argued that "the negro was too intimately a part of our life to not avail ourselves of the facts concerning his life." Future university president Henry Woodburn Chase instructed his charges that "industrial education was the only salvation for the negro," while a local Presbyterian minister, Rev. W. D. Moss, outlined "the religious characteristics of the race."[21] A concluding lecture by Stuart Willis, "What We Can Do," urged his fellow UNC students to "understand the Negro, assist in Sunday Schools, give illustrated speeches, and the like."[22]

In 1914 the Y sent ten UNC students, two at a time, to the local Quaker schoolhouse to conduct lessons in "spelling, reading, writing, history, and rudiments of mathematics and grammar" for black adults. This became known as the Negro Night School or the Orange (County) Night School. The Y reported that between fifteen and twenty local African Americans attended regularly.[23] A 1917 article in the *Tar Heel* revealed the Y's ambitious Night School plans for the coming school year. UNC students planned to teach nightly classes for African American men covering reading, writing, spelling, math, history, and debate. The paper reported "17 boys present during the first night."[24] The writer pegged the educational level of the men at the "4th and 5th grades" but added that they "proved themselves to be very intelligent. For instance, one of them asked . . . what Great Britain was going to do for Ireland when the war was over"; a good question indeed.[25]

UNC students had a growing number of opportunities to consider the state of race relations after World War I. Even though white paternalism informed nearly all of these efforts, they still reflected UNC's efforts to gather "facts" and legitimize southern race relations as a topic of study. In 1918, John Little of Louisville, Kentucky, helped spark campus interest in the race "problem" by presenting a "highly instructive and entertaining illustrated lecture" to UNC students at Gerrard Hall. Little was known for his work on behalf of racial uplift in the Louisville area. "Flashing scenes, taken from the localities where he has worked," Little used illustrations to impress the large student audience with the need for their work in the black community. "The filthy conditions existing in their homes, their crowded manner of living, and their appalling ignorance were graphically described by the lecturer," the *Tar Heel* reported.[26]

A newer perspective was starting to emphasize the need for sharing information between members of the black and white elite, but Little insisted that the status of race relations "presents a problem which must be solved by the white people alone. We must uplift the negro and help ourselves by helping him rather than attempt to neglect him or crush him under our feet." Following Little's address, UNC official Francis Bradshaw announced the initiation of a seven-week course on "negro problems," taught by four UNC professors, that would take place on subsequent Sundays. His appeal, combined with Little's lecture, prompted "over 280" UNC students to enroll on the spot.[27]

The "course" consisted of a lecture series presented over the next several weeks that clung to paternalistic notions of white problem-solving. Faculty members Eugene Branson, Charles Mangum, Arthur Raper, and G. M. McKie all shared their expertise on topics ranging from housing to morality to physiology. Together they show the good intentions of the faculty to use their expertise to promote some kind of racial "uplift," as well as the deep sense among some UNC faculty that African Americans could do little for themselves.[28] All four professors agreed that the black community—whether because of poor education, low morality, or natural disadvantage—needed the white community's urgent help. They also agreed that lifting up the black community was in the white community's best interest, too. Because they were white men employed at the state university, it was therefore part of the university's self-proclaimed mission to bring this expertise to the black population in order to benefit the entire community.

Sociologist Eugene Branson gave the introductory lecture for the Sunday courses, giving a "short but very interesting address" to the 270 students who attended. He argued that two reasons explained the sudden interest in race relations: an awakening to the economic shifts taking place in the South, and a heightened sense of "spiritual obligation" among some white southerners. The northern migration of black workers during the war years, Branson explained, "shocked" the white South into a greater awareness of conditions among black southerners. The migration, he claimed, had "paralyzed farming in wide areas and industries in certain corners." The new attention devoted to black southerners was already producing important health information. Branson noted that "our deadly epidemics originate in negro cabins and come into our homes in our clothes baskets." The danger of disease through poverty prompted Branson to take a spiritual turn: "The negro has long lain at our doors, as Lazarus at the doors of Dives, the rich man: that he has had the crumbs that fall from our table and we have left the dogs to lick his sores." He concluded, "I am not willing to leave out of my scheme of thinking, or ethics, or religion any one of God's creatures—black or white, dumb or human—that can in anywise be made better by my help."[29] Despite his good intentions and academic authority, Branson here revealed a racial sensibility rooted in white supremacy, a sensibility that associated "black" with "dumb" and "white" with "human."

Professor Charles Mangum of the School of Medicine presented information covering housing conditions among African Americans and an examination of brain and skull formations. The *Tar Heel* reported that the address "carried a feeling of hopefulness mingled with pity," a description that captures the white southern progressive view perfectly at this time. Mangum's lecture offered a mixture of physiology, morality, and bourgeois values. Reflecting on his own twenty years in Chapel Hill, Mangum asserted that "the negro" living in the town had "made progress, though slow, along all lines, especially commending the adoption of a higher moral standard among them." As he explained: "Wherever the negro has a well kept home his living condition is usually good, and he is a good citizen." Black homeowners, he added, "make much better citizens than renters." From here Mangum's thoughts segued into physiology and race: "The negro is prone to copy the white man's actions; he has no initiative and lacks self-control." As "proof" of this claim, he drew the students' attention to "the peculiarity of the negro's brain. His forehead, where the brain is undeveloped, is flat, while the white man's forehead has a bulge, where the power of self-control, thinking, and planning lies. On the other hand, the back part of the negro's head, where the animal instincts have their being, is fully developed."[30]

Mangum made the case for better education in hygiene to reduce the death rate in the black community. The black community, he concluded optimistically, was "highly appreciative and eager to cooperate with the white for the betterment of their conditions."[31] Mangum acted on his own plea for more education for the black community; outside the university, Mangum was involved in maintaining the local Orange County Training School, a school for manual education for black students. By 1920, the school boasted roughly three hundred students and had received favorable attention for its work.[32]

At the next week's lecture, Charles Lee Raper, dean of the Graduate School, continued the theme of white expertise employed on behalf of racial uplift by asserting that education for the black community "must be provided by the whites who control the government." According to the *Tar Heel*, Raper said that "physical health and hygiene should be emphasized in the education of the darkies. This is not only for their moral and physical uplift, but also for the protection of the whites." Raper presented a program of "practical" education in which "literature and classics should be omitted altogether, while such things as cooking and sewing should be taught the girls, and agriculture and manual training taught the boys." In conclusion, Raper proclaimed that "the schools for the negro should develop the disposition of the individual and teach a sympathetic attitude towards the whites as well as towards their own race. The schools should develop good citizens and workers, not doctors and lawyers, for the vast majority of negroes must be workers."[33]

Attendance at the Race Study Class lectures showed that interest in race relations was high at UNC. The lectures reveal a Progressive Era earnestness consistent with the pre-1920 perspective: UNC experts presented the "facts" of black community problems and called for improvement, but with the assumption that reform was a one-way street of white people helping blacks and that reform would never threaten white power. Genuine racial interaction to the benefit of the entire community did occur in Chapel Hill at least once during the 1920s, as a response to an emergency situation; unfortunately, no one at UNC seemed to take away any larger lessons from the experience.

In 1921 the *Tar Heel* reported that a dangerous fire had burned down homes and an African Methodist Episcopal church in the predominantly black neighborhood located at Chapel Hill's border with the neighboring town of Carrboro. According to the paper, "Only the combined efforts of the white and colored residents and the students of the University were able to save the surrounding buildings from destruction." The student paper added that the main obstacles facing those fighting the fire were its rapid outbreak (most likely the result of a kerosene lamp explosion) and racist town planning—namely, "the fact that no water mains had been installed in that section of the town." Yet the article revealed a brief, successful moment of interracial cooperation: "Students and townspeople threw bucket after bucket of water upon the surrounding homes, and the fire was confined to only two buildings. Owing to the crowded condition in that section and to the trouble and time entailed in drawing water from the wells, the fire once spreading to an outlying dwelling would have certainly swept the district if it had not been for the co-operation of the townspeople and the students." Once again Frank Graham was the university's man on the scene, and the *Tar Heel* reported that "the colored people of the community wish to express . . . their thanks and appreciation to the students and especially to Prof. Frank Graham for the assistance rendered in saving the surrounding homes."[34]

In other *Tar Heel* articles from this time, one can also see very apparent limits to UNC's concern for local black well-being. One 1918 article reported that the university janitors, an all-black group, had joined the radical labor organization Industrial Workers of the World and were now out on strike. Ed Stewart, described as "chairman of the strike," announced that "there will be no more bed making and no more hot water until we get a ten dollar [per week] raise." The article also indicated that Charles Woollen, the university official in charge of the physical plant, had "sent to Durham for strike-breakers, as the situation is fast becoming serious." Meanwhile, UNC students circulated a petition "asking that the janitors be not reinstated."[35] In addition, Howard Odum and Guy Johnson were apparently little troubled by the fact that black gang labor had made the impressive campus building expansion a reality. In fact, Johnson considered the proximity of gang labor to be a real boon as he and Odum collected traditional black folk songs: "Many a student and professor listened, spellbound, as a group of diggers sang a work song, with picks whirling in unison on the upstroke and a mighty 'hunh' of exhalation at the end of the downstroke. At twilight and dawn plaintive calls and 'hollers' could be heard in the barracks where the workmen lived only a hundred yards . . . from the residences of Odum and Johnson."[36]

Student writers for the *Tar Heel* took obvious delight in publishing articles mocking local African American residents. For example, in 1921 the paper published a wisecracking account of a local shooting incident in Carrboro and Potter's Field (an African American neighborhood of Chapel Hill). The article, titled "'White Likker' and City Negroes Mix," regaled its readers with the story of how "young negroes, acting upon the inspiration of the popular extract of corn, 'shot up' the neighborhood." The young men entered a local restaurant and ordered. When the bill arrived, "the inebriate ones became very excited and unlimbered their artillery with little discrimination as to direction or range." After a call to the police, the young men fled the restaurant, but then "went up and down the street firing their pistols and terrifying the inhabitants." The article concluded, "It is thought that the negroes were from Durham and were bent upon showing up-country niggers."[37]

In 1922, the *Tar Heel* found humor in the vaccination of university maintenance staff—"15 husky janitors"—against an outbreak of small-pox. "The broom-weild-ers [*sic*] were none too anxious to have their tanned skin pricked by the needle" and had to be persuaded to line up and receive the vaccination. The *Tar Heel* reporter again made light of the situation: "The janitors wanted to roll the bones to decide who would be first," but then a young man volunteered. "When Dr. Nathan applied the needle to the squirming darky, the other janitors seemed to enjoy the fruitless effort of the victim to keep a stolid countenance, and he became the target for several bits of African humor: 'Sam, Yo' lookin' pale, sho nuff,' 'Is dat a earthquake or Sam's knees knockin'?' 'Would a glass a mule he'p, Sam?' 'Looka dat boy jump! He'll bump his head on the ceilin' directly.'" But eventually it became their turn and the article reports that they all went through "the same convulsive shivers, shim-myings, eye rolling, as did Sam."[38]

Andy Johnston, the janitor of Caldwell Hall, home to the medical school, was both beloved and mocked in the pages of the *Tar Heel*. In 1927 the paper published an account of "Dean Andy," as he was called, selling and then buying back his body from the medical school. From the first sentence on, the account was rife with racial stereotypes: "Yas, Suh, I shore feels like I used to be," the paper reported Andy as saying. Believing that the medical school paid sixty dollars for cadavers, "Dean Andy" decided to go ahead and sell his body, "get the use of the money now, and also have the use of his body until he was dead." However, "the Dean had not counted on the most outstanding characteristic of his race interfering with his transaction, and that is their spasmodic religious faith." Andy grew concerned that if his cadaver was all sliced up, that the driver of the chariot to heaven might be put out at having to "gather me up in fragments." Fearful that he might just miss out on his chariot ride to salvation altogether, "Dean Andy" went back to the medical school and bought his body back.[39]

Charles Mangum, head of the School of Medicine, did not find the story funny. He dashed off a short letter to the paper stating "that the material in this article is without foundation in fact and is therefore both untrue and libelous in character. . . . Our medical schools do not buy bodies," he growled.[40] The *Tar Heel* backed off the story by conceding the facts were untrue and by attempting at least to pay some tribute to "Dean Andy." But here, too, stereotypes drove the effort. The follow-up article admitted that "Dean Andy" had been "embarrassed, brought to grief, yea, maligned by a *Tar Heel* reporter who drew his facts for the article . . . from none other than the thin, sinuous clouds of imagery." The article offered an explanation that connected shuffling African American behavior with gaining white affection: "Dean Andy is that type of antebellum darkey whose mild, courteous manner, meticulous regard for his duty, and complaisant, accommodating mien create a keen affection and respect for him among the students and members of the faculty of the medical school." But now, unfortunately, this story had caused "the venerable darky" to cast a "distrusting, antagonistic eye" on the college reporters.[41]

Clearly, therefore, the campus culture at UNC during the 1920s included abundant conventional racist stereotyping. But there is also evidence of a gradually emerging, countervailing movement on campus, led by those increasingly willing to probe the boundaries and limits of inquiry on race issues.[42] UNC's embrace of academic freedom made it possible that this new line of inquiry would eventually question the "fact" of white superiority and the legitimacy of segregation, no small achievement for a southern university at this time.

In January 1923, Howard Odum's *Journal of Social Forces* announced that the journal would be investigating the rise of the new Klan "in the scientifically sympathetic way." Odum then went ahead and offered his view that the Klan represented bad leadership that the journal would dissect through scientific inquiry. The journal, he noted, would "strive to estimate the tragedies that lie in the wake of those who are so easily misled by an inadequate leadership, and . . . strive to point the way constructively to the renunciation of false stands taken for whatever reason." Countering the Klan's claims that their objectives were "Americanism, Democracy, and Christianity," the journal would "show that they are un-American, un-democratic and un-Christian in every true sense of background, bottomground, structure, and ideals."[43]

Following Odum's prompting, university scholars used their work to criticize the Klan sharply and frequently. Sociologist Guy B. Johnson's critique of the Klan eventually led him to question segregation itself. In the May 1923 issue of *Journal of Social Forces*, Johnson noted that while the Klan had garnered a lot of publicity of late, "very little has been written in the way of unprejudiced analysis" of the group. His aim, therefore, invoking his own authority as an expert, was to "determine the salient sociological factors behind the origin and growth of the new Ku Klux Klan and to estimate the significance of those factors." Johnson found two: the Klan's use of publicity agents and the national reaction to World War I, which left "in its train a wave of crime, moral laxity, unemployment, and national hysteria." Therefore, the rise of the Klan was not simply a product of propaganda, nor was it just a "psychic reaction" to "postwar conditions." The Klan's rise was, rather, caused by a combination of the two; although, of the two, Johnson tended to think the latter was the stronger cause. The war had resulted in a heightened sense of "Americanism" that naturally led to postwar suspicion of "foreigners." It had also produced "an intensification of race feeling"; white Americans had become "more suspicious of the growing power of the negroes."[44] At the same time, however, "the negroes are less patient in their endurance of discriminatory treatment." This impatience had been generated by "the increased racial consciousness which the negro derived from his participation in the war." The war, therefore, "served to accentuate race antipathies rather than to reduce them," a phenomenon that "has been no small factor in precipitating the Ku Klux movement."[45]

While the Klan gathered a national following in the early 1920s, Johnson pointed out that the factors propelling its popularity rang "doubly true of the South." Again he cited the "rising consciousness of the negro race" that was, he added correctly, "slowly surpassing the capacity of present racial adjustments."[46] Johnson saw that the black southerner would continue to insist "with increasing strength that his 'place' is going to be a better place or he is not going to stay in it." As a result, the "southern Klansman looks with misgivings as he watches the color line grow gradually dimmer to the negro. He realizes that if the modern radical negro has his way, the race problem of today is nothing compared to the race problem that will come."[47] Again, by acknowledging African American demands stemming from the black experience during World War I, Johnson's formulation of the "race problem" was at this point significantly different from the analysis presented in the Y lectures discussed earlier, which conceptualized the problems of the black community as problems that only white people could solve.

Johnson was equally perceptive in his analysis of the likely white

southern reaction to changes in race relations. Asking white southerners to "contemplate the future of the Southland with the negro possess-
ing a degree of social and political equality" was a daunting challenge.
He added, "One might as well ask . . . 'What was before God?' as to
ask the typical southerner to contemplate the negro on a plane of social equality." He then quickly backed away from that grim scenario by
adding the standard CIC line: "The thinking, forward-looking southerner can see some ray of hope, some way out of the problem, as he
has shown in his attempts at interracial cooperation." Johnson remained
concerned, however, because "the masses" were "blindly afraid of 'social
equality.'" He concluded: "When we talk of crushing the Ku Klux order,
we display an amazing ignorance of human nature. It is not enough to
say that the great body of uninitiated Klansmen are merely in sympathy with the movement. *They are the Ku Klux movement!*" (his emphasis). The tension in Johnson's analysis was palpable in 1923 and would
grow more pronounced as the 1920s turned into the 1930s. What was
this "ray of hope" that "thinking, forward looking" southerners saw if
"human nature" sustained the Klan? It is difficult to see any such ray in
Johnson's analysis.

Later in 1923, Johnson expressed the same points even more dramatically in a revised version of his *Journal of Social Forces* article that
featured the value of interracial cooperation more prominently. The revised article was published in *Opportunity*, the National Urban League
newspaper. In it, Johnson forecast that "as the American Negro becomes
more and more the master of his own fortunes, it is almost inevitable
that those who believe in his natural inferiority shall seek, by force and
violence if necessary, to keep him 'in his place.'"[48] Here, too, Johnson tied
a better future to "clear thinking" by claiming that the "forward-looking
people among both races . . . have entrusted themselves to the belief that,
whatever the outcome, nothing can be lost by encouraging all efforts toward inter-racial co-operation and good will." Danger lurked not simply
in the acts of violence perpetrated by the Klan but also in the "social attitudes of hatred and prejudice" that would "affect the social heritage of the
next generation. . . . Can not," he asked, "the heritage to the coming gen-
erations be one of sympathy, respect, and co-operation? Those who think
clearly and are unafraid say—yes!"[49] Johnson's emphasis on the importance of "clear-thinking" people, his call for cooperation with the black
community, and his hopes for the next generation captured the UNC and
interracialist ideals perfectly. As experts, UNC faculty placed themselves

among the ranks of the "clear-thinking" people. As interracialists, they increasingly interacted with black leaders. And as teachers they were of course concerned about the next generation.

At a time when most white southerners took Jim Crow's permanence as a given beyond contemplation, Guy Johnson's analysis led him to predict a difficult future for segregation. In a 1924 article in the *Journal of Social Forces* examining the implications of black migration, Johnson noted that increasing urbanization would produce a "more rigid southern caste system." But he then promptly cast doubt on the future of this caste system: "Any attempt to solve the race problem by a caste arrangement," he predicted, "merely postpones the day when the white man must face the issue squarely and settle it, not according to his own convenience, but by making concessions to the powerful and race-conscious blacks."[50]

At least once, the university's criticism of the Klan came at a physical price. In 1925, shortly after George Washington Carver had spent two days speaking to UNC students and giving scientific demonstrations of his research, UNC students of the Dialectic Society sponsored a debate between W. A. Hamlett of Atlanta, editor of the Klan newspaper, *The Kourier,* and Josiah W. Bailey, a well-known lawyer and a future UNC trustee and U.S. Senator.[51] According to the *Tar Heel,* Bailey used his time during the debate to "knock the Ku Klux Klan on every occasion."[52] Then, following the debate, Klansmen in Raleigh attempted to attack Bailey. As Bailey described the scene to Eugene Branson, "I was the victim yesterday morning of a Ku Klux conspiracy, and was assaulted on the streets. I managed, however, to defend myself successfully—and no harm was done." He explained, "My Chapel Hill speech made them mighty mad; but I very much enjoyed making that speech, and am looking for an opportunity to make it again."[53]

As Michael O'Brien, Daniel J. Singal, Michael J. Milligan, Wayne Brazil, Fred Hobson, and other scholars have pointed out, the work in the first few years of the *Journal of Social Forces* represented a courageous effort to encourage new thinking and analysis on race relations.[54] That it came from within the South and was led by native-born white southerners like Odum, Johnson, and Arthur Raper is even more remarkable. There is no question that the scholarly approach encouraged by the journal was a product of the school's academic freedom. Beyond the *Journal,* Odum and Guy B. Johnson published *The Negro and His Songs* (1925) and *Negro Workaday Songs* (1926) to much acclaim.[55] The readership of these books and the *Journal of Social Forces* was still small and selective, but these years represented a promising start.

Yet perhaps nowhere on campus in the 1920s was UNC's academic freedom to consider new thoughts on race more evident and provocative than in the student publication *Carolina Magazine*. The monthly magazine earned its heralded reputation when future UNC Press director William T. Couch became its editor in the 1924–1925 academic year.[56] The student editors of and contributors to *Carolina Magazine* explored daring interracial themes in their own work and invited African American writers to showcase their work in the publication.

In the October 1926 edition, UNC student R. K. Fowler published a short story titled "Slaves." The story line was fairly simple, including an Old South versus New South generational conflict and a hint of interracial—and therefore taboo—sex. When a teenaged white girl's guardian/uncle (a symbol of the old landed elite) breaks off her engagement to the son of a merchant (a symbol of the new South), the young girl gets revenge by having sex with the black son of the family's domestic servant. Fowler, of course, did not describe the sex between the two; rather, he made clear in the final scene that it was about to happen.[57]

The ensuing controversy quickly became an issue of academic freedom. When the UNC student council called for *Carolina Magazine* editor Julian Starr to resign and for Fowler to be dismissed from the school altogether, President Chase assembled a faculty committee that included Frank Graham, Howard Odum, and historian R. D. W. Connor to review the case. Meanwhile, the *Carolina Magazine* board defended itself with a strong invocation of UNC's academic freedom. To be more precise, they pointed to UNC's commitment to defend scholars' freedom to do what they had been trained to do. To the students on the magazine's board, the possibility of UNC failing to defend Fowler and Starr was far worse than any potential outrage caused by the story itself.

The magazine board's outlined notes show their position: "Publicity due to the Council's action more dangerous than story. More provocative stories were published almost unnoticed last year." They insisted, as creative writers, on having the same "principle in matters of science, religion, economic, and political thought." Fowler was a UNC-taught creative writer who was writing creatively in a university publication. As such, he had done exactly what he had been taught to do. In a set of their expanded notes, the *Carolina Magazine* board sounded the theme of academic freedom as a defensible imperative: "If we find it necessary

for the sake of policy and fear for our appropriations to shackle this freedom, let us honestly recognize that just so far as we are ceasing to be a
real university, and above all let us not cover our action with a pious pre-
tense of morality."[58] The faculty committee voted to overturn the student
government's decision.[59] Starr and Fowler stayed.

Journalist Gerald W. Johnson, who had just left the chair of the
UNC Department of Journalism to write for the *Baltimore Evening Sun*,
defended the magazine and summed up the significance of the controversy by pointing to the value—and, for some, the problem—of academic freedom. Johnson pointed out that Addison Hibbard, a UNC English
professor and dean of the College of Liberal Arts, had made a niche
within his field by arguing that "the white professional writers of the
South are abandoning both sentiment and comedy as the only possible
settings for the Negro in fiction, poetry and drama, and are beginning
to treat him with sharp and questioning realism." Johnson added that
"apparently there is a certain tendency in the same direction among student writers."[60] This was exactly how academic freedom was supposed
to work. Hibbard brought his expertise into the classroom and had produced student writers experimenting with the new approach to creative
writing.

Johnson also cited a recent incident when a University of Virginia student editor had written a story with a similar theme of interracial sex that had prompted protestations in Charlottesville. But whereas
one might have expected Johnson to lament the reactionary tendencies
among the student readers at the University of Virginia and UNC, Johnson saw in the incidents a silver lining for the entire South. "The very
violence of the reaction makes it certain that the subject was vehemently
debated on each campus and awakened echoes in other colleges in the
region," Johnson concluded. "The unmentionable has been mentioned,
the darkest phase of the race problem has been effectively, if momentarily and somewhat luridly, illuminated. One generation of college students has come into realization that discussion of the subject is possible
since intelligent men hold divergent views upon it."[61]

The issue for Johnson was not whether interracial sex was acceptable, but whether, in an academic setting, students and faculty—
"intelligent men"—could discuss, debate, or write about interracial sex,
a point at the heart of academic freedom. He found it significant, and
guardedly encouraging, that the story had prompted an open discussion
of the sensitive issue of "social equality." He added, "As to whether this

innovation is advantageous or pernicious there may be debate, but there is no blinking the fact that it has come and that it is an innovation."[62]

However, Johnson's analysis shows the predicament that UNC's academic freedom created with regard to southern race relations. The Race Study Class lecture series of the late 1910s was premised on the belief that better facts and open inquiry would lead to an improvement in African American living conditions. UNC leaders accepted that form of change as positive. On the issue of "social equality" with African Americans, however, UNC supporters like Gerald Johnson had to insist that open discussion would not likely threaten the racial order: "It does not necessarily follow," he maintained, "that it foreshadows any perceptible change in the Southern social attitude."[63]

Johnson's insight reveals how the political reality of the 1920s South complicated UNC's defense of academic freedom. Staunch segregationists could reasonably ask: what, then, was the purpose of open discussion, if not to raise the possibility of a "perceptible change in the Southern social attitude" on race relations? UNC's response relied on their assertion that open discussion would always be done in a responsible, trustworthy way and, as will be shown later, that sometimes academic freedom produced arguments for conservative ends—proving that academic freedom did not "necessarily" lead to change.

Starting in 1927, the *Carolina Magazine* started publishing a "Negro Number," turning an issue over to an African American guest editor and guest writers. Since the advent of the "New Negro" (the phrase taken from Alain Locke's groundbreaking 1925 essay), the academic community had taken greater interest in African American writers. What is remarkable about *Carolina Magazine* during these years is how quickly and intensely some UNC students recognized and embraced this new cultural development. Over the next five years, the magazine published some of the most heralded black poets of the Modernist movement, including Langston Hughes and Countee Cullen.

The May 1927 issue featured African American writers such as Hughes and Cullen, Lewis Alexander, Arna Bontemps, Angelina Grimke, Georgia Douglas Johnson, and sociologist Charles S. Johnson, who together offered provocative poems and commentary on the literature and poetry produced by other black writers. For example, Lewis Alexander, a Washington, DC–born poet, reviewed Langston Hughes's *Fine Clothes to the Jew*. He applauded Hughes's "sincerity" and noted that the work possessed "an originality . . . which is quite refreshing. He goes directly to the source for his material and reports his findings as he sees them. The result is quite delightful."[64] The result was also quite daring for a student journal run by white southern students. Alexander explains that in "The Porter," Langston Hughes "understands something of the economic revolution which is taking place in the mind of the Negro." As proof, Alexander cites lines from "The Porter": "Rich old white man / Owns the world / Gimme yo' shoes / To Shine. /Yes, sir!" Alexander notes that there was once a time "when the porter and other domestic servants of the white folks felt themselves superior to the Negro farm hand or the Negro laborer, or even the Negro mechanic." But now, as Hughes had shown with his powerful simplicity, "the porter realizes the servility of his position." The poem and Alexander's review both point to the African American worker's resentment of systematic economic discrimination.[65]

The 1927 edition also published Hughes's poem "Mulatto," in which Hughes addresses the topic of interracial sex in a different way from R. K. Fowler in "Slaves." Whereas Fowler's story features a white teenage girl initiating sex with a young black man, Hughes's poem deals with white men forcing themselves on black women. Lewis Alexander included the entire poem in his review and proclaimed it "the masterpiece of the book." The poem includes a harsh description of forced sex: "Juicy bodies / Of nigger wenches / Blue black / Against black fences. O, you little bastard boy, / What's a body but a toy?" Later in the poem, Hughes shifts to a different voice: "*Naw, you ain't my brother. / Niggers ain't my brother. / Not ever. / Niggers ain't my brother.*" But Hughes then ends the poem powerfully with the lines: "*I am your son, white man!* / A little yellow / Bastard boy." Alexander concludes: "Nowhere do we find a more powerful picture of a delicate Negro-White situation. Mr. Hughes has said in the space of one short poem all that can be said about the matter."[66]

Carolina Magazine continued with its annual Negro Number in 1928 and took another step toward recognizing African American talent by turning the volume over to Lewis Alexander. The issue again included Langston Hughes, as well as Countee Cullen, Alain Locke, and Arna Bontemps, among others. Perhaps the most daring piece in the May 1928 issue came when the students themselves editorialized on why they published a Negro Number of the *Carolina Magazine*. In this editorial, the students defined the "Negro Problem" as the product of racial injustice and oppression by white people. The editorial led off with a quick overview of the current labels used to discuss the topic of race:

"'The Negro Problem' we call it, spell it with capitals, and speak of it in whispers or when we are sure no negroes are near." But, it continued, in "back of the 'Problem' there lies a tangled mass of economics dealing with the necessity of cheap and non-competitive labor, of psychology dealing with the master-slave relation, racial domination on one hand and traditional racial subjection on the other, or sociology dealing with 'the alien menial in our midst.'" By defining the "problem" in terms of economics, psychology, and sociology, the students again bolstered UNC's claim to having the freedom and skill to research, learn, and then teach bold new perspectives on a matter central to southern life. Their approach to the subject sits in sharp contrast to their professors' lectures on physiology and the Negro-as-Lazarus lectures from the 1910s. This new approach also included African American contributions to the dialogue: as the editorial contended, "The so-called 'New Negro' is simply the intelligent negro given the chance to learn, to think, to express himself, and to do."[67]

The editorial next probed the inequities of segregation. The article listed the common southern white slogans—"Keep the negro in his place," "White supremacy," "the Unwritten Law," and "the Black Peril"—and noted that these phrases were all a product of the South's defeat in the Civil War, "when men desperately clung to the vanishing remnants of all that they held dear, phrases which have taken root in the hills, phrases which, throttling the lives of swarthy men of talent, have forced those men northward." The editorial pointedly asked: "How many years will it take to penetrate the mores and substitute for race-prejudice a sense of fair play and a doctrine of equal competition, which will remove the traditional, artificial restrictions from the negro?"[68] The editorial then juxtaposed the Fourteenth Amendment with state Jim Crow laws and concluded dramatically that "the equality so magnanimously granted by the Constitution (and so thoroughly withheld by us)" had to be made real "so that talent wherever it may be will not be driven from the south simply because the pigment of the skin is dark."[69]

The daring found in the *Carolina Magazine* was at times matched by the university's invitations to guest speakers. In March 1927, UNC welcomed NAACP leader James Weldon Johnson to campus.[70] Most white southerners viewed the NAACP with deep suspicion, if not outright hostility. It had not been very long since Eugene Brooks, an early leader in the North Carolina interracialist movement, had lumped the NAACP together with Bolsheviks and rapists as groups to be avoided.[71] (The

Daily Tar Heel cleverly described Johnson as the "negro poet," not mentioning his affiliation with the NAACP.) After an introduction by Howard Odum, Johnson also presented to UNC the newer, harder-hitting explanation of the "Negro Problem" of the 1920s. He took the time to define precisely what, in his mind, constituted "the race problem"— namely, "the gap between the actual status and the constitutional status of the negro." The "negro" itself was "not a problem, but a tremendous force." Their greatest obstacles were not genetics or heredity; they were rather the myriad of "'mental stereotypes' such as 'a negro will steal,' and 'a negro is lazy'" that whites held about African Americans.[72]

James Weldon Johnson's visit to UNC again elicited the unease that the subject of race relations created among university leaders, even as they treated his appearance as a purely academic event. Guy Johnson remembered that "a group of reactionary students actually discussed riding Johnson out of town on a rail," but that plan was averted.[73] Howard Odum received some criticism for his connection with the event. Writing to Gerald W. Johnson, Odum noted with some nervous bemusement that "we have had James Weldon Johnson before a half dozen sociology classes, three English classes, and Paul Green's groups and I have just learned that I am an open advocate of social equality."[74] Odum explained further, "I had nothing to do with bringing Johnson here, but I am surprised at friends Connor and Hamilton's militant attitude against it." Invoking the school's mission and academic freedom, he concluded, "I do not think any harm will come of it. . . . My feeling is that if they have been invited here that we ought to treat them in a straightforward manner. Either we ought not to have them or we ought to be straightforward and open about it."[75] In the end, Johnson was treated in a manner befitting a fellow scholar, a visit made possible and handled successfully by a university working to institutionalize the value of academic freedom.

The criticism Odum referred to came from UNC historians Robert D. W. Connor and J. G. de Roulhac Hamilton. Both wrote letters of protest to President Chase, although Connor apparently never sent his. Hamilton brought academic freedom's reliance on public trust into consideration by couching his racism within his concern for the public's reaction. For people like Guy Johnson, the university needed to protect academic freedom in order to develop expertise that society would eventually recognize as useful. Critics like Hamilton and Connor reversed the formula. For them, UNC first and always had to make sure that the public remained comfortable with the school's activities and usefulness, so it could maintain its academic freedom and expertise. Exercising academic freedom that the public found extreme or irresponsible threatened the entire enterprise and was not worth doing.

Hamilton was especially outraged that Johnson was allowed to take over "ordinary classes" and not just advanced seminars for the day. "The thing is without excuse," he complained. "It certainly is unwise; publicity would lead to an explosion that would shake the institution to its foundation."[76] As a devout segregationist and white supremacist, Hamilton could never let a black man like Johnson into the ranks of "experts." Therefore, Johnson's visit was not a legitimate exercise of academic freedom. Here, then, was an example of the messiness of academic freedom on the ground: the success of James Weldon Johnson's visit depended on the ability of campus leadership to balance the public trust the university relied on with the academic freedom it needed. And that balancing act did not take place in a vacuum.

As Hamilton's analysis warned, given the racist context in which they lived, interracialists like Odum and Guy Johnson had to be careful when expressing what exactly the academic freedom to discuss and study race relations would lead to; their opponents, on the other hand, only had to warn against losing public trust. Hamilton contended that the issue surrounding James Weldon Johnson's visit was not whether he approved of the visit; it was not whether he thought the visit was good or bad for the students. The matter at hand was simply a question of what people would say about it and how that would affect the university. He continued at length: "There are thousands of people in the state who would want no better opportunity to emphasize the point they have been making that the University is out of touch with the people, that it is contemptuous of the people of the state, that it is in control of Northern and Western men who have no regard for public opinion." Hamilton tried to argue that he had "no sympathy with such an attitude," but he in fact did. UNC's invitation of Johnson displayed "a perfectly unjustifiable disregard . . . of the conviction of the people of the state, and of the whole South, that there must be no yielding on the question of admission of the negro to equality." Whether white southerners felt this way out of "prejudice or wisdom" was, in Hamilton's assessment, "entirely beside the question." It was a fact. That fact, combined with the southern insistence that "it is quite within the right of the people who support the University to speak with authority on the question," meant that UNC should not have invited Johnson. Hamilton's concluding remark was revealing: "Personally, I think their position is right, and I am in full sympathy with it."[77]

Hamilton's contention that the basis for white southerners' views of African Americans (i.e., "prejudice or wisdom") was "entirely beside the question" would have left men like Guy Johnson flabbergasted. Having the academic freedom as a sociologist to examine white southern racial consciousness—that is, how white southerners came to believe what they believed—was entirely the question for Johnson. Further, in the interest of maintaining the public's trust, Hamilton had tossed aside the university's claim to expertise (including, therefore, his own) by ceding it to "the people" and their questionable ability to "speak with authority" on southern race relations.

James Weldon Johnson's visit left an indelible impression on at least one UNC student. D. D. Carroll, the associate editor of the *Tar Heel*, wrote a lengthy, thoughtful editorial on Johnson's visit that reflected university leaders' aspirations perfectly. "A few weeks ago, the student body at a Southern university saw a beautiful example of the progress which men may make," Carroll began. Careful to characterize Johnson as a "scholarly negro," Carroll described how the poet spoke before "students of a state institution in a section where prejudice toward the blacks is most people's false 'culture.' But from the brief visit of this representative of a misjudged race," young white southern students had "struck from their minds the shackles which ignorance, beg-brained organizations, and economic injustices forged long ago." Carroll continued: "To a fellow man whose color has long provoked the scowls of Southerners, the student body of this Southern university extended a hearty welcome; these white leaders of tomorrow forgot their savagery and achieved a smile. . . . Today the scene is remarkably changed." Carroll proclaimed James Weldon Johnson "a national leader of his emancipated race" and "an exalted leader" at that.[78] Carroll concluded that UNC had "acted her motto—*Lux et Libertas* [Light and Liberty]. . . . The faculty can do much to sustain liberal thought on this subject. Will it?"[79]

For the time being, UNC's leaders felt confident that their academic freedom to examine the issue of race relations was helping lead the South toward a better racial situation. The contrast between the YMCA lectures on race relations in the 1910s, with their condescending views of African American potential, and the views expressed in *Carolina Magazine* at the end of the 1920s clearly indicates the dramatic shift that took place not only in race thinking in the academy but also in the political and economic context of the post–World War I years. Whereas men like Eugene C. Branson associated African Americans with Lazarus left to eat crumbs, Guy Johnson had already sensed Jim Crow's indefensibility, the student editors of the *Carolina Magazine* presented actual African Americans as brilliant writers, and the *Tar Heel* proclaimed James Weldon Johnson an "exalted leader."

2

"Go Ahead and Do Harm"

The Academic Study of Labor Relations

In 1924, Howard Odum eagerly anticipated launching a new study of conditions in North Carolina's textile industry and mill villages, under the auspices of the Institute for Research in Social Science (IRSS). The project's scope fit perfectly within the core mission of the IRSS, which was to initiate a "cooperative study of problems in the general field of social science, arising out of state and regional conditions."[1] Writing to his colleague Harriet Herring, Odum looked forward to the trust and cooperation he expected from the textile manufacturers: "I am sure no one would misunderstand us because we are working for the same purpose."[2] Others at UNC made similar assumptions. The year before, UNC president Harry Chase had written an article weaving together the school's expertise with the trust he presumed the state to have in that expertise. Chase wrote in the *Journal of Social Forces* that, even though he thought it unlikely, "it would indeed be tragic were an institution whose faculty is made up of competent specialists, and supported by the citizens generally, not to put at the immediate disposal of men and women . . . the benefits of its knowledge and skill in an immediate way."[3] Alan Tullos quotes sociologist Eugene Branson's assurances to Upton Sinclair that the university was "far beyond the reach of organized big business and the politicians of the state. We are free here to consider the foundational problems of life and livelihood in North Carolina, whether these concerns have to do with agriculture, manufacturing, capital, labor, whatnot."[4] By a wide margin, Branson, Odum, and Chase all turned out to be overly optimistic.

Once university researchers sought to bring their expertise to bear on the problems of industrial relations, they inadvertently initiated a bruising conflict with some of the state's textile industry leadership.[5] As UNC sociologist Guy B. Johnson recalled years later, "In some ways the conservative industrial faction was worse than the [conservative] race faction."[6] Attacks from textile industry spokesman David Clark, editor of the *Southern Textile Bulletin*, did the most damage to the university's research efforts and exacted a heavy personal toll on Chase and Odum. A relentless reactionary, Clark rejected the legitimacy of the university's search for industry "facts" and questioned the university's trustworthiness and its defense of academic freedom. Chase, worn down by years of attacks, eventually tried to narrow the parameters of academic freedom for his faculty by suggesting they funnel their expertise into safer channels, and Odum's goals for service to the state also grew considerably more cautious. By the end of the decade, it was often UNC students who championed the university's academic freedom to ask hard questions of the textile industry.

UNC began to consider the problems of labor in earnest when it hired Eugene C. Branson in 1914. Branson created the Department of Rural Economics and Sociology and a rural extension service that allowed him to begin investigating the living conditions of poorer North Carolinians. In 1916 Branson acknowledged that the growing millhand population was reaching a level worthy of investigation, but "the question of child labor in the country regions is a far bigger problem in the South."[7] This emphasis soon changed.

Tar Heel writers floated a rumor in 1919 that "a group of the University's ablest writers" were working together to produce a fictionalized yet "gripping story of modern industrial life." Even though they predicted being able to soon read "of titanic struggle between Capital and Labor, Bolshevism and Democracy opposing each other," it was apparently just a rumor.[8] Yet interest in the state of industrialization was increasing on campus.

In the midst of a brief post–World War I season of labor unrest in North Carolina, invitations to guest lecturers gave more evidence of the efforts UNC made to approach industrialization and labor relations as topics worthy of close academic inquiry. In 1920, L. E. Nichols of the American Federation of Labor (AFL), an organization energized by wartime promises to industrial labor, spoke before a UNC audience by invitation of the School of Commerce. Nichols outlined the organization's principles and assured listeners that his was not a radical organization along the lines of the Industrial Workers of the World (IWW).[9] The AFL has "no toleration for the IWW, Reds, Bolshevists, etc. . . . It is this propaganda of these IWW, etc., that has scarred the name of organized labor and I am here to discredit it on behalf of the American Federation of Labor." As the *Daily Tar Heel* reporter explained, the AFL "resents" the image of the worker being "not as Americanized as the man who sits at the desk as president of a bank. . . . No one has been more outspoken against radicalism and socialism than the American Federation of Labor."[10]

In August 1921, Governor Cameron Morrison sent troops to quell textile worker unrest in Concord, North Carolina, drawing even more attention to the troubled state of labor relations.[11] In November of that year, James Barrett—head of the North Carolina Federation of Labor and a man credited with having helped end textile strikes in Concord and Charlotte—gave a sharply worded analysis of the current labor situation. He first sounded a note bound to please UNC leaders by making "a plea for more conscientious study of the capital-labor problem." Then he rose to a strong defense of organized labor. "Under existing conditions," Barrett explained, "with capital organized as it is, the labor union is the only way. The organized laborer is not asking for control of the plant in which he works; he is only asking for a voice in the regulation of three things—wages, hours, and working conditions." Barrett also addressed the anxieties over "foreigners" in the labor force, but first "blamed the manufacturers who often discriminated in favor of cheap foreign labor." He concluded pointedly: "The labor problem will never be solved by abuse and bitter criticism on the part of the public and the newspapers."[12] The student newspaper applauded the university's invitation to Barrett as appropriate to the modern UNC's mission. His visit brought "to the University and student body a very vital connection with the thought and actions of life" beyond the campus. Barrett represented "a man, who in the greater world of affairs, is doing things that are a part of the great trend of the times," namely, "the great movements that in organized labor are vitally affecting the whole nation today."[13]

UNC's growing interest in labor relations as a topic of academic inquiry was bound to catch the always-nervous eye of Charlotte's David Clark, who emerged in the 1920s as one of the most outspoken critics of organized labor. He had been instrumental in instigating what George Tindall describes as a "propaganda campaign" against the workers during the 1921 textile strike.[14] Clark also grew into one of the most hostile critics of UNC; his attacks represented a full-blown challenge not just to the university's activities but to its very identity as a modern research university dependent on its academic freedom to perform its function.

Clark's animosity toward UNC seems to have begun in 1923, when Howard Odum's *Journal of Social Forces* published an article written by child-labor-law advocate Owen Lovejoy.[15] By that time Clark had successfully defeated federal child-labor legislation twice, initiating challenges to 1916 and 1919 child labor laws that were eventually found unconstitutional by the U.S. Supreme Court.[16] The mere sight of Lovejoy's name routinely sent Clark into histrionics, and this time was no exception.

David Clark's response to the Lovejoy article in *Social Forces* pointedly rejected the idea of academic freedom as a necessary function of university expertise. Clark adopted the skeptical view, present from the beginning of academia's professionalization, that expertise was clever cover for radical political agendas. He detected "dangerous tendencies" in the university's new interest in industrial relations and characterized Lovejoy, a leader of the National Child Labor Committee, as a "parasite" and a "professional agitator." Clark then folded UNC in with a slashing condemnation of labor leader and Columbia University professor Frank Tannenbaum, "an ex-convict and confessed Red," for an article he wrote for *The Century.* The article, "The South Buries Its Anglo-Saxons," outraged textile manufacturers, Clark claimed, and it "was conceived if not actually written at Chapel Hill."[17] (In 1924, Tannenbaum's articles were republished as the *Darker Phases of the South.* In it, he acknowledged Odum, Branson, and UNC sociologist Frederick Steiner "for the many suggestions and help given me.")[18] Clark complained that UNC was "going aside from its purposes and its intended work." The university, he maintained, "was never intended as a breeding place for socialism and communism but when professors and instructors turn aside from their duties as teachers of regular courses and seek to develop fads and fancies, great injury to our State may develop."[19] (Clark would not have been pleased to learn that Lovejoy had given a talk at UNC in 1922.)[20]

Clark's editorial attacked the issue of expertise that was so central to UNC's mission of establishing academic freedom. Clark flatly refused to consider college professors as "experts." Instead of chasing "fads and fancies"—what UNC professors would have called "research"—Clark

Howard Washington Odum, nationally recognized UNC sociologist.

defined the proper role of college professors as "teachers of regular courses." His column concerned John J. Parker, a promising attorney and UNC alumnus, so much that he recommended to Howard Odum that the university "either defend its action in accepting contributions from these people or . . . proceed to get rid of them as associates."[21]

Rather than defend his and his colleagues' expertise, Odum opted to play nice with Clark while worrying privately about what attacks like these portended. Gerald W. Johnson wrote to Howard Odum, urging him to stay strong. By insisting that the South had problems that needed fixing, the IRSS was "bound to do harm, praise God! Go ahead and do harm. The South needs a whole lot of harm done to its complacent self-satisfaction."[22] To Harry Chase, the anxious president of UNC, Odum predicted that he could earn the cranky editor's trust. "The whole matter is the saddest that I have run across," he noted. "I shall, however, make a personal friend of Mr. Clark and have him working with us. See if I don't? . . . Personally I am glad to have this kind of editorial. The more extreme they are the less harm, and the sooner we can get into common discussions of these common interests by all groups the better it will be for us."[23]

With Parker, Odum struck a tougher note: "The more I look at that editorial in the *Textile Bulletin* the more it seems to me there ought to be some way to prevent the recurrence of this kind of misinterpretation. If it were directed toward a person would it not be a matter of considerable libel? Is not the reputation of the University of far greater importance than that of one person?"[24] Odum and Harry Chase were just starting to learn that the "more extreme" criticism caused more harm, not less. Odum also failed to take advantage of the opportunity to defend the university's expertise, a defense that may not have convinced David Clark but that would have further edified the university's supporters regarding just what the mission of the modern university was and why it required academic freedom.

Responding to John J. Parker's concerns, President Harry Chase, on the other hand, pushed away any threat of radicalism by linking UNC's expertise and academic freedom to North Carolina's modernization and progress. UNC, he reminded Parker, had "steadily stood for the advancement of the industrial life of the state in important and far reaching ways. . . . If any one who knows the facts will think it over," they would clear the university of any charges of radicalism. Cleverly, Chase predicted Parker's certain agreement on the importance of academic freedom to the school's mission: "Freedom of discussion is one of the things for which the University has always stood, as you know, and for which it should continue to stand, as you will agree." Chase knew that university studies would "now and then" produce research "with whose view point as a whole there may not be general agreement." But, he continued, "I know that you would consider it just as great a tragedy as I would that for such reasons the University ever in anyway abridged . . . freedom of discussion. It is, after all, only by such freedom that truth comes, and I know you feel that every bit as strongly as I do."[25] Chase thus offered a clear assertion of the freedom to develop academic expertise as a morally defensible professional imperative, essential to the university's mission. Parker accepted the explanation along the lines Chase laid out: "I thoroughly agree with you that the University should maintain an atmosphere of freedom and that neither thought nor discussion shall be limited or restrained. . . . I think that the editorial in the *Textile Bulletin* must have been written without proper information."[26]

Through the 1920s, both Chase and Odum learned that people like David Clark were not necessarily concerned with having the "proper information." Responding the next year to an inquiry by Governor A. W. McLean about rumors of excessive drinking among UNC students, Chase complained that "it is quite hopeless to try to convince the detractors of the University who want systematically to try to do everything possible to injure it."[27] It was a hard, demoralizing lesson to learn.

Events in 1925 gave David Clark new opportunities to attack UNC's inclusion of labor relations as a topic of legitimate academic inquiry and its ambition to offer possible solutions through research. In September 1925, Clark read in the *Tar Heel* that the school's North Carolina Club intended to undertake a "study of North Carolina's social and economic ills with a view to seeking a remedy."[28] Clark, in response, again trotted out his objection that research into such things fell outside the university's mission: "The object of a University is to educate young men, not to reform the social and economic fabric of a state. The study of social and economic evils should be left to mature men and women and not to immature college students under the direction of professors who are inexperienced in business and notoriously impractical." Clark concluded by stoking fears of the university as a "breeding ground for reformers."[29] Whereas UNC leaders were open about their willingness to consider the need for reform, to conservatives like Clark reform meant radicalism, and he routinely linked the two to discredit the university mission and undermine the public's trust in it.

Clark launched another attack on UNC later in 1925 when Odum's IRSS proposed to the North Carolina Cotton Manufacturers Association that they conduct a joint study of the state's textile industry, focusing especially on the nagging problem of high labor turnover. Their research would include studies of mobility, personal morals, and cost of living among workers in mill villages.[30] Befitting the university belief in the social usefulness of expertise, the proposal pledged the IRSS's "desire only to render a public service. It is not interested in controversy. It has no desire either to prove charges or disprove counter charges. Its sole interest is to discover the truth and make that truth available not only for North Carolina but also for the entire South." UNC researchers "have had sufficient training in scientific research to arrive at conclusions based only upon actual discoverable facts."[31] The results of the investigation would be to "build up a body of knowledge on the whole subject of social-industrial relationships that will be useful to students of the industry, to the mills themselves, and to the people of North Carolina and the south." The IRSS would therefore "become a receiver and interpreter of facts" as well as a "distributor of facts and a contributor to Southern economic and social progress."[32] Odum and IRSS researcher Harriet Herring, a native North Carolinian with textile industry experience, worked on the proposal for more than a year; they remained optimistic, and perhaps naive, about its prospects.[33]

On the eve of the North Carolina Cotton Manufacturers Association's semiannual meeting in late 1925, Clark resumed his attack on the university by again linking its academic freedom with radicalism. "We believe that a college should attend strictly to the education of young men," Clark wrote, "and we can see no good reason for outside activities and investigations. . . . We know that such investigations breed radicals."[34] Harriet Herring traveled to Pinehurst to present the IRSS's proposal to the manufacturers, but they denied her the opportunity to speak before the association. Clark gloated over the rejection: "The business meeting turned down unanimously the request. . . . There was no mistaking the idea of the manufacturers that the university should 'stick to its knitting' and not engage in the pastime of breeding radicals and reformers."[35] Herring's work was redirected to conduct a more limited survey of welfare work in mill villages. UNC Press published *Welfare Work in Mill Villages: The Story of Extra-Mill Activities in North Carolina* in 1929, and President Chase sent several copies to textile manufacturers as an example of, as Guy and Guion Johnson recall, "patient, reasonable"—that is, safe—research.[36]

David Clark's charges reveal a perception of the university that would continue to produce problems for UNC through the 1930s as well. His criticisms did have a point: having the freedom to utilize their expertise in the service of possible change or reform was at the heart of the university's self-image. University leaders such as Chase and Odum expected the efforts of highly trained experts to be welcomed by a state and region in dire need of reform. How could anyone object to the university using its expertise to help lift the South out of its undeniable backwardness? If one rejected the claim that that was what the school was doing, then an objection could be made quite easily. By equating research and reform with radicalism, David Clark did just that.

What individuals like Chase and Odum were still struggling to learn was that the battle with Clark was not simply over what initiatives the university could launch in the short term. In order to achieve the kind of academic freedom that would allow expert research to be conducted and eventually put to the benefit of society, UNC needed to educate southerners on the value of its entire mission and gain their trust. A strong, steady defense of academic freedom and expertise would help achieve this trust, even if the university met with short-term defeats off campus.

In the eyes of other southerners, the very process of generating discussion of the IRSS proposal—even though the proposal failed—solidified UNC's reputation for academic freedom and expertise, and it legitimized questioning of the textile industry. The *Greensboro Daily News* editorialized that the firm rejection "stimulates curiosity as to why the approval was refused and as to what conditions the cotton mill men do not wish to be studied. . . . When the manufacturers oppose such a study they make it more difficult but they will not stop it. They will inevitably cause more persons to wonder why they oppose it."[37] The student-run *Carolina Magazine* weighed in along similar lines as the *Greensboro Daily News*: "We cannot conceive of a real university which does not definitely interest itself in accumulating, recording, and making available information concerning the living conditions of its people. And equally hard is it for us to conceive of an intelligent mill owner who would not either provide for himself, or cause some agency to provide for him, a comparative study of living conditions." The writer recognized correctly that this matter went to the core of UNC's identity: "A university cannot keep its self-respect as a university and avoid the responsibility of making knowledge available for the use of those who know or think they know the value and use of knowledge."[38]

Nonetheless, by the end of 1925, President Chase indicated that the university would not pursue the matter any further.[39] Both Chase and Odum had been bruised badly by fights with David Clark over academic freedom and with Christian fundamentalists over the issue of evolution.[40] Odum wrote in early 1926 that he thought it best to remain "very much in the background awhile."[41]

But if Chase and Odum thought backing down would placate David Clark, they were sadly mistaken. Clark continued to campaign against what he began calling "the Meddling Departments of the University of North Carolina."[42] He also warned of retribution against UNC: "The university will feel it when the next legislature meets. . . . The manufacturers can and will cause the legislature to cut the appropriation of the university if they persist in making studies unwelcome to them."[43] (Clark later tried to deny he made this comment, but the *Raleigh News & Observer*, which published the quote, reaffirmed its accuracy with their reporter.)[44]

Raleigh journalist Nell Battle Lewis, normally an ally of UNC during the interwar years, chastised the university for backing down from the textile industry. She complained that UNC had received its "orders" from the textile leaders and "accepted them without protest." She pointed directly to the expertise available at UNC and concluded sadly that "there is no phase of the life in North Carolina about which less authoritative and unprejudiced information is available than about the textile industry. And as long as the cotton manufacturers have their way this will continue to be the case."[45] A writer in *Carolina Magazine* chimed in: "So unless Nell Battle Lewis will write us an article on this subject, we fear the manufacturers will go unexposed for some time yet."[46] *Carolina Magazine* was correct: hard-hitting investigations of the textile industry were not forthcoming from the IRSS.[47]

Being criticized by a friend like Nell Battle Lewis no doubt stung, but at the same time other university friends continued to defend the school's expertise and its need for academic freedom. In March 1926, the *Greensboro Daily News* published a lengthy, glowing article on the work of the IRSS. The author began by pointing out again the crying need for expertise in a changing, modernizing South. Think, the writer asked, of the hundreds of local government officials, the "poor fellows who puff and strain in their efforts to cope with the problems of the average small town." Where could the local government official "get information on the particular questions that bother him?" Thankfully, North Carolina had some leaders who saw that the modern university "ought to be a great repository of learning made available to any citizen of the state who needs it."[48]

The *Greensboro Daily News* countered Clark's message of fear by painting a frightening image of a future without the guidance of UNC's expertise. It noted how, historically, industrialization had produced social unrest and violence. The paper cited Lancashire, England, as an example: "Before Lancashire settled down into a stable industrial region dreadful things happened there—brutal contests between capital and labor, attended by all manner of violence, destruction of property and lives, and the engendering of bitter and lasting hatreds." The pattern repeated itself in New England later. The conclusion was clear: "Looking back now, it is easy to see how much of it might have been prevented by just a little wisdom, foresight and tolerance. . . . The only question is, are we going to have the wisdom, foresight and tolerance that those others lacked?"[49] This was a clever rhetorical maneuver: whereas Clark highlighted the dire consequences of "radicalism" at the university, the *Greensboro Daily Times* turned the tables by pinning the responsibility for future violence on the intransigence of people like David Clark. Far from being a "breeding ground of radicals," the university's expertise and academic freedom were potential sources of stability for North Carolina and the entire South.

Despite this strong defense, Chase and Odum continued to withdraw from the field. In one remarkable incident, the two men squelched an IRSS project in dramatic fashion. In April 1927, Chase wrote to James A. Gray, a UNC trustee and an executive at Winston-Salem's R. J. Reynolds Tobacco Company, making vague reference to "the matter we discussed the other night" as "making a favorable progress." Chase said that "in a few days I think I shall be able to let you know of its accomplishment" and thanked Gray "for letting me know about this situation as you did."[50]

It turns out that "the matter" referred to in Chase's letter was a small study begun by IRSS researcher Robinson Newcomb, an Oberlin College graduate. Newcomb started a research project on the African American business community of Winston-Salem; as he recalled, he "interviewed in every Negro business establishment. I found out what they were selling, how much, and so on." But to determine just how much economic potential a black-owned business could have, Newcomb needed to find out the income level of local, working-class African Americans. He hoped to get an idea of the wage levels of black workers at R. J. Reynolds, but the company refused to share its information with him. Undeterred, Newcomb began waiting outside the factory gates on payday, where he would find the company's African American workers leaving for the day. He explained that "the men were paid in cash in envelopes. They tore the envelopes apart, took out the money and threw the envelopes on the street. I got the envelopes [and the receipts left in them] for a few weeks and so learned what the wages were."[51] Newcomb then went on to complete his study, but his clever research strategy "made the R. J. Reynolds Company mad" and prompted James A. Gray to lean on Chase.[52]

Chase and Howard Odum complied with chilling thoroughness. In early May 1927, Chase reported back to Gray:

> Our understanding reached the other night . . . has been carried out. All copies of the manuscript of the study of the negro business concerns in Winston-Salem have been recalled and destroyed, with the exception of one copy which Mr. Fries wrote Mr. Odum he had personally destroyed. The questionnaires and notes which formed the basis of this study have also been destroyed. I have personally seen to the destruction of this material so that there would be no question about it. The study begun in Winston-Salem has been abandoned, and I believe, therefore, that the situation is undoubtedly cleaned up in accordance with our understanding.

This is to say, it was cleared up in accordance with Gray's wishes. Concluding, Chase reached a new low in groveling: "I want to say once again how much I am obliged to you for calling this matter to my attention, and I am certain that such an incident will not be repeated."[53] Chase explained euphemistically to reporters that Newcomb's work was "unsatisfactory to the Institute at the University, and it was not utilized."[54] Odum fired Newcomb on the grounds that he was conducting research beyond his proposed study.[55] He later instructed IRSS researcher T. J. Woofter to explain "about Newcombe's [sic] Winston-Salem work that it was unreliable and, therefore, not usable. I am afraid that if we put it only on the basis of controversy he will add this to his martyr complex and start another story about us being afraid of something."[56] In fact, Chase and Odum were afraid of something: they were afraid to push too hard against the state's manufacturing elite.

Still, in 1927, Clark was back again, stirring up fears of subversion stemming from UNC and painting the modern university as providing cover for political radicalism. In an April 1927 article in the *Southern*

Textile Bulletin, Clark explained that "in the South, with our freedom from foreign blood, people are patriotic and go quietly about their business with little realization of the tremendous undercurrent of communism and anarchy that prevails in certain circles in other sections." Clark detected communism infiltrating the YMCA, the YWCA, Washington bureaucracies, and the Federal Council of Churches of Christ in America. "While the communistic forces utilize the Church and other agencies whenever they can do so to their advantage, they really seek their destruction," he explained.[57] Clark was johnny-on-the-spot in December when Paul Blanshard, "a college professor and a socialist," organized a meeting in Greensboro to coordinate efforts to reduce North Carolina workers' minimum weekly hours from sixty to fifty-four. Clark seemed almost giddy about a handful of UNC professors being present at the meeting.[58]

Blanshard, an investigator for the socialist-oriented League for Industrial Democracy, had been in contact with Howard Odum for some time, trying to convince him to join forces for yet another study of the textile industry. Not surprisingly, Odum refused, not because of his own rejection by the textile industry but rather because there were already too many studies going on at the time, he said. Undeterred, Blanshard came to Chapel Hill in early 1927 to consult the ongoing research being done by IRSS members Harriet Herring and Jennings J. Rhyne. After completing his work, Blanshard still hoped to woo the famous UNC sociologist, so he sent Odum the manuscript of his article in hopes of an endorsing quote. Odum refused and instead gave it a sharp critique as being unbalanced and riddled with factual errors.[59] Blanshard went ahead and published two articles critical of the textile industry and life in the mill villages in the *New Republic* in September 1927.[60] His hopes for following up his articles with a movement for labor reform led him to call the Greensboro meeting in December, which was attended by UNC professors Frank Graham, Harry M. Cassidy, Thomas Holland, and G. T. Schwenning, along with Nell Battle Lewis.[61]

David Clark pounced, using the happy confluence of UNC professors, the socialist Paul Blanshard, and proposed workers' rights legislation to launch a new round of attacks against the radicalism UNC encouraged through its academic freedom. He tied the professors' attendance at the meeting to their work as faculty members and hinted again at a radical conspiracy. For Clark, the role of a modern university professor included at its secret core a radicalism that threatened the South. Academic freedom was therefore part of the conspiracy. "Some day, but possibly too late," he growled, "the business men of America are going to realize that the greatest menace of this country is the modern college professor." This new villain, "while drawing a salary for teaching, feels that part of his duties is to cure all the ills of the State and to regulate the conduct and the affairs of the public." Once again, research and reform meant radicalism. "Into our colleges have come radicals, communists, atheists," Clark charged. "If the average business man could sit for one week in the class rooms of some colleges and hear the insidious doctrines that are being taught he would feel like taking a stick and driving out the vipers that infest them." Clark went after Blanshard specifically, linking him to UNC and paying special attention to the fact that in a recent article, Blanshard had criticized other universities because, in Clark's words, "they refuse to follow the lead of the University of North Carolina and become the refuge of radicals and socialists."[62]

Clark complained, "No one has ever explained to us why men who are employed to teach in universities and colleges feel that curing the social evils of the State are [sic] part of their duties," a statement that ignored a small mountain of articles and hours of speeches delivered by university leaders since the beginning of the decade.[63] University leaders in fact constantly explained that the university's mission had changed from the classical emphasis of the nineteenth century to the twentieth century's mission of public service through expertise and academic freedom. Nonetheless, Clark once again anticipated a confrontation with the university: "The time has come for a showdown and the people of North Carolina must decide whether or not a lot paid to teach in their colleges shall claim the right to make laws and regulate the industries."[64] This was more Clark hyperbole. University researchers never claimed the right to make laws or regulate industries. But as Chase and Odum had learned by then, Clark was not especially interested in having all his facts straight; he was interested in weakening the state's trust in UNC. For that purpose, rumors and allegations were more useful than facts. For good measure, Clark added that the "never ending stream of these radicals, atheists, and sexologists as lecturers at our colleges and universities" prompted him to wonder "if there is not more of an organization behind this movement than has been realized."[65]

Discouraged by the constant fighting with Clark and the fundamentalists (and already entertaining new job offers),[66] Chase in early 1928 began to backpedal from his earlier defense of UNC's academic freedom. In March, Chase wrote a long memo to Howard Odum, Frank Graham, and Dudley DeWitt Carroll, "just a basis for discussion," outlining his rapidly narrowing definition of academic freedom, specifically in the social sciences.[67] "A man who enters a university faculty in any of the fields of social science," he declared, "takes upon himself the obligation to be a scientist, and not a social reformer." He continued:

> The whole theory of university education in America draws such a distinction. The social scientist is human: he has his sympathies and prejudices, but he is not engaged by a university for these, but for his competencies as a scientist. If his sympathies and prejudices color his work, if he desires to advocate this or that cause of social reform, the institution has the right to say to him, "You were not engaged for this. You have no right to maintain yourself at the expense of the university in order to forward your own views and sympathies. If you desire to engage in the advocacy of this or that social cause, you must sever your connection with the institution and work through other channels."[68]

Chase began to swing to David Clark's view that research not welcomed by the state should not be welcomed by the university either:

> As a matter of fact, [university] men do engage in the advocacy of such causes as better educational facilities, the promotion of health and sanitation, civic improvements, church causes and the like, and there is no thought of impropriety. On the other hand, it is equally true that no one would question the fact that no member of a university faculty can with propriety advocate certain things. Some of these are general; e.g., the overthrow of government by armed forces. Some are more local in character; e.g., certain phases of the race problem in Southern states— mixed schools, for example. Where can a line be drawn?[69]

Chase had again arrived at the awkward position of saying that it was okay for university professors to advocate for some things, but not for others (even when the advocacy was a product of work done from within their own disciplines). This was largely the same position his critics took, and it placed UNC far from what its mission had been at the beginning of the decade, when Chase himself hoped the fruits of the university's expertise and academic freedom would proceed "wherever and in whatever form it is our privilege to see the need."[70]

Even more significantly, Chase attempted to redefine a scholar's unpopular views as the product of "sympathies," a word he repeated throughout the memo, always in a negative light. "Sympathies," in Chase's view, were not objective in the way that "expertise" was, a common assumption in the 1920s. But Chase then threatened punishment for vaguely defined offenses, these products of misplaced "sympathies," and in the process conferred tremendous power upon administrators such as himself: "No faculty member has any right to allow his personal sympathies for any controversial cause to involve his colleagues and his institution in a situation that means general embarrassment, restricted educational opportunities for students and threatened careers for his colleagues. . . . If his sympathy for such a cause becomes sufficiently strong to raise in his mind a real conflict with his institutional loyalty, he should obviously sever his connections to the institution."[71]

This passage restricted faculty members' academic freedom to whatever a college president determined was not embarrassing or a product of "sympathy." With this remarkable redefinition, Chase ran the danger of undermining UNC's entire mission, considering the university had enemies willing to distort facts about university professors and their activities in order to cause such embarrassment. Guy and Guion Griffis Johnson concluded later that Chase's memo was "probably meant as a warning."[72] Economics professor Harry Cassidy, who had attended the Greensboro meeting and who elsewhere had disputed textile industry claims of high worker wages, left UNC at the end of the school year amid accusations of a political firing; Chase had deemed him "not ripe for promotion."[73]

A comparison of Chase's positions in this memorandum with those of another leader in American education—Arthur Lovejoy, a founding member of the AAUP—shows how far the UNC president had retreated from the bold pronouncements in his 1920 inaugural address. In 1930, Lovejoy reaffirmed the idea that the academic freedom that was key to unlocking the utilitarian value of the university was "rendered impossible if the work of the investigator is shackled by the requirement that his conclusions shall never seriously deviate from generally accepted beliefs or from those accepted by the persons, private or official, through whom society provides the means for the maintenance of the universities."[74]

Chase had to know he was tacking in a different direction from the one he had charted out at the beginning of the decade. Unfortunately, he returned to his conclusion, which in essence defined the university's mission as whatever Chase determined the public would tolerate, a point he tried to finesse. "To what causes does the above apply? There is no possible general statement. They will vary from time to time, from place to place." Chase's next comment attempted to establish limits reflecting the lay of the land politically in 1928: "In North Carolina they certainly involve, for example, advocacy of particular forms of taxation, of the organization of labor, of social equality between races, of a socialistic regime, etc."[75] As this book argues, labor and race issues were the two key issues UNC researchers and leaders identified as problems most in need of the university's expertise to solve. If UNC scholars under Chase's orders avoided addressing them–especially those trained to study labor and race relations—the university's modern mission was in danger of becoming meaningless.

The relentlessness—and, at times, the disingenuousness—of the university's opponents, especially the Christian fundamentalists and David Clark, caused Chase to wonder privately just what the university was capable of in such a climate and whether "the University can try to render service of an expert kind in public matters without having to pay for it politically." He pondered in amazement the treatment of individual professors:

> Even Mr. [Eugene C.] Branson, with his years of intelligent service, is very much in bad just now with certain elements in the state. I don't know of a more conservative man than [D. D.] Carroll [head of the School of Commerce]. In fact, I sometimes think he leans a little backward in his conservatism, and yet I suppose half the mill men in the state would tell you with perfect sincerity that he is a socialist, a radical, and perhaps a Bolshevik. I don't know a better Christian gentleman than Odum, or a man with greater passion for the South, and yet you know some of the things he had to go through.[76]

Chase now found it "very curious the way everything seems to focus on the University." But instead of redoubling his efforts to defend the university's academic freedom and maintain the public's trust in UNC, Chase speculated gloomily on the future: "It seems to me it would be a great pity if the University were forced to retreat within the walls of its campus, and yet that is a possibility."[77] Retreat, in fact, was precisely what Chase recommended. He lamented the "many things we would like to do and don't do, just because we don't think they are wise in the present state of public opinion."[78] Harry Chase had lost sight of the fact that reassuring a worried public while enabling the faculty to offer expert service to that same public without fear of retribution was his job.

Despite the hand-wringing, the times were on the side of UNC's efforts to shine some kind of light upon labor conditions. Even David Clark could not hide the fact that the textile industry in the late 1920s was faltering badly. Following the heady post–World War I promise of industrial harmony, the Piedmont's textile industry changed throughout the 1920s in significant ways.[79] The sense of mill-owner paternalism was disappearing quickly, to be replaced by "efficiency studies," frequent job cuts, and speed-ups. Phillip J. Wood notes that even the state's vaunted educational reforms were undertaken with an eye toward maintaining a ready supply of cheap, young workers.[80] By the late 1920s, textile workers had developed what George Brown Tindall described as a "cotton-mill caste" identity: "Mill children went to mill schools; mill workers went to mill churches; and on Saturday afternoons they met an ill-concealed contempt from the people downtown."[81]

The millhands also grew more receptive to calls to organize, from unions such as the AFL, the United Textile Workers, and, before long, the communist-led National Textile Workers Union (NTWU). On March 12, 1929, tensions between workers and mill owners boiled over. Starting in Elizabethton, Tennessee, and moving rapidly into North Carolina, textile workers struck quickly and effectively. In response, Elizabethton business leaders kidnapped two labor leaders and dropped them off separately in North Carolina and Virginia with stern instructions not to return. Meanwhile, in mid-March, a representative from the NTWU, Fred Beal, made his way to Gastonia, North Carolina, and began to organize there. Gastonia workers faced implementation of the "stretch out" (forcing workers to operate more machines simultaneously), two 10-percent wage cuts, and a reduction of the work force by nearly one-third. By April 1, a majority of the Gastonia workers at the Loray Mill, led by Beal and the NTWU, struck over a range of issues: a minimum wage, a forty-hour week, equal pay for women and children, ending the stretch out, better living conditions and lower rent in the mill houses, and union recognition. When the mill superintendent refused to even negotiate, Gastonia and especially the Loray Mill became the focal point for communist union organizing.[82]

The communists' presence gave mill owners and the state and local governments the opportunity to wave the red flag and warn against revolution. Governor O. Max Gardner, a textile plant owner and a UNC graduate and trustee, ordered the state militia in, and the owners threatened retaliation against

Button supporting Gastonia textile workers, 1929.

the strikers. In a tense, swirling set of circumstances, some frightened strikers went back to work even while the NTWU continued to gain new members. Community leaders organized a Committee of One Hundred to handle security matters once the state militia withdrew. Local union strength ebbed and flowed through April and May, but as June neared, it seemed that the strike had failed. Production levels had returned to near normal, and the strikers had been replaced. After the strikers were evicted from their mill cabins, they erected a "tent colony" on an empty lot owned by one of the few businessmen in Gastonia supportive of the strike.[83] Finally in June 1929, matters came to a head as the local police and unionists exchanged gunshots, leaving police chief D. A. Aderholt mortally wounded. Unionists were charged with the killing, and a local judge ruled that the trial's venue should move from Gastonia to Charlotte; but when the trial took place in August, violence was reignited.

During the spring semester of 1929, the *Daily Tar Heel* only mentioned the events in Gastonia a few times, coming out as openly proworker (but anticommunist). In so doing, UNC students reflected the perspective that industrialization was supposed to lead to progress; when it did not, failures needed to be acknowledged honestly and objectively. "From the very first the strikes at Gastonia and Charlotte were doomed to failure," the paper editorialized, because the mills had the power of the state behind them. Once the state troops were called in, "the strikers were placed at a tremendous disadvantage." The *Daily Tar Heel* criticized Gardner for sending troops in: "There was no valid reason [why] the troops should have been called out; their presence during a strike always mitigates the situation in the interests of the employers to a decidedly unjust degree." At the same time, the editorial rebuked the workers for allowing communist organizers like Beal to become involved. The communists "prejudiced the people of the state against the workers" and therefore undermined the strikers' cause. Meanwhile, the cause remained justified, because "anyone familiar with North and South Carolina mill villages admits that the workers are living under highly deplorable conditions. . . . The only hope for the mill worker lies in organization. Individually he hasn't the slightest voice in setting the wage that he will receive and the conditions under which he must live and work. Organization of mill workers in Carolina is inevitable; but the workers should be extremely careful how they organize."[84]

The tension and conspiracy theories gripping the Piedmont in mid-1929 pulled in one of UNC's ablest researchers, Harriet Herring. When Herring received notice of an AFL-sponsored conference being held in Burnsville, North Carolina, to study "women workers in industry," she and Luther Hodges, an up-and-coming figure at the Marshall and Fields textile division (and a future governor), attended one session. A full lineup of liberals and leftists spoke. The list included A. J. Muste of the Fellowship of Reconciliation, Paul Porter of the League of Industrial Democracy, and radical economist Broadus Mitchell. But Hodges wrote Herring afterwards that "we" (presumably the Marshall and Fields company) had "just received (confidentially) from one of the Auxiliary [Detective] Agencies a complete report on the meeting at Burnsville which you and I attended. It was reported quite complete, including the register of all in attendance. (Thank the Lord I made my mind up earlier that I would not register.) These people had one of their men planted and this person gave a report on each speech made during the afternoon. . . . This person also reported some things that [labor organizer Alfred] Hoffman said outside the conference room."[85] It must have been frightening to a person like Herring, dedicated to impartial research and dwelling in the relative safety of academia, to have been spied upon. But the situation revealed just how hostile the business community was to labor activism.

Two months after the Burnsville meeting, the discovery of a deranged juror caused the Aderholt murder trial to be dismissed. Angry Gastonia locals, led by a policeman and likely organized by the Committee of One Hundred, rampaged through the union encampment destroying members' property, kidnapping and beating union leaders, and threatening further violence before calling it a night. The NTWU initially responded by calling for its own show of force, a mass meeting of protest. The union's call for the mass meeting led to the killing in broad daylight of union member and balladeer Ella May Wiggins, a twenty-nine-year-old mother of five. Wiggins and a truckload of union members were driving to the meeting from nearby Bessemer City, unaware that it had been cancelled, when their truck was trailed by a line of cars and pickups filled with angry Gastonians. Finally, one car circled around the workers' truck and then stopped suddenly, causing the truck to come to a crashing halt. The scene turned into an ambush: gunshots poured into the truck. As the workers scrambled to escape, Wiggins was shot in the chest and killed. George B. Tindall notes that Wiggins's murder "occurred in broad daylight, with no fewer than fifty witnesses," but those charged with the shooting were not brought to trial, as a grand jury cited "insufficient evidence."[86]

The murder of Ella May Wiggins signaled an end to the NTWU's efforts in Gastonia, but not to labor-related violence in North Carolina in 1929. When labor unrest appeared that fall at the Baldwin and Clinchfield mills in Marion, North Carolina, workers turned to the United Textile Workers for support against working conditions they described as a "sweatshop" and mill village conditions that were deplorable.[87] Historian Phillip Wood describes the working conditions in Marion as "even worse" than those in Gastonia.[88] Owner R. W. Baldwin met the Marion workers' demands with derision and laughter. In response, the workers walked out and shut down the mill. The strike led to a series of violent incidents that included Baldwin getting hit over the head with a walking stick and company toughs evicting union members from their homes, occasionally with fire. Finally a confrontation between strikers and the police left three workers dead, and three more died later as a result of their injuries. As in Gastonia, the local police were implicated in the violence. As the trial proceeded, Benjamin Stolberg, writing for *The Nation*, described Sheriff Oscar F. Adkins, charged with one of the murders, as "the typical fat boy. . . . He sits in the courtroom accused of murder, watching the proceedings there with a smile of apparent indifference."[89] Even though the United Textile Workers did momentarily earn a few concessions, dozens of active union members were not rehired. All observers understood that the key factor in ending the strike was the violence that the mill owners, the town fathers, and the state were willing to unleash against the workers.[90] The strike "was lost, miserably and with a vengeance."[91] Finally, a local jury acquitted Sheriff Adkins and his deputies in time for them to go home for Christmas.

UNC's response to the labor unrest of the late 1920s revealed little campus sympathy for communists. The absence of a communist presence at Marion left one *Daily Tar Heel* writer to conclude: "The battle is between labor and capital entirely." Communism only "served to becloud the issue at Charlotte and Gastonia," but its absence at Marion gave North Carolina the opportunity to settle the struggle between labor and capital in an equitable manner. "The true causes of contention present themselves at Marion with a stark reality. Upon the governmental agencies of the state now rests the burden of proving to the nation that North Carolina is capable of administering justice to the forces of both capital and labor in the titanic struggle in which the Marion calamity is an important event."[92] The facts, in other words, compelled a modernizing state, the "progressive democracy" Governor Cameron Morrison had promised at the beginning of the decade, to act also on behalf of workers, because it had clearly supported capital during the recent conflict. The students asked: would it? The signs from Marion were not promising.

UNC students, in the meantime, proved willing (more willing than some of their professors and administrators) to keep publicly pointing out the gap between the promises of industrialization and its failures. In December 1929, the student paper analyzed a speech delivered at North Carolina State University by Charlotte's Benjamin B. Gossett, scion of a powerful textile family. Gossett explained that because the industry as a whole was operating at a loss, it needed "greater cooperation of the mill-owners" in order for profit to return. The *Daily Tar Heel* countered this point by noting that "unionization, which represents the sort of cooperation among the employees that he declared imperative for the employers," was, in Gossett's words, "nothing less than disastrous for workers and manufacturers alike." Gossett also defended the mill-owned workers' villages, describing the owners as "providing their workers with excellent homes and surroundings." Again the *Daily Tar Heel* replied: "Anyone familiar with mill villages in the south realizes that they are certainly not composed of 'excellent homes and surroundings.'" When Gossett accepted the workers' right to organize as long as unionization did not "conflict with the best interests of society," the *Daily Tar Heel* retorted that "perhaps unionization is in conflict with the interests of capital, but it is certainly *not* in conflict with the best interests of the workers, who constitute the bulk of our society." Moreover, "no mention was made of the strong-arm tactics of many manufacturers, who discharge every employe [*sic*] who joins the union. Through unionization alone," the editorial concluded, "can the interests of the workers be safeguarded, and we believe that once labor is in a position to be assured of receiving its just portion of the profits in the textile industry, it will cooperate fully with the manufacturers in attempts to increase these profits."[93]

David Clark responded to the *Daily Tar Heel's* strong defense of the rights of labor by poking fun at the "baby radicals" at UNC. He once again rejected the idea that UNC faculty represented legitimate expertise in labor and industrial matters or that labor relations were an area of legitimate academic inquiry. Clark was certain that some "crack-brained professor" had taught the students that "labor unions would be a fine thing for Southern mills." As a result, "A group of young boys, without business experience but with a prejudice against industry inspired by the teachings of radical professors proceed to tell Mr. Gossett just what is wrong with the textile industry."[94]

Clark again trotted out conspiracy theories aimed at undermining trust in UNC, shifting the terms of the debate this time away from challenging the university's expertise and toward academic freedom as an invitation to liberalism and radicalism. He had recently been influenced by *Sinister Shadows*, Edwin Marshall Hadley's virulently anticommunist conspiracy-theory novel, published in 1929. Despite its status as fiction, Clark insisted that the book was a "powerful and true exposure of the radical and communistic organizations which reach into our colleges" and especially of those in "almost every faculty" who were "trying to convert students into Communists." Clark found common cause with Hadley, noting defensively that "when we or anybody else say anything against the activities of these radicals, they pretend that the attacks are against free speech or the institution to which they are connected."[95]

Unfortunately the *Daily Tar Heel* followed Clark's lead into the debate over UNC's liberalism. At first the paper rejected Clark as being incapable of objectivity. The editors dismissed his views, noting that "even very young minds in all their plasticity cannot fail to recognize . . . the extreme prejudice underlying the opinions of such journals as the Bulletin. . . . Depending upon the good will of the mill owners for its very existence," the *Southern Textile Bulletin* "must necessarily devote all its energies to furtherance of their interests." The student paper reiterated that its aim had been to point out the inconsistencies in Gossett's address—that the facts, a commodity always so important to UNC, contradicted his statements. But, in conclusion, the *Daily Tar Heel* invoked the good intentions of UNC's liberal professors rather than their expertise:

A University professor evinces strictly humanitarian interest in the welfare of a group of Americans living under deplorable conditions; he is branded a "crack-brained radical" by journals such as the Bulletin, devoted to the selfish promotion of the interests of those responsible for such conditions. Utilizing every form of scurrilous and cowardly attack, persons of the calibre of David Clark . . . let no ethical considerations interfere with their determination to discredit those who would improve the conditions under which the workers live. College professors who exhibit liberal tendencies are represented as "twisting the minds" of their students, ruining their careers. The methods employed by the Southern Textile Bulletin . . . are utterly reprehensible.[96]

By defending UNC researchers as nice people, the student writers missed an opportunity to defend their professors on the grounds of their expertise and authority. Academic freedom gave UNC professors the chance to become experts but not necessarily to become liberals. Clark and other critics always had a more difficult time countering the recognized expertise of UNC professors, especially when those experts were trained to study the social effects of an industrializing society. The best Clark could do was simply to reject the notion that facts offered by UNC's researchers counted as expertise. But in this case the facts were clear to everyone, not just UNC professors: by the end of 1929, North Carolina's economic modernization had not led to the "progressive democracy" Governor Cameron Morrison had predicted at the beginning of the decade.

The decade ended with UNC's interest in labor relations lacking consistent direction. The university's leaders had backed away from the fray. In 1930 Harry Chase stepped down from the presidency and left UNC altogether. Howard Odum had already signaled his intention to avoid controversy. But UNC students continued to show their willingness to ask hard questions. Moreover, they continued to have the freedom to ask those questions. And elsewhere on campus a familiar voice, Frank Graham, was emerging, stepping into the leadership void to defend the university's mission and its commitment to the social usefulness of expertise through academic freedom.

Part II

The 1930s

3

"A Complex and Baffling Age"

Frank Porter Graham Ushers in a New Decade

UNC leaders, faculty, and students who embraced academic freedom as an institutional value in the 1920s assumed that its fruits would lead to useful change and a more progressive state and region. This was a formulation that did not strike them as controversial, because the South was in undeniably poor shape as the 1920s ended. UNC leaders and students in the 1930s increasingly invoked the term "liberal" to describe the political nature of the changes they hoped would come to the South. Frank Graham, for example, frequently conflated the values of academic freedom with liberal values, leaving behind the unfortunate impression that academic freedom meant liberalism. The two certainly did share core assumptions that patient, steady progress would come from tackling social and economic problems head on. But UNC's advocacy of academic freedom did not mean that its defenders insisted that their work be used for liberal causes. The expertise that academic freedom facilitated sometimes led university professors and officials—Frank Graham included—to take conservative positions on the hot-button issues of the day. Still, UNC's critics continued to assume that academic freedom meant liberalism through the 1930s and well beyond.

UNC's efforts to establish academic freedom in the 1920s helped publicize difficult conditions for workers, the injustices of segregation, and the talents of African American writers. Although tangible results were often difficult to measure, the fact that academic freedom allowed UNC scholars and students to discuss and investigate these difficult social issues was significant. Howard Odum and Harry Chase may have backed away from vigorous defenses of UNC's academic freedom by the end of the decade, but other members of the UNC community, such as Guy Johnson and the writers at *Carolina Magazine*, had not. UNC's efforts constituted a promising, if not totally successful, attempt to convince southerners that the expertise facilitated by the university's academic freedom could be put to constructive use in addressing the thorny issues society faced.

As the university and the South left the 1920s behind, academic freedom continued to shape UNC's regional involvement with race relations and labor activity. But the Great Depression and a bold new political climate fostered by Franklin Roosevelt's New Deal presented new challenges and a different set of circumstances; as a result, academic freedom functioned differently at UNC in the 1930s.

When Frank Porter Graham assumed the presidency of UNC in 1930, a glowing article in the *Washington Post* heralded both his defense of academic freedom and his progressive, liberal views. "Liberals at the university," the *Washington Post* noted, "are nothing new," and Graham's presidency "gives to his own ideas a seat of authority." In addition to Graham's inauguration being a glorious day for southern liberals, his presidency promised a "new day of freedom in North Carolina, the South, and in education."[1] Graham's leadership added immensely to UNC's reputation as that rare place in the South where academic freedom was possible and where liberal, progressive views were welcome.

The almost uniform praise heaped on Frank Graham since his presidency has reached mythical, even biblical, proportions; Oregon senator Wayne Morse once described him as "Christlike."[2] Native North Carolinian and UNC alumnus Charles Kuralt called Graham "a saint," adding that if "we ever get so self-absorbed that we forget about Frank Porter Graham, we will have forgotten everything noble about our past."[3] Interviews conducted more than half a century later attest to Graham's influence. Phil Hammer, a campus leader and editor of the *Daily Tar Heel* in the mid-1930s, recalled that after a dispiriting first semester of college, far away from his family in New York City and short on money, he rallied by throwing himself into campus activities. His turnabout

Frank Porter Graham.

was inspired "largely because of Dr. Frank Graham." In 1932 "the world seemed to be falling apart," but in Frank Graham, Hammer found "a man who [was] doing something." Hammer added that among the students, "everybody thought he or she had a personal relationship to Dr. Frank, in a way, and everybody did."[4]

Worldly graduate students also fell under Frank Graham's spell. The legendary southern historian C. Vann Woodward earned his doctorate at UNC during this time. Woodward rented a room next door to Graham's house and occasionally walked to campus with him. He recalled years later, "I was devoted to him and would do anything he told me."[5] Adds William Friday, who arrived at UNC near the end of Graham's presidency, "he was my folk hero, too."[6] Friday sees Graham as "playing a role then of a social conscience," a man whose sheer force of personality appealed to and nurtured the more progressive aspirations of North Carolinians.[7] Graham, he believes, was "acutely aware" of his symbolic importance to progressive-minded southerners.[8]

In the glow surrounding his inauguration in November 1931, commentators focused not just on his likability, decency, and liberalism, but also on a hopeful quality that defied easy definition. Given the dire

Graham, beloved by southern liberals, walks across the UNC campus with El-
eanor Roosevelt and student (and future pollster) Louis Harris, 1942. (Courtesy
of Hugh Morton Photographs and Films, North Carolina Collection, University of North Carolina at Chapel Hill Library.)

economic circumstances, the stakes for selecting the right president for
the university were high. Upon Harry Chase's departure from UNC,
Governor O. Max Gardner remarked that the "election of a president
of this university is of more importance to North Carolinians than the
election of any governor or any senator at any time."[9] Local newspaper
editor Louis Graves explained that Graham's popularity was ultimately
"due to an underlying essence that quite defies analysis."[10] The *Daily Tar
Heel* added, "All who have sought to describe and portray the man have
failed, and will fail . . . to capture a spirit . . . that, while appreciated, it is
never fully understood."[11] David Cohn observed that many of Graham's
followers "do not entirely understand him; some are mildly dubious of
his objectives; but they fight for him because they trust the man's integrity."[12] When the selection fell to Graham, Max Gardner was relieved
that North Carolina had found "a leader whom we need only to know to
trust and to trust implicitly."[13]

An unapologetic, gradualist liberal, Graham believed that a spirit of openness, inquiry, and community made UNC great. He also believed that UNC's influence held great potential to help the entire South become a more productive, more democratic society. Graham was born in 1886 into a family with deep North Carolina ties. He had a warm, loving mother, and his father was a Charlotte educator. Among his eight siblings was older brother Archibald "Moonlight" Graham, whose own life story appears briefly in the 1989 movie *Field of Dreams*. Frank was an energetic child who excelled in sports despite his small stature. Following his father's scholarly inclinations, Frank became a voracious reader at an early age. As a teenager, a case of the measles and bad eyesight slowed Graham's educational progress. Nonetheless, he came to UNC as an undergraduate in 1905.[14]

Graham threw himself into college life, participating in a range of activities from baseball to student government to debating societies. He was elected to Phi Beta Kappa in his junior year before embarking on an even more hectic senior year, during which he was at one point editor of the *Tar Heel*, senior class president, and president of the campus YMCA chapter. After graduation, Graham spent a year in law school at UNC before moving to Raleigh to teach high school for two years. Returning to Chapel Hill, he completed a second year of law school and gained admission to the bar. In 1913 Graham became secretary of the campus Y, and in 1914 he began teaching a course in history at UNC as well. Teaching history ignited a new passion within Graham, and he completed a master's degree in history at Columbia University in 1916.[15]

When the United States entered World War I in April 1917, Graham, inspired by his hero Woodrow Wilson, managed to get into the Marines despite weighing only 125 pounds, measuring five feet six inches tall, and having poor eyesight. Tragedy struck when Graham's brother David was killed at Belleau Wood in France in 1918, deepening Frank's desire to see action. But it was not to be; by the time his regiment was prepared to see combat, the war had ended. When new UNC president Harry Chase invited Graham to become the school's first dean of students, he accepted, happy to be back at UNC and in Chapel Hill. One year later, in 1920, Graham was back in the history department as an assistant professor.[16]

In September 1920, Graham embarked on what became a long career of campaigning on behalf of the university. The university leadership made an appeal to the state government for $20 million on behalf of the entire state university system. Graham organized students, alumni, civic clubs, and labor unions, and he lobbied governor Cameron Morrison on behalf of the cause. Throughout the campaign, Graham made numerous contacts throughout the state and honed his message explaining the university's service to the state. Despite concerns that the state could not afford educational reform as well as infrastructure improvements (the state also had a $50 million highway improvement plan in the works), Governor Morrison pledged to support the $20 million effort.[17]

Graham then spent two years completing coursework for a doctorate in history at the University of Chicago. Working under fellow North Carolinian William E. Dodd, Graham became absorbed in the historical development of southern industry. His new passion for the study of industrial development led to him abandon the Ph.D. to attend the London School of Economics, with its noted economists Harold Laski and Richard Tawney. Both men taught economics with a social conscience and with varying commitments to socialism. Graham also studied under Leonard Trelawney Hobhouse, who was known for his sharp critique of the socialism in vogue among British intellectuals of the 1920s.[18] Despite the scattered approach of Graham's graduate education in the 1920s, it taught him the importance of examining the social implications of economic development, the value of honest historical reappraisals, and the absolute necessity of openness in a democratic society to allow disturbing facts—both past and present—to see the light of day. When the evolution crisis came to a head in the South, Graham was ready to speak out.

As the controversy over the Poole Bill reached its decisive moment in 1925, Frank Graham, still studying at the London School of Economics, weighed in with a strong defense of Chase and UNC's academic freedom. In a letter published in the state's major newspapers, Graham made the case that the university's academic freedom encouraged a healthy sense of inquiry that would lead to progress. Chase, Graham said, was determined to "preserve the spirit of the old and build the structure of a greater university where their children can seek to develop, untrammeled by tyrannies, their best physical, intellectual, and spiritual selves."[19] With "vigor, variety, and freedom," Chase's presidency contributed to UNC's greatness. Indeed, Graham continued, "the danger is often the other way. Inbreeding of ideas and methods is not good for either the faculty or the students. New contacts, outside points of view, conflicts of opinions, comparison of standards and methods, cross-fertilization of minds—these are essential conditions for wholesome freedom and progress." The people of North Carolina, Graham was sure, "like all truly progressive peoples of the past and the present," were "eager for other contacts, methods, and ideas, out of whose clashing vigor and variety come progress."[20] Chase, Graham argued, had "raised the University standard to be seen of all our people. Freedom to think, freedom to speak, and freedom to print are the texture of that standard." For Graham, the university's academic freedom went beyond intellectual principle; it was the "spiritual possession of the people," to be used by UNC faculty and students to help North Carolinians "fight against the false fear of truth and the foes of freedom, whatever be their power."[21]

UNC rural sociologist Eugene Branson applauded Graham's ringing defense of Chase and the university, acknowledging along the way that defending academic freedom was still risky. "It is a timely, able and courageous statement," Branson wrote. "It bolsters President Chase, the University, and the great cause of freedom at a time when the State and the South need courageous support." Branson hoped, therefore, that Graham would wrap up his studies abroad and come home: "We need you . . . more than ever."[22]

Back in the history department for the beginning of the 1925–1926 academic year, Graham's graduate training had produced in him a singular focus: the challenge to extend democratic values as far as possible. As Numan V. Bartley summarizes, progressives like Graham remained "committed to the proposition that only the empowerment of the masses of citizens could provide the foundation for a soundly structured liberalism."[23] Child labor, low wages, and long working hours all became issues of economic democracy for him. As president of the North Carolina Conference on Social Service, he helped write what became a new labor law in 1929. The law, signed by new governor O. Max Gardner, was considered one of the most liberal worker compensation laws in the South at that time.[24] The law provided $6,000 to the dependents of a worker accidentally killed on the job, plus a small weekly payment. According to the *New York Times*, "the need for such a policy in North Carolina" had "long been evident," and it allowed the state to stay "abreast of progressive states in the protection of the rights of employed in the matter of personal injury."[25]

The explosion of southern labor unrest in 1929 gave Graham the opportunity to call for a more informed—and therefore, by his logic, more progressive—course of southern industrialization. The murder of Ella May Wiggins, the single mother and activist gunned down during the Gastonia strike, prompted Graham to write to *News & Observer* columnist Nell Battle Lewis to express how moved he was by the "sheer power of the figure of this woman shining out from the facts. . . . Her death is upon us all."[26] With regard to the economic difficulties ahead, Graham—writing straight out of the UNC catechism—urged the open admission of problems and an inquiry into the facts: "All of us, owners, workers, teachers, preachers, citizens, need to begin digging more deeply into our study of economics, history, sociology, psychology and the philosophical and spiritual sanctions of our human life and personality." Projecting this vision across the region, he also summed up UNC's mission perfectly: "Information will lessen bias and understanding will remove hate of people."[27] Graham also revealed the incrementalism that was an important part of the liberal view when he added that by "gradually and intelligently pegging away, a little here and a little there, with due regard for the rights of all," the South could achieve progress in worker-owner relations.[28]

The hard times that sparked labor unrest also caused serious difficulties for the university. Even before the stock market crash of October 1929, Governor Gardner called for "retrenchment and reform." Concerned about growing state debt and unwilling to raise taxes, Gardner pushed hard for cuts in the state budget. The governor trimmed $1.5 million from the state budget in the first six months of his term and promised that more reductions were on the way.[29] As the economic crisis deepened, however, the state assumed greater responsibilities for roads and schools as municipalities suffered from dwindling local tax revenues. This put an even greater strain on Gardner's efforts to trim the state government's finances. UNC, like other state institutions, felt the pinch. The state cut the school's appropriations by 25 percent in 1929–1930 and another 20 percent in 1930–1931. These cuts not only put a severe damper on any dreams of expansion; they threatened to drive out quality faculty, many of whom were already turning down more lucrative offers out of loyalty to UNC.[30] In February 1930, in the midst of this deepening crisis, Harry Woodburn Chase announced his decision to leave UNC at the end of the academic year to become president of the University of Illinois.

No one was more surprised than Frank Graham by his election

to the presidency of the university on June 9, 1930. Graham tried repeatedly to take himself out of the search, telling the Board of Trustees that historian R. D. W. Connor was a better choice. His supporters kept his name in among the nominees anyway. Even his mother, Katherine, weighed in, writing to her son: "It would give me and your father a great deal of pleasure if you would allow yourself to be considered as a successor to Dr. Chase. . . . The University needs you."[31] The momentum for Graham continued to build. Finally, on the fourth ballot, the trustees selected Graham.[32]

As the new president, Frank Graham had no time to waste. Just days into his presidency, Graham hit the road to make the case all across North Carolina that the state's charter university needed to stay afloat.[33] When the state legislature reconvened in January 1931, he appeared before the Joint Committee on Appropriations. Biographer Warren Ashby sums up Graham's message succinctly: "Depressions are temporary; schools and colleges are the permanent source of economic, social, and spiritual well-being."[34] At the time of the hearing, the committee was considering a nearly 33 percent cut for the 1931–1932 academic year. Graham talked the committee down to a 17.6 percent cut, only to find out later that the appropriated amount was to be slashed by an additional 24 percent, which would have resulted in a bigger loss than the original 33 percent. Graham met with Governor Gardner and seems to have pried loose a promise that there would be no further cuts.[35]

Completely absorbed in his efforts to retain the school's funding, Graham put off his inauguration until November 11, 1931. But understanding the importance of the moment, he finally began to make plans for his inaugural address that summer. Escaping to Columbia University to prepare, Graham pushed aside his always long to-do list and poured his energies into writing. As Graham explained to a friend, he "wrote down whatever there was in me which came from my own studies, thinking and experience during the last ten years. I wrote and rewrote for a week and had to stay up until after three o'clock one morning and four o'clock another morning in order to get what was in me [onto paper]."[36]

The address, clocked at seventy-eight minutes long, revealed a man making an impassioned yet sophisticated case for the modern university and its importance to the modern world. Today's university, Graham began, was "so dynamic in its life that no occasion, however local or international, is outside the range of its radiation. The campus and the world interact upon each other with generative and regenerative power." The modern university was "so intimately a part of the context of every real problem of the modern world, that any life strand found at hand anywhere running through the life of the world enters into the texture of the modern university."[37]

Graham, a dissertation away from getting his doctorate in history, gave his large Kenan Stadium audience an overview of the history of education. Echoing John Dewey's insights of the early 1900s, Graham took special notice of the rise of the newer social sciences, prompted by "the increasing complexity of modern society." While granting that even the traditional sciences "gave questioning admission to the newer social sciences," Graham remained confident that "more and more the new social sciences will prove their value in this complex and baffling age."[38]

Themes of complexity and change dominated the address, pointing always to society's need for experts with the academic freedom to help sort out the problems of this modern world. "The very fluidity of ideas and the organic nature of life processes" meant that the modern university constantly had to be prepared to adapt the means by which it advanced knowledge and its own social usefulness. "In no other way than by the integrated view can we understand the wider implications of the specialized knowledge" that the modern expert produced, with its "power to destroy or rebuild the structure of the modern world."[39] Graham also stressed UNC's commitment to democracy and its ability to serve the state. It was the "function of the state university not only to find its bits of truth and teach the truth gathered from scholars everywhere, but to carry the truth to the people that they may take it into their lives and help to make it prevail in the world of affairs." The university, he proclaimed, "comes from the people and should go out to the people."[40]

From here Graham pivoted into a full-blown defense of UNC's academic freedom. "Without freedom there can be no university," he said. He then spelled out the "various course and . . . wide meaning" that academic freedom actually took when embraced by an institution such as UNC. It meant for the students a "growing sense of responsibility and student citizenship" through their ability to "govern themselves in campus affairs" as well as the "right of lawful assembly and free discussions by any students of any issues and views whatsoever." For faculty, academic freedom meant "the right . . . to control the curriculum, scholastic standards, and especially matters pertaining to intellectual excellence; to teach and speak freely, not as propagandists, but as scholars and seekers for the truth with some sense of responsibility for the teacher's part in the development of the whole youthful personality." The faculty under Graham's administration would have its freedom to "help shape university policies by votes, representation, advice, and, may we hope, a large sharing in the life of the University and the people of the state." Graham held next that academic freedom also meant "freedom of the scholar to find and report the truth honestly without interference by the University, the state, or any interests whatsoever. . . . Without such freedom of research we would have no university and no democracy."[41]

Having set out as clear a defense of academic freedom as UNC had seen since Chase's battles against the fundamentalists in 1925, Graham then explained that his purpose in spelling out in detail his understanding of academic freedom was "for the sake of fairness." He understood from the outset of his administration that as president he had to work always to help keep academic freedom alive and productive. If the trustees could not accept his definition of academic freedom, the "only recourse for changing such conceptions is to change administrations. This is not said defiantly but in all friendliness and simply as a matter of openness and clearness."[42]

Frank Graham ended up serving UNC as president until 1949. Throughout his long presidency, he held to the belief expressed in his inaugural address that the openness of academic freedom would help produce the changes the South needed. In addition, it is easy to see now that academic freedom under Frank Graham made liberalism at UNC increasingly popular in the 1930s, even if liberal ends were not necessarily the purpose of having academic freedom. But, again, at issue here is not whether UNC in the 1930s was, or became, a liberal school. It continued to have plenty of conservatives among its students, faculty members, and trustees. And the surprising twist in the story of Frank Graham's presidency is that despite his well-known liberalism, his defense of academic freedom at the university was at times used for conservative ends.

4

"A New Negro Is About to Come on the Scene"

Leadership vs. Caution in the Struggle for Racial Equality

On a crisp autumn afternoon in 1935, Paul Green, a famous UNC playwright and a dedicated liberal on race issues, decided to join a couple of faculty friends and take in the Duke-Auburn football game up the road in Durham. Green was well known for writing sympathetic African American characters into his plays and for presenting the grittier, uglier side of southern race relations. In 1930, for example, he staged an early version of his play *Potter's Field*, based on the hardships of life in Chapel Hill's black community, to help raise funds for the local African American school, the Orange County Training Center.[1] For this and other efforts to improve race relations in the region, he earned the admiration of southern liberals of the 1920s and 1930s. His diary, however, reveals that not everyone appreciated his views on race: "On way to car after game a funny incident happened. A drunk Carolina student leaned from his car, quoted a bit of Negro Tommy's speech at me and said, 'Go f— yourself.' Who he was I do not know."[2] As Paul Green's experience at the football game reveals, being a white southern liberal—especially one considered an "expert" on southern race relations—could be a trying experience.

During the 1920s, UNC faculty, students, and administrators had used the university's academic freedom to relate to African Americans in new ways. Through the CIC, UNC had established new contacts with black leaders and gained more perspective on the black experience. Some UNC faculty and students had embraced the work of black authors as writers to be read and appreciated for their vision, their technique, and their talent. Prominent African American leaders such as James Weldon Johnson, George Washington Carver, and Robert Moton had visited the campus and interacted with UNC students. UNC leaders entered the 1930s expecting more of the same.

Academic freedom enabled Paul Green, Frank Graham, and the school's famous team of sociologists to deconstruct the mythic narrative of segregation's virtues. Green wrote about "feeling the need of concerted effort towards racial justice, abolition of present chain-gang system, better pay for teachers, etc., etc."[3] Guy Johnson and his graduate students continued to take a hard, candid look at conditions affecting the local black community. For instance, the research he and others conducted on black poverty provided a "scientific" explanation for the evidence of the devastating effects of a Jim Crow political economy. Student Mayne Allbright applauded the selection of Frank Graham as president, saying it was a sign of good things to come for southern race relations. "On the Negro question," Allbright said of Graham's leadership, "a constructive attitude of scholarly research and gradual race improvement."[4] Allbright perfectly summed up UNC's ambitions at the time; but the 1930s proved to be far different from a mere extension of the 1920s.

There was no doubting the mountain of obstacles to be overcome as white southern liberals surveyed southern race relations at the beginning of the 1930s.[5] They saw even deeper black poverty caused by the Great Depression, the appalling Scottsboro Boys case in Alabama, and new evidence suggesting lynching was on the rise again. Throughout the South, the criminal justice system continued to put to death African Americans convicted on the flimsiest of evidence and by no jury of their peers, a situation that Paul Green described as "the southern indoor sport—execution of more Negroes."[6] In North Carolina, violence stalked the efforts of the black professional class as they attempted to do their jobs, such as the two Durham lawyers who faced "about ten shots" and "rocks hurled" outside the Henderson courthouse as they attempted to defend two African American men charged with assaulting a white woman.[7] It is with good reason that historian Augustus Burns says the 1930s for black southerners were "years of trial, with little hope."[8]

Out of this despair, a spirit of militancy arose. African Americans pushed even harder for a "forced entrance of the future" on their terms.[9] New, assertive voices emerged from within the black community, speaking on a range of issues including antilynching legislation, the inequities of Jim Crow education, the humiliations of living under white supremacy, and the need for increased black political participation.[10] In 1933, C. V. Cools of New York urged a Raleigh audience to become politically engaged. Unless "they 'got into politics,'" Cools proclaimed, "their efforts would amount to naught." At the same event, Lawrence Oxley— the director of the state's Division of Work among Negroes and later part of Franklin Roosevelt's "Black Cabinet"—insisted that "if we organize and lay before the people our wants and our needs there is no reason why we shouldn't obtain our objectives. For instance, we should have at least one judge and possibly another election official."[11] The next month NAACP leader Walter White visited Raleigh and, according to the *News & Observer*, declared that "Negroes should be more outspoken and courageous in seeking equal educational opportunities . . . urging the need for shaking off traditional lethargy and working diligently for a new order." White hammered home the point that "North Carolina never discriminated against a Negro by giving him lower taxes than white people, but he can't get the same education that is accorded white people." The white community, he warned, needed to give the black southerner "a better break in order to keep him from being forced to accept the tenets of communism."[12]

The tension between African American assertiveness and the constant threat of white retaliation compelled UNC's liberals to emphasize anew the importance of gradualism. During the 1930s many at UNC already fit historian Tony Badger's astute characterization of post–World War II southern liberals: people who "professed optimism but advocated caution."[13] UNC's liberals continued to find fault with Jim Crow, to call for more respect for the black community, and to work out new relationships with black leaders. But the institution's liberalism remained chained to the assumption that if change threatened segregation too severely or suddenly, disaster would surely follow. The school therefore continually invoked its authority—bolstered always by its academic freedom—as a key component of its strategy for keeping progress gradual and safe. It continued to conduct "expert" studies of racial conditions and to offer learned counsel as a check against those advocating a sudden reordering of race relations. Academic freedom therefore helped southern liberals at UNC advance their research on race relations and unearth new information on actual conditions—that is, to add to UNC's expertise—while at the same time helping the school discourage radicals and the new generation of black activists from challenging segregation's survival.

Throughout the decade, UNC's fear of a violent explosion underlined its cautious approach on race. For example, in 1931, soon after a controversial campus visit by the poet Langston Hughes and in the midst of a failed campaign to pass an antilynching law in North Carolina, Howard Odum wrote a piece for *The Nation* that reveals an almost frantic view of southern race relations (especially for someone who prided himself on his professional composure). Odum cited his Columbia University mentor, Franklin Giddings, to highlight the challenges facing the antilynching movement. For Giddings (and Odum), the concept of "folkways" was the key to understanding any social change. Odum quoted Giddings: "Every time, the folkways will defeat the stateways if they are against the stateways. . . . I have been unable to find any instance in history in which a law, a governmental enactment, has won its way against the folkways."[14]

The tension between folkways and stateways ran parallel to the tension between fear and the hope for a better future. And fear, Odum insisted, drove the lynch mob to lynch. Next, however, Odum said that those who, like himself, wanted careful progress were also afraid of the larger irrational, uncontrollable fear lurking within the white South: "Of this fear the great body of people who are horrified at lynching are afraid. . . . We are afraid to protest. We are afraid to legislate. We are afraid to enforce law and liberty. We are afraid to teach. We are afraid to preach. Afraid of the public, afraid of the demagogue, and deep down, rationalizing amid the fears, we are afraid to do anything. . . . We are all afraid."[15]

In light of this bleak assessment, little resembling "progress" seemed forthcoming for southern race relations. Nonetheless, as the 1930s began, UNC leaders continued to try to assert their influence on southern race relations, citing the usual mission values of expertise, interaction, leadership, and the freedom to investigate. Similarly, the North Carolina CIC, an organization with strong UNC ties, carried the approach of the 1920s forward into the new decade, pledging in 1931 their efforts to "know the facts and then to make these facts known to those who can do something about it."[16]

Meanwhile, in Chapel Hill, local evidence of white-on-black violence at the beginning of the decade indicated that this approach might not have been able to do much good and that UNC's claim to leadership in race relations was dubious. In 1931 the *Daily Tar Heel* ran a disturbing story about Sam Barber, a "local colored waiter," who had driven into town in his run-down Ford to buy some kerosene for his lamp so he could sit through the night with a gravely ill child. As he parked his old car, "Cop R— accosted him brusquely and demanded, 'Sam, get that car fixed! It makes too much noise.'" Then:

> Sam, hardly looking up asks what's the matter with it. Cop R— incensed at a reply tells Sam to go to the garage and have it fixed. Sam still wonders what's the matter. Cop R— asks Sam who he's talking to. Sam tells him. R— says he will lock him up. Sam tells him that his child is dying. R— repeats that he will lock Sam up. Sam says go ahead. R— grabs his arm and starts to drag him off. He knows but ignores the fact that Sam ought to be back at the bed of his dying child. Another colored person, a bystander, protests and appeals to R— on account of the child. R— gruffly lets Sam go. Sam buys a dime's worth of kerosene and goes back to his dimly lit room to watch his child pass away.[17]

The scene, the *Daily Tar Heel* reported, was "typical of the discriminating injustice and harsh, unreasoning pressure" the local police imposed upon the black community. From the writer's perspective, this could hardly be called progress in southern race relations. It was, rather, a stinging indictment of UNC's liberalism, because those who called Chapel Hill home most certainly did not see their southern town as "typical." Chapel Hill, the author noted, "is liberal. Chapel Hill is tolerant. Chapel Hill leads the state. It is all quite true, perhaps, comparatively speaking but often and much too often this enlightenment is so shallow as to be almost farcical."[18]

This author expressed a concern that UNC was not doing enough to foster better conditions for stable race relations—a concern that began to dog university leaders during the 1930s. As the years passed, a more disturbing question loomed: could they do enough? If a Chapel Hill policeman saw fit to rough up a grieving African American father because of a noisy car, what hope was there that UNC's efforts and expertise could persuade other white southerners to consider a new day in race relations?

Incidents like the one involving Sam Barber caused UNC leaders to become increasingly convinced throughout the 1930s that the threat of local violence loomed. The reaction to Langston Hughes's campus visit in 1931 provided more worrisome evidence that racial tensions might soon erupt in violence. Hughes came to UNC at the invitation of Guy Johnson and Paul Green, visiting some classes and giving a well-received public lecture. The controversy arose on the eve of Hughes's visit, when an off-campus periodical, *Contempo*, published a poem and an article Hughes had written about the unfolding Scottsboro Boys saga. In both pieces, Hughes mocked the southern justice system and white pretensions to superiority, especially in light of the fact that at least one of the two white women involved was a prostitute.

In addition to the dozens of angry letters Frank Graham received about Hughes's appearance, the *Southern Textile Bulletin*'s David Clark came just shy of advocating a lynch mob. "In most places," Clark wrote, "any man who wrote such articles would be driven out, in fact, would be fortunate to escape bodily harm." Instead, "this negro," Clark continued, who "writes such words about white girls . . . is to be welcomed at the University of North Carolina by certain students and probably by certain professors."[19] For his part, Hughes came to Chapel Hill, had his visit, and left, remaining on the whole unconcerned. Taking Clark's threats in stride, he wrote teasingly to A. J. Buttitta, coeditor of *Contempo*: "See what you have done? I can't come back!"[20]

But the seeming unpredictability of day-to-day racial coexistence kept university leaders like Robert B. House so on edge that a local bus ride became fraught with potential danger. In May 1932, House wrote to the Carolina Coach Company to complain of a traumatic experience that he and his wife, Hattie, had endured while riding the 10:00 p.m. bus from Durham to Chapel Hill. "A drunken Negro," House wrote, "who openly boasted of the possession of liquor was sprawled out in the back of the bus from the time he got on it . . . until he got off. . . . His conversation was lewd and offensive and he set the tone for the entire group of Negroes who continued to talk lewdly and offensively all the way to Chapel Hill. Is there nothing for a man and his wife to do but either stay off of the bus or to submit to such conditions?"[21] No doubt the experience genuinely unnerved House, but his discomfort at having to "submit" to "conditions" established by an African American is also palpable in his letter.

H. H. Hearn, general manager of the bus company, wrote back to explain that the driver had "not been able to get dinner because he was visiting his mother earlier in the day." Therefore, the driver ate late and boarded the bus at the last moment, and "did not notice that any of them were intoxicated." Once under way, the driver, concentrating on the "safe handling of the bus," was unaware that "this kind of talk had gone on until you spoke to him at Chapel Hill." Despite having established that the driver was, on the whole, a conscientious employee who loved his mother, Hearn still found the driver negligent. Had the driver been "more intent on his work . . . he could have heard the same language as Mrs. House and you were compelled to listen to, and . . . he would have been perfectly justified in ejecting the passenger."[22] Revealing the influence that UNC officials like House wielded—he was named Dean of Administration in 1934—Hearn then asked if House recommended that the driver be fired, a serious matter given the ongoing economic depression.

House, consistent with the emerging UNC view in the 1930s, responded by invoking the fragile state of race relations. What concerned him was that he had "observed chances for something like a riot where students and Negroes are mixed." Intoxication threatened everyone's security, "particularly where two races are concerned." House relented on the bus driver, who "appeared to me to be a competent and an efficient man, courteous and polite in his bearing. . . . I am by no means seeking retribution for the past occurrence, and I should hate to see him suffer."[23] The driver received a warning and a reprimand from the company.

In the 1930s, when the subject was race relations, UNC leaders repeatedly tried to contextualize these incidents as matters involving caution, trust, or the need for more expertise, all values central to academic freedom. They reiterated their view that the expertise that academic freedom fostered enabled them to see more acutely than laypersons just where the dangers lay. As Robert House's disturbing bus ride reveals, they were constantly on the lookout for reckless behavior on and off campus that could provoke a violent reaction or an "outbreak" that would then constitute a "setback," two words they used frequently when discussing the state of southern race relations.

The theme of trust came out again as UNC defended the actions and individual rights of English professor E. E. Ericson, whose political activities nearly sparked "something like a riot" in October 1936. It was widely known on campus that Ericson held progressive views on race relations.[24] When Communist Party vice presidential candidate James

Ford, an African American, spoke in Durham, Ericson attended the lecture. Afterwards, along with others, Ericson met Ford for dinner.[25]

Ericson's attendance at dinner with Ford sparked outrage throughout the white South. In dozens of columns and letters, critics attacked the professor, UNC's academic freedom, and its liberal reputation. They were angry that a state employee had dined with a communist; that a white professor had publicly dined with an African American; and that the university defended Ericson. Dr. Roy W. McKnight, the president of the Mecklenburg County chapter of the UNC Alumni Association, called for an ideologically driven purge not unlike the one that the University of Mississippi was going through at the same time and that the Universities of Georgia and Texas would experience in the late 1930s and 1940s.[26] And yet while McKnight's complaint suggested a willingness to set clear limits on academic freedom, it also showed that he had accepted the principle itself as imperative to the institution, unlike David Clark, who routinely rejected the notion. McKnight started out by allowing that faculty were entitled to a certain scope of action:

> I believe a university professor should enjoy the right of freedom of speech and liberality of thought, but when a faculty member's conduct and philosophy of life become so opposed to American tradition, especially to Southern tradition, as to be offensive to the sensibilities of the thousands of alumni and to the taxpayers of the state then it is time for the university administration to start a general house cleaning. I can see no place in the faculty of the University of North Carolina for such an individual, nor can I understand why the administration permits and apparently condones such offenses.[27]

In the end, McKnight, like J. G. de Roulhac Hamilton and Harry Chase in the late 1920s, defined academic freedom as something that could be enjoyed only if the public was satisfied—not something that was all the more essential when the public was dissatisfied.

Frank Graham used the incident to reassert UNC's position of leadership as a trustworthy community of honorable experts operating in a climate of academic freedom and in the service of the state. Graham situated UNC's academic freedom between potentially reckless forces on both sides of the issue, reinforcing along the way the university's gradual approach to racial progress. In a letter he sent to correspondents upset over the Ford dinner, Graham described Ericson as "a man of un-impeachable personal character, high competence as a scholar, distin-guished ability as a teacher, who has a conscientious devotion to his work and the welfare of his students. . . . I have not asked and do not intend to ask for his resignation."[28] As a university employee, in other words, Ericson did what he was hired to do. He meanwhile had the free-dom to associate with whomever he chose. But Graham understood why the critics were so upset. Therefore, he offered these words of caution:

> Our interracial relations in the South are so delicate and so highly charged that we must first of all be fair and wise in so far as God gives us to be so. Any person who touches or jars these relations should do so with humility of mind and a prayer in his heart. We are making progress slowly with more and more understanding and appreciation of the values of a finer coop-eration between the races. Any happening that upsets or mars that understanding, I deeply regret, but we must be careful that we do not permit a greater mistake of dealing unjustly with any human being.[29]

This passage went to the heart of UNC's philosophy on changing race relations. It implies that Ericson was not careful, but it also warns critics against making a "greater mistake" by impeding "progress" as defined by UNC. Hounding Ericson out of the state would diminish UNC's ac-ademic freedom, would not lead to "more understanding," and would upset the "finer cooperation between the races" even more than Eric-son's dinner supposedly had.

Still, daily racial coexistence, even in Chapel Hill, was fraught with potential explosiveness. The "outbreak" UNC leaders constantly feared finally happened on a hot summer night in 1937. On Saturday, August 21, Chapel Hill was readying for a break from the normally busy life of a college town. One week remained in the university's summer session, and the fall term was not scheduled to begin until September 13. But late that night, police were summoned to Yarborough's Service Station on West Franklin Street, where Chapel Hill turns into Carrboro. A nasty fight had left a young African American, Tom Atwater, bloodied from being hit over the head with a beer bottle by a white Carrboro man, James Horne. Chapel Hill chief of police W. T. Sloan took Atwater to a doctor, while Carrboro officers arrested and held Horne. Carrboro, with its largely white textile millworker population, lay adjacent to the poor, largely African American neighborhoods of west Chapel Hill. Inverting the usual early 1900s scenario of white crowds gathering outside southern jails demanding justice, in this case a growing number of angry African Americans appeared outside the Carrboro jail where Horne was being kept. Chief Sloan reported that he and the Carrboro officers finally "dispersed" the crowd, but it reassembled at Yarborough's Service Station. Fearing for the prisoner's safety, Carrboro police chief R. H. Mills moved Horne to the jail in Hillsborough, about twelve miles away.[30]

Chapel Hill and Carrboro police returned to Yarborough's, where they found about three hundred African Americans gathered. Chief Sloan reported that the crowd, still angry over Atwater's beating, began throwing "rocks and various other things" at passing cars.[31] He called the Durham Police Department for help in restoring order. When "some white boy" made the ill-advised decision to pull into Yarborough's "to inquire as to the trouble," the crowd surrounded the truck, rocking it back and forth and trying to overturn it. The truck somehow got away and headed toward Carrboro. Shortly thereafter, Sloan noted, another truck "driven by white people" and "barricaded with railroad ties" sped by with "rifle and various othe[r] artillery" blazing into the crowd. The truck then turned around and came back for another pass, "still shooting." The African Americans gathered at the service station returned the gunfire "very promptly." After the truck passed by the second time and both sides exchanged more gunfire the Durham police arrived, and the crowd dispersed.[32]

The clash horrified UNC officials. It also prompted the development of a research agenda that ultimately revealed more starkly the inner workings of a racially unjust society. Sociologist Guy B. Johnson wrote to Frank Graham that discussions among white leaders were ongoing and that he intended to assign some of his better students to study the disturbance. "As soon as we accumulate some facts concerning Negroes and the recent race riot," Johnson said, "we will be in a position to discuss the problem of what to do about it."[33] Johnson's statement was not exactly a rousing call to action, but it was a textbook representation of the UNC approach. Their expertise would produce facts that would lead to solutions, stability, and progress.

Over the next few years, UNC's research in response to the riot found that beneath the appearance—or behind the myth—of a stable, progressive, segregated village, the local African American community confronted many interconnected difficulties. The research conducted by Charles M. Freeman, a graduate student in sociology, confirmed that the black community was "almost wholly dependent upon the University and the white families" for work. African Americans worked mainly as "porters, waiters, delivery clerks, collectors of laundry, clothes pressers, janitors, lawn workers, gardeners and draymen."[34] Not surprisingly, as the university budget suffered during the 1930s, so, too, did the black community.[35] The dollar value of real estate owned by African Americans declined steadily, from a total of $290,520 in 1927 to $183,871 in 1938, a reduction of 36.7 percent.[36] Nearly half of Chapel Hill's African American population received federal aid in the first year of the New Deal. Both the Red Cross and the King's Daughters handed out flour and cloth to needy local families, white and black. An accounting of those helped by the Emergency Relief Administration and the local chapter of the King's Daughters showed that nearly 65 percent of local aid had gone to Chapel Hill's black community.[37]

In the months following the riot, Lee Coleman, another graduate student in sociology, conducted a series of interviews with local African Americans. Many cited police mistreatment as one of the biggest problems in local race relations. Following are some typical findings: "In cases involving negroes, especially negroes and whites in the same case, the negro suspect or offender does not get an equal chance with the white," and "the local police usually assume that the negro is guilty and the white man innocent."[38] There was no denying that the West Franklin area of town, adjacent to the white working-class neighborhoods of Carrboro, could be rough; so calls for a greater police presence were mixed in with respondents' condemnations of police brutality. James Britton, a filling station employee, put it simply: "The recent wave of fights and killings could be stopped if the police would regularly patrol the negro sections." Another interviewee said the police department should designate specific officers to patrol the "negro section . . . both for protection and for arresting negro drunks and rowdies who are the ones who start the trouble between the races."[39]

Underneath the actions of those apparently causing the trouble—youths of both races, racist white policemen—remained the entrenched, persistent economic difficulty that was a part of everyday life for most African Americans. The university and the town were home to several large PWA and WPA projects, including the Chapel Hill Post Office, UNC's Woollen Gymnasium, and a new university medical building.

New Deal programs brought job opportunities for local African Americans, but not necessarily stability, let alone improvements in local race relations.

Lee Coleman's interviews reveal a widely shared understanding in the black community that low wages were the root of their immediate difficulties. Interviewees' responses also convey an air of disbelief that their well-educated white neighbors did not understand this. C. T. Boyd, pastor of the local Church of God, put it bluntly: "White people apparently do not realize how hard it is to live on the wages paid." Boyd had heard that "local servant wages are very largely agreed upon and set by the [white] women's clubs." He suggested that a committee of "colored people" should "come before them and present their side of the question."[40] Kate Tinnie agreed: "It's hard to see how white employers can expect so much and pay so little."[41] James R. Cobb noted, "All wages in Chapel Hill [for negroes] are too low, but there is a rank unfairness in local PWA work." The wage scale set by the government for different skill levels was, Cobb claimed, "frequently circumvented" according to race. Having worked on the construction of the Woollen Gymnasium, a PWA project, Cobb told how "negroes are classified as unskilled for pay purposes, but are often put on semi-skilled jobs. White boys, on the other hand, are usually listed on the pay scale as mason's helpers or in other semi-skilled classifications, whereas they may often know how to do only the lowest kind of work."[42]

Following the riot, town leaders continued to invoke stereotypes and call for greater community efforts to combat local African American laziness, underscoring the challenge UNC leaders faced in changing the perspective of even the local white community. The state employment service announced grandly that it had hired ten black workers from Durham to work on the Woollen Gymnasium, "as the result of the disinclination of Chapel Hill Negroes to work."[43] A local judge, speaking in the wake of the riot, encouraged Chief Sloan to make arrests under the town's vagrancy laws as a means of keeping black workers on the job.[44]

Local African Americans bristled at these generalizations about their supposed indifference to work. For Kenneth Jones, the problem was not a black unwillingness to work but white willingness to exploit a mobile supply of desperate black workers:

Great numbers of negroes come here from other places. . . .
If they are willing to work cheap, the white people hire them

without any kind of investigation. After a few weeks' trial they find them unsatisfactory and discharge them, but meanwhile these negroes have sent for their families, and when they are turned off they either become public charges or they turn to crime for a living. . . . This situation could be prevented by a little care on the part of employers. They should require references of applicants, find out why they are unemployed and why they have come to Chapel Hill . . . and not let them settle down here unless they are of desirable character and can add to the productive population.[45]

It is not hard to see why, by the end of the decade, some African Americans came to see a degree of falsity in UNC's claim to race leadership, especially when the white community's response to racial problems was to have UNC study the situation, but also to arm themselves. After the riot, Chapel Hill police chief Sloan wrote to the town aldermen: "I personally don't think that we will have a repetition of such an affair, but I think it very advisable to equip ourselves with necessary equipment to cope with a situation that might arise, such as machine gun [*sic*], tear gas bombs, and amunition [*sic*] etc. I think that we were very fortunate that the University student body was not here at that time."[46]

Low wages and a growing population led to a housing crisis in Chapel Hill's black neighborhoods. Shortly after the 1937 riot, *Chapel Hill Weekly* editor Louis Graves—unintentionally revealing the status of UNC faculty—wrote: "The white people of Chapel Hill ought to realize that trouble in the negro quarter is traceable to deeper causes than the lack of adequate police protection." Graves described how recently a "member of the faculty, had to go for the family servant in his automobile. He knocked on the door of the house where she lived. When there was no response he opened the door and knocked on a partition wall, and while he stood there he heard voices from several rooms." Later, Graves continued, the faculty member "remarked to the servant that there seemed to be a lot of people in a very small house. She told him that thirty-five men and women lived in the house, and that she paid a dollar a week for the privilege of sleeping on a cot in a room with two or three other persons."[47]

University research also showed how white political power kept local living conditions for African Americans in a shabby state. John Chapman observes how, through the early decades of the 1900s and the rise

of Jim Crow in Chapel Hill, "white neighborhoods gained public services at the expense of black neighborhoods."⁴⁸ Many of those interviewed
by Lee Coleman said that in addition to low wages, the poor housing,
high rents, and woefully inadequate city services in black neighborhoods were essential problems. C. T. Boyd Jr. pointed out that city garbage collectors skipped many African American blocks. "This service is
supposed to be available to all citizens," Boyd noted. The condition of
the streets themselves reflected a racist allocation of public resources.
"With a few exceptions," Boyd added, "the negro streets are very rough
and ill-kept."⁴⁹ James R. Cobb agreed. The black neighborhoods of Chapel Hill needed better street lights and better "upkeep" generally. "This
is only within their rights as taxpayers," Cobb asserted.⁵⁰

A number of local African Americans linked the prospect of future
progress with greater input from the black community itself. James R.
Cobb, for instance, captured perfectly how a liberal university environment, enlightened through academic freedom, was supposed to benefit
the entire state: "The university should make an example out of Chapel
Hill in its treatment of the negro. . . . By maintaining a liberal and fair attitude it can set an example for its own students to follow when they go
back to their respective home towns." Charles Craig, an active voter who
was also a member of the local Janitors' Association, the North Carolina
CIC, and the PTA, took his ideas a step further. He envisioned a "permanent negro advisory committee." As he explained it, "the city and county
officials usually build negro schools, pave streets, change school policies, etc. without consulting the group most concerned in the changes.
There have been some serious mistakes in the past through the lack of
such consultation. Such a committee could act as consultant, present
ideas and plans of its own, and serve as a channel for presenting pleas
by other negroes." Kenneth Jones agreed and called for "better cooperation and respect from city officials in general." But Jones added that because of the "attitude of some city officials, Chapel Hill negroes hesitate
to make any kind of complaint, even to report a street light out."⁵¹

To make life for the local black community even more difficult, the
threats of local racial violence remained. In December 1938, two African American brothers from Carrboro were held pending accusations
that they had raped a fifteen-year-old white girl a mile outside of Chapel Hill. One brother was soon released after the young woman indicated he was not among her attackers; the other remained in custody, but
still not charged. The *Daily Tar Heel* noted that armed UNC students

The *Daily Tar Heel* staff at work, ca. 1936.

roamed the town on the night of the arrest. John Creedy met a fellow student that night "walking the main street of Chapel Hill with a loaded shotgun."[52] Later, the student paper described "an angry crowd of Chapel Hill townspeople and students" who had "spent most of a day scouring the countryside for two Negro boys. They were armed with guns and bloodhounds. Cars and even an airplane were used to search out the fugitives. . . . This 'posse' was a product of a so-called enlightened college town."[53]

Following the 1937 unrest, UNC's freedom to investigate enabled them to learn a great deal about a local black community they had largely taken for granted, while the prospect of more violence reinforced their belief in gradual, careful change. Meanwhile, others at UNC focused their efforts on helping the struggling rural African American population and used their expertise to present scathing analyses of southern racial injustice.

Graduate student Olive Stone came to UNC in 1935 precisely

because of its liberalism on racial matters, as well as its highly regarded sociology department.[54] Stone would soon become the secretary for the Southern Committee for People's Rights, a fledgling civil rights group, but first she found quick academic success by publishing an article in the *Journal of Negro Education* in 1936. The article stated that "no segment of the population of the United States is so disadvantaged as the present Negro farm population. . . . The Negro farmer finds himself hedged about by the fact that he is a member of a minority race, discriminated against, in varying degrees, at all levels of attainment." She continued, "one must examine the economic nature of that position." Speaking of race and class in the South, Stone said that "it is next to impossible to treat them separately. And history has shown that neither taken alone can unlock the door to the Negro problem." Stone described the South as "a region where racial prejudice has been used as an economic and political weapon to prevent change and to avert dissatisfaction, where it has become a crippling divisive force in the use of public funds and facilities for health, education, transportation, etc." But, she added "racial discrimination is not just a haven of refuge for preservers of the *status quo* in eras of revolt. It is a practice kept oiled and working by regular and steady application in everyday life."[55]

However, Stone detected signs of positive change stirring in the rural South. "For an increasing number of Southern farmers, white and Negro, the days of climbing the Jacob's ladder of wishful thinking are over. They are organizing from Virginia to Texas, from Arkansas to Florida, into tenants' and croppers' and small farmers' unions and militantly protesting rather than passively acquiescing to the marked inadequacies of ladder relief, ladder credit, and ladder opportunities of an economic and social nature."[56]

Stone connected her view of the future with a remarkably modern interpretation of African American history, leading her to predict that the new assertiveness would continue. Black history, Stone argued, was "replete with the militant and courageous efforts of considerable numbers of Negro farmers to better their condition. . . . Slave revolts . . . organized demonstrations, and strikes, the use of civil and constitutional channels, agrarian, racial, and finally class protests fill every period of Negro history. . . . Each stage has prepared the way for the next." These movements now struck "fear into the hearts of those who trusted in ignorance, poverty, isolation, and the force of habit to avert such an eventuality."[57]

Despite the work of UNC faculty and graduate students such as Olive Stone, Lee Coleman, Charles Freeman, Paul Green, Guy Johnson, and others, university leaders grew increasingly concerned that the facts demonstrating the inequities of Jim Crow did not seem to be leading to reform or progress, which was the raison d'être of academic freedom. Consequently, UNC leaders often remained frozen by uncertainty over how exactly to proceed. After dutifully studying the local black community, it was not until the end of the decade that UNC took concrete steps to effect change. UNC officials helped fund and develop a new community center for African Americans, and with partial funding from the WPA, a new neighborhood that became known locally as Pine Knolls took shape as a home for African American UNC employees.[58]

Beyond Chapel Hill, UNC leaders found a small measure of success through their organizational approach to improving the quality of life for black North Carolinians. Graham, Odum, and Guy B. Johnson enthusiastically endorsed a mid-1930s proposal—initiated by N. C. Newbold, who headed up the state's Division of Negro Education—to create a new division of state government that would help improve education for the state's African Americans. The new agency would combine resources and personnel from the state Department of Public Instruction, UNC, Duke University, and the North Carolina College for Negroes.[59] In April 1935, Newbold received word that the General Education Board was sending $2,565 to cover half of the $5,130 budget submitted for the first fourteen months of the agency's activities.[60] The Division of Cooperation in Education and Race Relations was born.

Division activities ranged from promoting health care education to celebrating black culture. In 1936, the division sponsored a medical instruction clinic for fifty African American doctors. White physicians from the medical schools of UNC, Duke, and Wake Forest lectured on pulmonary diseases. A similar clinic conducted in 1937 concentrated on fractures, heart problems, diabetes, and various other ailments.[61] The Division of Cooperation also sponsored dental clinics that were run along the same lines as the medical clinics.[62] The clinics reflected the standard liberal values of the time: expertise, cooperation with the black community, and, division leaders hoped, progress in the form of better health.

As part of their efforts to recognize black culture, the division used funds to supply library collections with books "by or about Negroes." They promised to support the work of African American artist William

Arthur Cooper, who was to undertake a project to paint the portraits of one hundred North Carolina African Americans. The division also sponsored the writing of "brief sketches of the life and work" of leading black educators in the state. They hoped to broaden the history-writing component of their work to include histories of North Carolina's black colleges. Colleges that already had institutional histories sent them to be added to the Duke and UNC libraries.[63]

Division of Cooperation members saw their work as civilized and uplifting, but not every North Carolina resident agreed with them. N. C. Newbold received hate mail for associating with black educators and certain UNC faculty members. In 1937 he passed along to his UNC friends a copy of a semiliterate tirade he had received: "I am more than surprised to see your name connected with such Communistic people," the offended party wrote. "As you know Dr. [Guy] Johnson admits his membership in the Communistic party and . . . am convinced that you and [North Carolina College for Negroes president] Dr. [James] Shepard are also members." As for the division itself, "If this is not a disgrace to our State then nothing could be." The writer threatened to "appear before the legislative bodies and place this entire underhand, tratorous [sic] and disgraceful plan before them and ask the immediate removable [sic] of every State Employee connected and the elemination [sic] entirely of your dept. and your removable [sic] from the boundaries of our State."[64] Katharine Lackey, Frank Porter Graham's bright and capable secretary, could not resist replying to Newbold: "I thought Chapel Hill had the market cornered on the 'red,' but I see they are shooting at you too! I don't think it will bother Dr. Graham a great deal; from frequent exposure he has become immune."[65]

The Division of Cooperation's work was commendable, of course, and it amounted to more than most southern agencies or universities were willing to do. But it was also work done within the parameters of segregation, according to the pattern of white southern liberalism in the 1930s. However, academic freedom at UNC allowed a few courageous, insightful individuals to question whether segregation could ever be made equitable and just. For instance, the candid comments elicited from local African Americans in the sociology research following the 1937 riot indicated a new willingness to speak the truth about life under Jim Crow. Academic freedom at UNC facilitated the emergence of at least a few people who were willing to listen.

In various ways, UNC kept track of the increasing evidence that black impatience and resistance were growing in the 1930s. In a mid-decade letter to Guy B. Johnson, William J. Trent Jr., dean of Bennett College in Greensboro, recounted the arrest of newly hired professor Warren Scott for refusing to ride in the "colored" car of a train to Greensboro. Scott, a professor of religion, was traveling for the first time in the South. Finding the conditions of the coach reserved for African Americans unacceptable, he moved to the car reserved for white passengers. The conductor asked if Scott was "a foreigner or not." He was not. Then the conductor insisted he move to the "colored" car. Scott refused, "but was quite polite about it." Next, after "several unsuccessful attempts to unseat him," the conductor notified the police. While making the arrest the "everpresent sheriff with his two guns . . . proceeded to grasp Scotty by his coat collar and pull him along." Professor Scott resisted "such treatment" and was "threatened with a gun [by the sheriff]." Trent concluded: "And so off to jail." Scott was released on bail, whereupon he promptly retained a lawyer. The Southern Railway opted not to press charges, and the case against Scott was dropped. "The next week," Trent added, "Scott bought a car."[66]

In 1936 the UNC student paper informed its readers that black resistance was taking on the appearance of a mass movement. In February, the *Daily Tar Heel* ran a story about African American shoppers in Durham boycotting the local A&P and Kroger grocery stores to protest the stores' unwillingness to hire black workers. The story noted that the boycott would spread to include Pender's Grocery Store, a regional grocery chain, where, boycott leaders promised, "the placard 'DON'T BUY WHERE WE CAN'T WORK'" would be "paraded before the store."[67] In December 1937, the (white) Theatre Owners of North and South Carolina, Inc., passed a resolution to ban movies that depicted black and white actors acting on "equal social basis"—"whatever that is," said *Carolina Times* editor Louis Austin,[68] mocking the often-invoked white fear of "social equality" with African Americans. In response, college students from North Carolina A&T and Bennett College announced a boycott of Greensboro movie theaters.[69] Austin was thrilled. The students' action, "bespeaks a new day. . . . Here is hope—hope that a new Negro is about to come on the scene."[70] By February 1938, hundreds of Greensboro African Americans had joined the students in the boycott, and the Winston-Salem *Post*, which served as the local black newspaper, announced that it would not run advertisements from the theater corporation. Austin called upon black students throughout the state to join the A&T and Bennett students in the boycott: "Every time you spend a nickel with one of these theaters you are cutting the throats of your fellow students in Greensboro. . . . The refusal of Negroes to pull together in their fights has often been the cause of unnecessary defeats."[71]

As the *Daily Tar Heel's* stories on the boycotts indicate, the UNC community could not help but notice these events. Some UNC students showed new interest in the students at Bennett and North Carolina A&T, both historically black institutions. UNC alumnus George Stoney recalls that when he was a student, he met with African American students from nearby colleges in the mid-1930s through the campus YMCA. He noted that they were still careful not to have treats or sodas together, so as not to violate the segregationist custom of not eating with a person of the other race.[72] But Junius Scales, who came to UNC in 1937, four years after Stoney, recalled meeting and dining with black students through his membership in the American Student Union. For Scales, it was "a tremendous experience, to meet black students my own age and to sit down and have a meal. It was unbelievable. . . . It was quite thrilling in '37 or '38."[73]

Through the 1930s, some UNC liberals grew increasingly critical of segregation itself and not just its flaws. In 1935, Paul Green confided to his diary that "intelligence, justice, liberty have not the least connection with a man's color or whether he is waited on by a servant or waits on himself, whether his father owned three acres of land or three thousand or more. Again, a child knows this, and yet our system is such that we live and die with no other method in effect."[74] By the late 1930s, some people at UNC were starting to associate "progress" on race issues with the end of segregation instead of its careful reform. By creating the space for this view to emerge publicly, UNC's commitment to academic freedom deserves some of the credit for this progress.

Janet Seville, a graduate student in sociology, published a call to "drop the labels" in the November 1938 issue of *Carolina Magazine.* Seville argued that the effect of segregation was to "reduce awareness of other possibilities to a perception of skin color." The "labeling goes on and on. Each group sees itself in terms of individuals as people, sees the other in terms of the label." Jim Crow, Seville argued, not only injured black people; it failed all southerners. "The present position of the South in the national spotlight as the Economic Problem No. 1 indicates the inadequacy" of segregation, she argued. The South would never achieve progress until it could "drop the labels."[75] One reader found Seville's argument threatening and responded by issuing a threat of his own: "Yesterday afternoon about 1:30, a high school girl was criminally assaulted by a nigger. About 7:45 that evening a married lady living near Greenville, N.C., received the same treatment from a nigger assailant. I sincerely hope that those nigger-loving scalawags who called themselves Southerners in their articles in the Carolina Magazine . . . will read . . . and decide 'what kind of South' they are going to have if they 'Drop the Labels.'"[76]

By the late 1930s, some of UNC's institutional allies were raising questions openly, if cautiously, about the future of segregation. A committee of the Division of Cooperation submitted a report in early 1938 summarizing the current state of advanced education for black North Carolinians. North Carolina, the report began, "provides no educational facilities for its Negro citizens . . . in the professional fields of medicine, law, engineering, social work and pharmacy, and . . . no graduate work in the arts, science, or vocations." Next, the authors (which included black educator Charlotte Hawkins Brown) placed special emphasis on "the almost insuperable economic difficulties which stand in the way of establishing separate graduate and professional schools for Negroes . . . of the same quality as that which now prevails in the institutions available to white students." Following this point to its logical conclusion, the committee was "of the opinion that . . . the best way of meeting the graduate and professional needs of Negro students is to admit them to facilities available in the existing higher grade institutions of the State." This meant integration; but the committee report quickly backtracked by recommending first a "thorough canvass" to determine "whether or not it is practicable to initiate such admissions, experimentally." Before the report concluded, the authors switched directions entirely by urging the state to pour more money into building up opportunities for black graduate education, including providing "fellowships in institutions outside the State for Negroes who are eligible to pursue graduate and professional studies."[77] However timidly, a committee created by the state had broached the possibility of ending segregation. Soon the specter of ending segregation at UNC itself emerged.

In Division of Cooperation meeting minutes from 1938, UNC dean Francis Bradshaw commented that "this kind of meeting could not be held in places like Germany where people are weeded out on the basis of their racial stock."[78] These remarks are especially telling considering that some applicants to UNC were indeed "weeded out" because of their race. In 1933, Thomas Hocutt applied for admission to the UNC

Pharmacy School, because the state provided no graduate pharmacy education for black North Carolinians. Upon being denied admission, Hocutt took UNC to state court. As the Hocutt case approached its hearing, Frank Graham made an impassioned appeal for a more concerted effort to improve advanced education for African Americans. Graham wanted it made perfectly clear that Hocutt, in his view, probably was capable of matriculating successfully at UNC were it not for the state law that denied him entry. He hoped that, in the likely event that the court would rule against Hocutt, state leaders would work together in earnest to address the gaping inequities in the state's segregated educational systems. Graham noted that "for many years and in numerous directions the University of North Carolina has worked with the leaders of the Negro race in this state and in the South for the constructive promotion of the common good of both races."[79]

Judge M. V. Barnhill dismissed Hocutt's case, citing his failure to fill out a complete application, but the message was clear: the state was not about to let UNC budge on segregation, and Graham felt he had no choice but to obey state law. Southern liberals found it demoralizing that UNC, of all southern universities—and under Frank Graham, of all people—was not willing to do more to oppose the law mandating segregated schools. Virginius Dabney observed, "The University of North Carolina is concededly the most liberal state institution in the South in its attitude toward the Negro race. There is no likelihood that any other Southern college or university for whites will acquiesce in the admission of Negroes so long as the school headed by Dr. Frank P. Graham maintains its present uncompromising attitude."[80]

Later in the 1930s, young black North Carolinians and UNC officials alike closely followed the court case *Missouri ex rel. Gaines v. Canada*, Lloyd Gaines's case challenging the lack of graduate education for African Americans in Missouri. The case threatened to draw embarrassing attention to the callous and unfair reality of segregated school systems. Reactions to the *Gaines* case even before its conclusion shed light on the new assertiveness in the African American community, aimed now at UNC. The university reacted by reminding applicants of the state law mandating segregated schools; but UNC also revealed the conservative side of academic freedom by dismissing the arguments of black applicants as lacking sufficient expert authority to speak on what constituted progress in the immediate future of race relations.

In 1938, Frank Graham began to receive letters from African

Americans echoing themes from the *Gaines* case. In August, C. Durham Grandy of Greensboro wrote: "It may interest you to note, Dr. Graham, that there is nowhere in the state of N.C. a single first class university available to Negroes. That there is not one in the seventeen former slave states, a single university that will today receive Negroes into the medical school, supported by state funds. That there is not [one] that will receive Negroes in the graduate school."[81]

Edwina Thomas of Winston-Salem wrote to Dean W. W. Pierson asking for an application to one of the university's graduate programs. Thomas must not have indicated her race, because Pierson sent her an application, which she completed and returned. In all likelihood, Pierson then read on Thomas's application that she was a student at the all-black Talladega College in Alabama. He sent her a polite explanation of why he could not admit her. "It is my understanding," Pierson wrote, "that it is the public policy of the State of North Carolina and the University of North Carolina not to admit members of the colored race to the University. Such admission would entail a reversal of a social policy of long standing and would require action to that effect by the trustees of the institution." He would "withhold therefore a ruling as to your academic eligibility for admission."[82]

In May 1938, Edwina Thomas took her case to Frank Graham. "As I am unable financially to cope with the expenses of graduate schools outside of my own state," she explained, "I should like very much for you to advise me as to just what I can expect from the State of North Carolina in the way of help financially if I am to be denied admission to the State University because of my race."[83] In his reply, Graham pointed out the existence of a recently appointed governor's commission, most likely based on the Division of Cooperation's investigations, to study funding for graduate education for black students. At the moment, he was optimistic: "I think . . . you can count on some such provision within the coming year. We will be glad to cooperate to this end."[84] When Governor Clyde Hoey called for a special legislative session to be held in the fall of 1938, Thomas tried again with Graham. Sadly, Graham had to report to Thomas that the special session would not be discussing educational funds for black North Carolinians.[85] For a man like Graham, dedicated to racial uplift and education, such situations must have caused heartache. He believed that North Carolina would only change slowly, but he also knew full well that crucial opportunities for bright young black southerners were lost as time went by.

The U.S. Supreme Court ruled in favor of Lloyd Gaines in December 1938, holding that either the University of Missouri had to admit him or the state had to provide another university for him to attend that was of equal academic quality. The court's decision prompted a new round of inquiries to UNC from black North Carolinians. When Hubert Barbour, a prospective medical student from Johnson C. Smith University in Charlotte, wrote to Graham following the *Gaines* decision, Graham found himself having little to say. Barbour pointed out politely that the situation had now changed as a result of *Gaines*, because North Carolina did not have a medical school for African Americans: "Being a native of this state and due to a recent decision handed down by our Supreme Court I am eligible to enter your Institution." Barbour then backed off just a bit, allowing that UNC may not be ready to start admitting black graduate students right away. Instead, he offered Graham an alternative: "If I cannot enter in the fall of 1939 I should like to know if any appropriations can be made by my state for me to enter an Institution in another state."[86] Again Graham reported that committees were meeting, reports pending, and further developments looked hopeful. But he said nothing about Barbour attending UNC.[87]

The most celebrated of these inquiries came from the sharp mind of Pauli Murray. Murray began her attempt to enter UNC before the *Gaines* decision was handed down.[88] Her letters to and from Graham ended up making headlines in 1939. Murray was already running past the logic of the *Gaines* ruling and anticipating one of the issues that would surface in *Sweatt v. Painter* in 1950 and later in *Brown v. Board of Education* in 1954: separate meant unequal. The "Negro schools in North Carolina," she wrote Graham, "have not been given those facilities which will place them on a par with white schools." Whereas Graham had indicated that patience and separate but equal graduate schools were still a "wise long-range solution," Murray wanted to know "what guarantee have the Negro students of North Carolina that their graduate facilities will be any higher in quality than their undergraduate schools?"[89]

Graham conceded Murray's point about the poor quality of black education in the state, but he gave no ground on admitting her to UNC. "I am aware of the inequities which you point out," he assured her. But, as Graham saw it, "the only way to obey both the state Constitution and the United States Constitution is to make adequate provision in separate Negro institutions." Moreover, the "only way to change . . . the state Constitution . . . is by referendum of the people." Segregated public schools were part of the state constitution as amended in 1875, any change to which, as Graham noted, ultimately required the approval of the people. But the same Frank Graham who campaigned tirelessly and successfully in 1920 for a bigger educational budget, and again in the early 1930s to save UNC's appropriations, now expressed fear at the thought of a campaign for the end of segregated schools. Instead, Graham invoked his and UNC's cautious leadership: "Negro leaders and the white leaders who have been the friends of the Negroes in the struggle for justice are strongly of the opinion that the most unfortunate thing that could happen at this time would be a popular referendum on the race issue." It went without saying that Pauli Murray was not counted among Graham's group of "leaders"; therefore she lacked the authority or expertise to be taken seriously. Barely a year past Chapel Hill's own race riot, he concluded, "the possibilities of an inter-racial throwback do not have to be emphasized in our present world."[90]

Graham listed his many efforts to achieve "a more adequate provision for Negroes in the public schools, higher standard Negro undergraduate colleges, and a substantial beginning in the provision of graduate and professional work." Graham knew that phrases like "more adequate provision" and "a substantial beginning" rang hollow to young African Americans. "This may seem to you to be an inadequate and minimum program," he admitted, but there still remained, he repeated, the possibility of "a throwback against whose consequences we must unceasingly be on guard in the best interests of both races, who after all go up or down together."[91] Graham's view that both races were moving up and down together must have exasperated Murray; as she could have pointed out, one group was already "up" and the other already "down."

Still, Pauli Murray thanked Graham for his "very fine letter" and agreed that of course "the issues which you have raised . . . will require further study." But Murray added a thought that would run through the next generation of the civil rights movement: "We of the younger generation cannot compromise with our ideals of human equality. We have seen the consequences of such compromises in the bloody pages of human history, and we must hold fast, using all our passion and reason."[92] Pauli Murray ended up attending and graduating from Howard University Law School in 1944, before launching a brilliant career as a lawyer, writer, and civil rights leader.

Graham's letters to Pauli Murray offered very little in terms of concrete results for black students. His repeated fears of a "throwback" and his frequent invocations of "moving forward carefully" suggest that little was going to happen anytime soon, again reflecting the conservative side of the university mission. This formulation also gave him a measure of control. As he had explained earlier in response to the Ericson controversy, if either side pushed too hard there would be trouble unless they did what he as the leader of UNC suggested and took matters slowly and carefully. UNC leaders would have celebrated the existence of "passion and reason" among their own students, but those same traits among young African American activists made UNC liberals nervous. Graham and his colleagues genuinely feared another outbreak of violence in response to African American assertiveness. The *Daily Tar Heel* reported that UNC had taken on "an antebellum note" on the heels of the *Gaines* decision and the Murray letters. One student was quoted as saying, "I've never committed murder yet but if a black boy tried to come into my home saying he was a University student . . ." Other students "vowed they would tar and feather any—'nigger' that tried to come in class with them."[93]

Despite these hostile reactions, UNC's academic freedom still allowed for a few at the university to call openly for the end of segregation. Murray's visit to UNC in the spring of 1939 no doubt encouraged their efforts.[94] Historian Howard K. Beale, considered an expert on academic freedom, spoke out in her defense, as did UNC alumnus and Raleigh newspaperman Jonathan Daniels.[95] *Carolina Magazine* editor John Creedy supported immediate admission of black students into UNC: "Apart from the question of what a Negro ought to be is the fact that many of them are the equals in every way of the whites." Creedy, like Pauli Murray, had grasped the basic fact that they still lived in a semidemocratic society. He hoped that the "younger generation in the South" would be able to solve the problem differently from "Adolph Hitler and his fellow maniacs" by using "our own hearts and later with our votes and the votes of others of the new generation—which gives no tradition the right to say it nay."[96]

Glenn Hutchinson, a graduate student in sociology, added a biting, satirical look at the state of "equal opportunity" in segregated southern education. Writing in *Carolina Magazine*, Hutchinson started with an anecdote about an African American child standing at the classroom blackboard trying to solve a math problem posed by his teacher: "If two and two equals four when does one dollar equal four dollars?" Understandably, the child did not know the answer. His teacher then explained: "You see, Johnny, this is the way the white folks here in the South figure. Lots of big people like governors and legislators say we have got to have equality of opportunity in white and Negro schools. So they give us one dollar for every pupil and the white schools four dollars for every pupil and that is equality." Little Johnny went back to his desk muttering, "Dem white folks must be crazy." Careful to establish his credentials and perhaps taking a swipe at Howard Odum's all-white sociology courses on "The Negro," Hutchinson noted that he was

> a southerner born and raised in the heart of blackbelt Georgia, but I am not proud of that southern attitude. . . . How much nearer we would come to an intelligent understanding of the social problems that confront us in the South if the viewpoint of the Negro could be expressed in our classrooms. What would be more helpful to students in the sociology course on "The Negro" than for Negroes to be admitted to that class to bring the touch of reality to the search for understanding? In admitting Negroes to our graduate and professional schools their gain would also be our gain.

Concluding, Hutchinson proclaimed that "I would be really proud if the University of North Carolina would be the first in the South to crack open that iron gate which we have closed in the face of the Negro."[97] A group of ten graduate students published an open letter stating they had "no objection to the admission of Negroes to the graduate and professional schools of the University. We feel that the Negro as a citizen has every right to equal educational opportunities with every other group of citizens."[98]

Hutchinson also published in *The Crisis*, the NAACP publication, a summary of the controversy over the possibility of black graduate students integrating the university. Hutchinson pointed out that this debate at UNC was significant because "Chapel Hill has achieved something of a reputation of being the leader of southern liberal thought." He noted the absence in North Carolina of graduate training for black students—an important point in light of the *Gaines* ruling—and sounded a note of pessimism in response to Governor Hoey's contention that black graduate programs could be started "without the expenditure of a very large sum of money." Hoey, Hutchinson complained, "either has a very low opinion of the graduate and professional schools of his own university, or is sadly mistaken in believing that anything approaching 'equality of opportunity' can be provided 'without the expenditure of a very large sum of money.'"[99]

Despite the fact that "many liberal professors and students" at UNC "expressed themselves in favor of immediate admittance of Negroes to the graduate school," another challenge remained, Hutchinson said: the white southern public. "Those who are familiar with southern folkways realize that every other possible course will be exhausted before the color bar is taken down," he predicted. So for the moment, the fear remained that "each state will set up a weak graduate school for Negroes and thus seek to satisfy the letter of the law."[100] Because North Carolina lacked the funds to create a truly equitable dual school system, Hutchinson concluded, "there is left but one alternative, and that is to admit Negroes to the white colleges of the South." But, he continued, "as Shakespeare says, 'Aye, there's the rub!' But why should there be any 'rub'? . . . What was rubbed off the white teacher who first taught Frederick Douglass, the great emancipator, or Booker T. Washington, the great educator, or Paul Lawrence Dunbar, the great Negro poet? . . . Is it not time that our southern white colleges proved that they are really doing a good job in education by helping their students to rub out the rub of race prejudice?" Like Olive Stone, Hutchinson grounded his analysis in a modern view of southern history: "I am thankful that there are many native southerners, however, who are just as anxious to fight against race discrimination and race persecution as their grandfathers were to fight for slavery."[101]

In a letter to the *Daily Tar Heel,* history professor Howard Beale agreed with Hutchinson's view and tied UNC's reputation to his view of the promise of liberalism: "Most of us who know this university, especially those of us who know her reputation over the country, are proud of her tradition of liberalism that gives her prestige in the nation. This tradition has not been created by boasting of it in the abstract, but by successively meeting concrete issues as they arose in accordance with the best tenets of liberalism." But Beale also cut right to the heart of the limits of white southern liberalism during the pre–*Brown v. Board of Education* days: "The southern liberal, faced with the practical difficulties of the Negro in his midst, constantly faces a dilemma. . . . Yet the issue must be faced. . . . Liberalism cannot be pursued in all categories and then denied whenever the Negro appears." Beale predicted accurately that "sooner or later southern liberals must choose between their liberalism and their own or their neighbor's emotions on the Negro."[102]

The debate continued in other venues, where again one finds powerful arguments for integration met with invocations of caution by UNC leaders. Paul Green recorded the reaction to a talk he gave at Graham Memorial auditorium on the topic: "Urged chance for Negro graduate students at University. Silence—cold. Well, it will come. But we must work."[103] At an "inter-racial meeting" held shortly after the *Gaines* decision, students and faculty from the North Carolina College for Negroes, Bennett College, and UNC passed a carefully worded resolution urging "the legislature to consider a policy whereby qualified and carefully chosen Negro students could be educated in graduate and professional levels by the means and forces already existing in the state."[104]

Some comments made by Harry Comer, a popular member of the administration and executive secretary of the campus YMCA, reflect the increasingly difficult bind in which UNC officials found themselves as a result of the *Gaines* case. In a spectacular example of southern liberal wavering, Comer's comments ran the gamut from advocating integration to worries over a race war, all in the span of a few weeks. In February 1939, Comer "flatly stated that he would like to see Negro graduate students in the University 'by the beginning of the spring quarter, or at least shortly after that.'" Then, as the *Daily Tar Heel* noted, Comer "quickly modified his statement by explaining that it would be almost impossible under present conditions." Next he backed down some more: "We are not at that point now. The atmosphere would be unwholesome. It would be extremely uncomfortable for the Negro students at the University."[105] Privately, Comer revealed his fear to Graham that "I do not think a referendum on the state law to allow Negroes in the white schools would begin to carry, and fully believe also that such a referendum would come little short of precipitating a 'race war' in North Carolina."[106] Similarly, William T. Couch, director of UNC Press, wrote in *Carolina Magazine* that "I do not believe that any good would come from the admission of Negroes to the University; and if any situation should develop under which the Negroes were admitted I think it is possible that extremely serious trouble might ensue."[107]

The Psychology Department wavered similarly before arriving at Comer's and Couch's conclusion. A student's interview of J. F. Dashiell, the department chair, revealed that within the scientific community "the whole problem of race is pretty much an open question." Dashiell, along with professors English Bagby and Robert J. Wherry, noted that psychological testing showed that it was enormously difficult to pin down inherent intellectual racial differences. Bagby went so far as to say that "psychologists have failed to show any inherited differences between races." But Professor W. J. E. Crissy invoked the UNC approach of caution, conveniently placing the source of potential trouble off-campus when he argued that "the Negro admitted to Carolina would be faced with a grave conflict between academic equality and severe social inequality. . . . Even with tolerant students, a Negro's entrance may take effect in the state's backwoods area by stirring up the wrath of the people who would see in such a state of affairs the University tending toward radicalism." Therefore, most of the department faculty "agreed in the opinion that the admittance of the Negro to Carolina classrooms would be undesirable from both the Negro's point of view and the students' point of view."[108] From multiple sources within UNC, therefore, the voices of authority highlighted their own expertise in arguing for caution and against change.

Frank Graham, with the *Gaines* case decided, returned to a theme he had sounded several times before: the need for southern states to upgrade their public education commitment to their black citizens. Graham resumed his efforts as a persistent, passionate advocate of improved funding for black schools, essentially attempting to make real for once the "equal" part of the *Plessy* ruling's infamous "separate but equal" principle. In March 1939, Graham, in a nationally broadcast radio debate with Senator Josiah Bailey, placed equality in education within the global crisis of democracy. "With democracy in retreat in many parts of the world," Graham hoped that a new commitment to "equitable" funding would "give a lift to the democratic hopes of the forgotten millions."[109] During the question-and-answer period, Graham spoke more directly about the need for more funding for black schools, much to the delight of his many supporters. Iola Pryce wrote to Graham and offered her "deepest thanks for the beautiful plea which you made for equality in education being extended to Negro children in the south. You may be sure that the hosts of people who love justice cheered your remarks, so courageously made."[110] From Howard University School of Medicine, Dr. Hildrus A. Poindexter wrote: "Those of us who have carefully followed the policies, principles of fair play, and action of your administration at the University know that you stand for true democracy with opportunities for all Americans. Nevertheless, when an educator, who without duress or political expediency, expresses voluntarily to the nation his belief in minority opportunities, he deserves commendation for his strong conviction and courage. As long as champions, such as you, speak out, democracy will still live in America in spite of the action of others."[111] Even Senator Bailey chimed in: "You have your critics in North Carolina, but I believe 90 percent of the people appreciate your fine qualities."[112] Still, it is worth remembering that this chorus of praise was offered for Graham's efforts to make segregation more fair—not for any efforts to dismantle it.

We have seen that the threat of interracial violence did indeed loom in the 1930s, occasionally breaking out into actual altercations. As the 1930s turned into the 1940s, that threat did not abate. Richard Wright, notorious in the white South for his white wife and for having been a communist at one time, spent the summer of 1940 in Chapel Hill working with Paul Green on a stage production of Wright's novel *Native Son*. At the summer's end, Wright and others planned to have a party to celebrate the play's completion. Carrboro resident and writer Daphne Athas recounts that the plan to have the party in Carrboro brought forth a warning: "The rednecks sent word through the grapevine" that "if you bring that nigger to Carrboro, we're going to kill him."[113] The party took place in Chapel Hill instead. Paul Green's daughter, Janet, recalls that her father was "alarmed by a crowd of angry white Chapel Hill citizens who told him they resented Wright's presence with white girls at a racially mixed party. They threatened trouble. One was my dad's cousin, and he had a gun. Dad calmed them down as best he could, but he spent the night beside Wright's rooming house, in case the mob came for him." According to Janet Green, her father "never told Wright of this and similar hostile incidents."[114]

UNC officials took special notice of Wright's presence. Comptroller William D. "Billy" Carmichael asked John Blake, a Chapel Hill police officer, to spy on those attending the dinner for Wright. Blake reported back to Carmichael, "As per your request I am furnishing you with what information I have on the party that was given Wednesday night for the negro author [Wright]." Blake listed four women, two each from Chapel Hill and Carrboro, as well as four men and one woman described as students. Blake added, "There were others that I was unable to find out who they were."[115]

For UNC leaders, the difficulties of trying to do right by their black fellow citizens without provoking a "throwback" continued to mount, especially after the *Gaines* decision. In February 1940, Dean R. B. House received an alarming memorandum informing him that there were

African American students taking correspondence instruction through the university. Dean House wrote back with an experienced administrator's mix of politeness and urgency. "I am convinced that we had better stop all proceedings right where we are and ask advice and permission from the University and State authorities before proceeding any further," House suggested, knowing full well what the results of such a request for "advice" would be. Continuing to give correspondence instruction to black students was risky "because we are in danger of violating the law by direct or indirect enrollment of Negroes. I ask you, therefore, to clear out and finish such individuals as you have in process now and to accept no further responsibility in the matter whatsoever until I bring you an answer from the President and the Trustees."[116] The fact that black North Carolinians were already taking correspondence courses at UNC would have, at a minimum, proved quite an embarrassment to school officials had it been made public.

By the end of the decade, there was indeed a "new Negro" on the scene, just as newspaper editor Louis Austin had hoped. Unfortunately, there were far too few "new" white southerners. UNC's ambitions at the beginning of the interwar period—to chart the path for improved race relations—ended up being frustrated as the 1940s began. They were confounded in the 1930s by the fact that neither their fellow white citizens nor young African Americans were especially interested in what UNC had to offer by way of gradual progress under its leadership. UNC's investment in its identity as a trustworthy institution, dedicated to academic freedom, underlined its commitment to the goal of gradual racial progress. But that commitment to gradualism also ended up compromising the university's efforts to lead when change came about in the form of growing black resistance and the *Gaines* decision (and later *Sweatt v. Painter* and *McLaurin v. Oklahoma State Regents* in 1950). Still, on campus, Paul Green, E. E. Ericson, student editor John Creedy, Glenn Hutchinson, Howard Beale, Janet Seville, and others dared to imagine, talk, and write about a future South without racial discrimination. By doing so, they at least forced the argument for integration out into the open. But the country's entry into World War II shifted much of the university's focus away from its self-proclaimed leadership role in race matters. The first African American students admitted into UNC did not arrive until the early 1950s.

5

"The Rankest Center of Communism"

The Left Comes to Campus

UNC campus events in the early 1930s seemed to confirm David Clark's suspicions that the university was the "refuge of radicals and socialists." In May 1931, British socialist Harold Laski, Frank Graham's former professor at the London School of Economics, delivered a lecture at UNC. The same week, Norman Thomas, leader of the American Socialist Party, visited campus.[1] In September, a small UNC branch of the Socialist Party set a fall schedule of biweekly meetings and invited "everyone interested in the discussion of social, economic, and political problems from the socialistic viewpoint" to attend.[2] In October 1931, a handful of students organized a John Reed Club. Named after the radical journalist whose life was profiled in the movie *Reds*, John Reed Clubs promoted proletarian art and journalism and had ties to the Communist Party USA.[3] In a 1932 *Daily Tar Heel* poll of students' preferences for president, Socialist Party candidate Norman Thomas placed second behind Franklin Roosevelt (and well ahead of the Republican incumbent, Herbert Hoover).[4]

That same fall, when communist organizers were making plans to organize textile workers in Burlington, UNC professors invited the communists to speak at Graham Memorial hall. UNC's academic freedom and liberalism instantly became focal points for criticism. The Burlington *Daily News* criticized UNC, "supported by funds from the pockets

Norman Thomas, American Socialist Party candidate for president of the United States, speaks to a UNC audience, 1931. Thomas finished second to Franklin Roosevelt in a 1932 UNC student poll of presidential preferences.

of the lowly taxpayers," for "allowing the communistic party to organize on the Hill." UNC professors, the paper complained, made the campus "a haven for communist[s], a party that openly opposes our form of government and the teachings of Jesus Christ." The *Daily Tar Heel* no doubt made few friends by lumping the *Daily News* editor in with other "bigots" as one who "digs deep into the storehouse of demagogy and . . . appeals to the common people, to class prejudice, to fundamentalists, to chauvinists, to section pride and prejudice, and to groups of the same backward unintelligent understanding as his own."[5]

UNC's involvement with labor activities and leftist leaders got the decade off to a contentious start in the ongoing struggle to define what academic freedom would mean. Unlike the 1920s, when the mere desire to investigate working conditions prompted cries of "radicalism" from critics like David Clark, during the 1930s there was no question that some faculty and students at UNC were active in leftist and labor causes. But whereas conservatives like Clark blamed academic freedom for the presence of activist professors, UNC leaders insisted that the commitment to academic freedom kept inappropriate activism out of the classroom and research while allowing the faculty their rights as individuals to follow their political convictions in other arenas.

UNC sociologist Eugene C. Branson, far from being a radical, had absorbed the university mission fully. While the university was not beyond error, he explained in a letter to his son, "where [Clark] says or implies that the University of North Carolina is teaching in its classrooms any of the things that he so bitterly opposes . . . the charge simply isn't true." He continued:

> If perchance these various questions come up in classrooms and in student-group meetings our aim is to see that both sides have a full hearing. We act upon the belief here that the University is a fact-finding body and not a propagandist agency for any set of economic or social doctrines. Who shall deny students the right to think? The professors? The trustees? . . . I deny that the University is the seedbed of riots and insurrections against the established order of things. . . . Exactly the contrary is true here. The University is struggling with all these wild rumors with all the wisdom it can command.[6]

UNC officials and faculty echoed Branson's point throughout the decade. Radicalism, whether anyone liked it or not, was in the air in the 1930s. Surely it was better, they argued, to analyze radical ideas and movements in the presence of responsible, educated, trustworthy UNC faculty members, and offer to their students and to the state at large "all the wisdom it can command," in Branson's words.

In the heated political atmosphere of the 1930s, however, it was a tall order to ask people to believe that a professor working alongside a socialist labor organizer off campus was not somehow going to be critical of free-market capitalism back in the classroom. UNC leaders were aware of this predicament. In Paul Green's *The Enchanted Maze*, for example, a 1939 play based loosely on UNC campus life, a troubled student faces expulsion for delivering a pro-labor speech before an audience that included pro-business trustees. The student explains that he felt it was his duty to defend labor: "Dr. Coleman himself has taught us in sociology fifty-four that labor has a right of collective bargaining, and free speech. And one day I remember he said the worker should share in the profits of his labor. Isn't that right, Dr. Coleman?" Green's stage directions for the embarrassed professor's response are succinct: "[*But* DR. COLEMAN *stares ahead of him without making an answer.*]"[7]

At UNC the principles of openness and honesty were critical to the university's ability to maintain its defense of its academic freedom. If university radicals did the job they were hired to do for the university and remained open and honest about their activities off campus, then Frank Graham stood a chance to retain the trust of North Carolina taxpayers, trustees, and legislators, as well as the legion of university supporters throughout the South. Over the course of the decade, not surprisingly, UNC often failed to convince critics who equated activism with radicalism that academic freedom was not somehow part of the "problem," as they saw it.[8]

Within days of his inauguration in early November 1931, turmoil greeted Frank Graham's presidency. As mentioned in the previous chapter, UNC playwright Paul Green and sociologist Guy Johnson invited poet Langston Hughes to deliver a lecture and speak to select classes on November 19, 1931. By all accounts Hughes's visit to the campus was uneventful. The *Daily Tar Heel* described Hughes giving a "straightforward, humorous story of his life."[9] Hughes did interject some race and class analysis into his classroom visits, however. He explained, for instance, how he had "no objections to humble labor but I rebel against a system which limits negroes to these jobs alone."[10]

Poet Langston Hughes (*left*) visits with Tony Buttitta in Chapel Hill, 1931. Re-percussions from Hughes's visit plunged new UNC president Frank Graham into a fierce battle over academic freedom.

The controversy arose mainly in response to the publication in an off-campus journal, *Contempo*, of Hughes's poem "Black Christ" and an essay he had written about the ongoing saga of the Scottsboro Boys. In "Black Christ" Hughes wrote, "Christ is a nigger on the cross of the South." His words about Scottsboro were similarly inflammatory. Pointing out that the nine Scottsboro boys had no chance for a fair trial, he sarcastically criticized the "dumb young blacks" for being "so indiscreet as to travel, unwittingly, on the same freight train with two white prostitutes." In the future, he suggested, "let the sensible citizens of Alabama (if there are any) supply schools for the black populace of their state, (and for the half-black, too—the mulatto children of the Southern gentlemen. [I reckon they're gentlemen.]) so the Negroes won't be so dumb again." Hughes also took a swipe at "the mill-owners of Huntsville," pointing out that if they paid higher wages, then white women would not "need to be prostitutes."[11]

Constant UNC critic David Clark went ballistic. In addition to threatening a lynching, Clark wondered aloud what could possibly explain the University's acceptance of such a person? Of course he had his answer already: "Communism demands social equality with negroes," he pointed out, "and must have been well-taught at Chapel Hill."[12] Others condemned UNC about as angrily. Thomas P. Graham, a relative of Frank's, wrote: "The whole State is being stirred about the unfortunate Langston Hughes affair." UNC in particular was "being criticized severely that this infamous negro was even allowed on the University campus."[13] He went on, "Unless the condition is remedied and at once, I shall give all my support to some other Institution that has nerve and power enough to stand in the fear of God, and in the ideals that built it. . . . All the alumni are behind you to a man," he added, but that loyalty came at a price: they "all expect you to take steps immediately to prohibit similar happenings and to weed out any Professors or Instructors with Communistic or Anti-Christian teachings."[14]

In defense, UNC spokesmen pointed out that Hughes's actual visit came off without incident—an example of academic freedom exercised calmly and responsibly—and that *Contempo* was not a university publication or published by university students. The latter was technically correct; coeditors Milton Abernethy and A. J. Buttitta were former UNC students. In the fall semester of 1931, Buttitta was not registered, while Abernethy had withdrawn from the UNC law school in October, citing a lack of funds. This means Abernethy was most likely still enrolled when he and Buttitta planned the publication, but not at the time when the controversial material was actually published.[15]

No one at UNC disputed that Hughes was a radical in the eyes of most southerners. Yet, they argued, his radicalism harmed no one when the actual radical himself appeared on campus to exchange ideas with faculty and students in an atmosphere of academic freedom. Of the event itself, university executive secretary Robert B. House pointed out that "while on campus, from all I can learn, [Hughes] conducted himself as a gentleman in every way."[16] UNC officials portrayed the uproar over Hughes's visit as another of David Clark's serial attempts to attack academic freedom and undermine the university. Speaking about Clark, House said, "simply examine the files of the Southern Textile Bulletin, pick out his numerous comments on the University . . . compare these with the actual facts and just see whether or not when Mr. Clark . . . knows what a fact is."[17] The *Daily Tar Heel* chimed in: "So Little David picks up his trusty slingshot, lays in a good supply of spitballs, and set out to destroy a mythical Goliath of communism at Carolina."[18]

Langston Hughes came and went from Chapel Hill, but the controversy did not leave so quickly. David Clark continued to hammer away, linking the school's academic freedom and liberalism to the infiltration of godless communism and radicalism. Soon after Hughes's departure, Clark noticed the latest production by the renowned Carolina Playmakers: a three-act production called *Strike Song*, co-written by James O. Bailey of the UNC English Department and his wife, Loretto Carroll Bailey. The UNC *Alumni Review* explained that *Strike Song* was an "impartial" production based loosely on the 1929 labor uprisings in Gastonia and Marion.[19] Loretto Carroll Bailey explained that she and her husband "sought in this play not to suggest a solution rising out of the industrialization of the piedmont south, but to present the situation as honestly as possible from several points of view."[20]

David Clark remained unconvinced, to put it mildly. Clark called *Strike Song* a "gross, willful, and deliberate misrepresentation of the textile industry." He complained that characters "upon the side of the strikers are painted in the best possible light whereas those upon the side of the mill are represented as unfavorably as possible."[21] Clark suspected there was more at work here than just a romanticized, pathetic version of the 1929 strikes. The play's inclusion of music caused Clark to wonder if perhaps the purpose of the play was to give striking workers new songs to sing. At one point the workers perform a song credited to slain

North Carolina striker Ella May Wiggins and sung to the tune of "The Battle Hymn of the Republic":

> The boss man wants our labor, and his gold to pick away.
> But the workers want a Union, and a shorter working day.
> He has told us that he hates us, just because we want more pay.
> The Union is marching on.
> Glory, glory, to the Union.
> Glory, glory, to the Union.
> Glory, glory, to the Union.
> The Union is marching on!

It is hard to imagine a song bound to produce more outrage in a pro-business, white southerner like David Clark than one with lyrics written by a communist and modeled after original lyrics written by an abolitionist. Clark insisted that the play represented "an effort to aid the unionizing Southern mills and its authors have used the weapon of misrepresentation to an extreme extent in an effort to further the cause. It is a gross and willful effort and is contemptible."[22]

UNC's interest in the new proletarian theater continued when Michael Gold, editor of the Marxist journal *New Masses*, visited campus in April 1932. Gold visited E. E. Ericson's sophomore English class, E. J. Woodhouse's government class, and drama professor Frederick Koch's playwriting class. In Koch's class, Gold spoke highly of the new theater movement in the Soviet Union and called for the development in America of "mass drama." A proponent of the workers' theater movement, Gold predicted the commercial theater was "soon to die," to be replaced by "mass drama" that would "present through the individual, the mass, and mass problems on the stage." Voicing the agitprop views of the 1930s theater left, Gold told the class, "In this manner alone can the theatre live as an actual social force rather than a seat of culture and entertainment."[23]

The controversy over Hughes's visit resurfaced in September 1932 when L. A. Tatum of Belmont, North Carolina, a "retired cotton manufacturer," according to the *Winston-Salem Journal,* presented a petition to Governor Gardner condemning UNC, citing Hughes's visit and decrying the "anti-religious invasion of higher education."[24] Approximately three hundred North Carolinians signed the "Tatum Petition," forcing Graham and other university supporters to endure another round of accusations that academic freedom and liberalism served as the gateway to radical infiltration of the south. S. F. Teague, a Goldsboro attorney, wrote to Graham: "As to the negro Langston Hughes . . . I do not think he is the type of person that I would want my alma mater to allow on its campus. I am sure that I would not want him lecturing to my boys. . . . In fact I can see no reason why a group of Southern boys would want a negro lecturing to them in their college."[25] W. H. Ruffin wrote to UNC dean Francis Bradshaw that he realized that Graham and other university leaders were not socialists, but their position on academic freedom "offers an opportunity to radical and destructive forces to concentrate their efforts in Chapel Hill." When someone like Langston Hughes visited UNC, "it can be compared to releasing a number of test tubes full of typhoid germs in the water supply of Chapel Hill."[26]

Graham, meanwhile, somehow ended up with a copy of a letter that told a very different tale from the newspapers' descriptions of Tatum as a rich, retired, conservative cotton man. Raymond Bellamy, a sociology professor from the Florida State College for Women, wrote to C. C. Weaver, an Episcopalian minister from Winston-Salem, detailing a previous encounter with Tatum in Florida. "Your information concerning the activities of Mr. Tatum has a strangely familiar sound," Bellamy began. Tatum "spent weeks and months—and I can almost say *years*—in our library, hunting through the books and picking out little isolated sentences which he could construe as being undesirable. He seemed to have a peculiar delight in hunting out obscene matter. . . . I have also been told that he makes a point of reading all the details about murders if they have a sex complication. . . . Frankly, I believe the man is decidedly unbalanced mentally."[27] Bellamy continued to spill the sordid details of Tatum's life in Florida: "It is common knowledge that he was a high official in the Ku Klux Klan." According to Bellamy, the local community shunned Tatum until he finally left. The Masons refused him, the Kiwanis ousted him, his local Presbyterian Church forced him to quit teaching Sunday school, and the Chamber of Commerce published an open letter labeling Tatum an "unwelcome stranger."[28] It is not clear what, if anything, Graham did with this information.

Support for the university remained solid among those who applauded UNC's liberalism and academic freedom. Locally, Rev. Albea Godbold of University Methodist Church urged Graham to take heart: "We glory in the tolerance, freedom, and democracy that prevail on this campus, and are grateful for a president who fearlessly champions these great goods of life." Godbold was not merely celebrating Graham as a fellow liberal. Rather, he made it a matter of special importance that Graham, as a liberal in a position of authority at the university, led according to their shared progressive beliefs, beliefs that included "freedom . . . on this campus. . . . God grant that narrow-mindedness, bigotry and prejudice shall not hamper the University of North Carolina," he concluded.[29]

Other letters echoed Godbold's. Jonathan Daniels of the *Raleigh News & Observer* wrote: "Tatum's activities, it seems to me, are rather dangerous at this time when the naturally large reactionary element in this State can secure ready support from those who do not want to pay high taxes." Like Albea Godbold, Daniels was not just defending liberalism; he defended UNC's liberalism and academic freedom together. There was, he added, "not anything closer to my heart than intellectual freedom and the welfare of the University."[30] The *News & Observer*'s Nell Battle Lewis called the petition the "return of Bryanism" from the previous decade and "foolishness, just plain foolishness."[31] J. L. Hamme added, "Doubtless the suggestion from any of the friends of the University, to produce counter petitions, would result in thousands as compared with hundreds."[32] Governor Gardner gave the petition the silent treatment, and within a few weeks Graham was writing to thank newspaper editors for their support as the crisis faded.[33] Graham wrote to J. Edward Dowd, editor of the *Charlotte News*, to thank Dowd for his assistance in UNC's "hour of need. You and other editors have reached out helpful hands from State to Chapel Hill, and believe me we were glad to take hold of them."[34]

Summarizing the university's latest fight with its reactionary critics, a student journalist, John Alexander, tried to set the controversy within the context of what life was actually like on the UNC campus. While Alexander admired his professors' liberalism, his analysis offers a useful reminder that one test for UNC's academic freedom was how much latitude it created for faculty and students on campus to do their work, not whether it made UNC a "liberal" university. Alexander related how the university had long been locked in "constant struggle against reactionary forces which have been overcome only thru [*sic*] great bravery and doggedness of purpose of our leaders who have been ever ready and willing to risk their positions in the cause of liberal education." But, Alexander continued, "there is very little going on in Chapel Hill . . . that would mark us as particularly liberal in the eyes of the nation. . . . Free

Life was not all studying and activism at UNC during the 1920s and 1930s: students relaxing, 1937.

love and atheism, the bogies that haunt the dreams of Tatum and Clark are practically unknown to the student body." Indeed, he argued, there was simply not much at UNC to distract the students "from the ways of righteousness, the Democratic party, or the sanctity of the home. On the contrary there is little here that might ruffle the most reactionary, crabbed, hardshelled, and dyed-in-the-wool, ultra conservative."[35]

Despite John Alexander's assurances, a tidal wave called the General Textile Strike crashed over the state in the fall of 1934, energizing university activists, prompting spirited campus discussions of the future of capitalism, and bringing UNC in for more criticism as being sympathetic to radical forces now even more evident in the South. The strike took hundreds of thousands of workers off the job throughout the South and brought the simmering frustration on both sides of the labor issue to a violent boil in September. Strikes literally surrounded Chapel Hill, occurring in Durham, High Point, and Burlington. The *Raleigh News & Observer* reported that six thousand textile workers were on strike in High Point alone. On September 5, High Point police, with the help of state National Guard troops, made more than thirty arrests, charging striking workers with forming a "flying squadron" of men to infiltrate the plant premises and forcibly shut down the Carolina Cotton and Woolen Mills.[36] The High Point arrests gained notoriety from the fact that the alleged mastermind of the flying squadron was Alton Lawrence, secretary of the state Socialist Party and a UNC graduate, class of 1933. Upon hearing that Lawrence had been arrested, Frank Graham, traveling in Georgia, wired the High Point police and expressed his willingness to "go bond" for Lawrence. Chief of police W. G. Friddle refused Graham's offer, stating, "I do not regard a telegraphic agreement to go on bond as a legal bond."[37] Without Graham's help, Lawrence was released September 9.[38]

Graham's willingness to bail Lawrence out made headlines and gave his critics another opportunity to accuse him of being a closet socialist. Leading the attack, as always, was David Clark: "We think it was very appropriate for President Graham to furnish bail because he is responsible for Alton Lawrence for being a socialist. He was not a socialist before he entered the University." Graham and his radical professoriate, Clark charged, "have been working for several years to install socialism, communism, and atheism in the minds of immature boys intrusted [sic] to their care and it was but to be expected that they would make converts of some of those who had weak minds."[39]

Once again Jonathan Daniels and the *Raleigh News & Observer* defended Graham. Graham, Daniels explained, "undertook to go on the bond of the young Socialist . . . not because he shares that young man's economic views, but because having known the young man as a student, he was 'confident you have committed no crime.'" Graham's willingness to stand up for the legal rights of this one person was inspirational because "in North Carolina today . . . there is real danger that the forces of government are more preoccupied with the preservation of the rights of property than safeguarding the rights of men." The "courage of one great liberal gleams . . . in the present darkness."[40]

The state's labor unrest took a new and explosive turn in Burlington in September, pushing Alton Lawrence's arrest off the front page. People had long considered Burlington immune to the economic problems and labor unrest afflicting the rest of the country because Burlington Industries had moved into the production of rayon, a material popular for new fashions and household uses, and demand for rayon was perennially strong.[41] But Burlington was swept up in the General Textile Strike anyway; on September 15, the Holt Plaid Mill was damaged by explosions that turned out to be caused by detonations of dynamite. Rumors quickly swirled, claiming that this was sabotage committed by striking workers. The rumors intensified when sticks of unexploded dynamite were found at the Stevens Manufacturing Company, also in Burlington. Within days, ten men were arrested, and by December seven of them were found guilty.[42]

On campus, the results of the trial sparked passionate interest in the workers' cause. UNC Press director William T. Couch, English professors James O. Bailey and E. E. Ericson, playwright Paul Green, and C. Vann Woodward, at the time a graduate student in history, headed up campus efforts to draw attention to the plight of the convicted workers. The "Defense Committee" charged that the workers' trial represented a miscarriage of justice. Couch and Bailey coauthored an article presenting their own facts, in the UNC way, and discrediting all the evidence against the workers.[43] In private correspondence, C. Vann Woodward revealed that he had visited the strike scenes with Communist Party organizer Don West, who was wanted for arrest in Atlanta and who used the name James Weaver.[44] Having explained that "the only way to learn about American labor is through first-hand observation," at Burlington Woodward saw "workers who wer [sic] bayoneted" and how "every method of fascism was used" against them. Despite his association with West, Woodward also believed that in this strike, "communism was pretty much eclipsed."[45]

UNC activists joined the cause by supporting the workers' appeal, although undercover communist organizers such as Don West were instrumental in keeping the momentum for an appeal going. Local efforts began in February 1935, when West organized a "forum" for Methodist and Baptist student groups to discuss what was being called the Burlington Dynamite Case.[46] Within days, four of the convicted workers made an appearance on campus at an event billed as a "mass meeting of students and townspeople."[47]

The appearance of the convicted workers on campus touched off a brief exchange between the editors of the *Daily Tar Heel* and Woodward, a member of the convicted strikers' defense committee. The student paper took a conservative turn, arguing that they "cannot help those Burlington strikers who were convicted of dynamiting." The students, "we are sorry to say, have neither the money nor the community influence to aid them to get an appeal that may be fully justified." The editorial did not dispute that the students had the right to help, if they so chose. But instead it reminded readers of the trust the university needed to maintain with the public. Echoing J. G. de Roulhac Hamilton's argument from the 1920s, the editorial argued that campus displays of radicalism, especially futile radicalism, would not serve the university well. In light of the "prejudice that already exists against the University, it is an imprudent move to call such a meeting. That prejudice has grown out of the same feeble, misdirected, and ostentatious efforts that characterize such strivings toward social justice as this."[48]

C. Vann Woodward took the editors to task. On the matter of labor relations, Woodward had done his homework: "I happen to know that the interests of these strikers are pretty much 'jeopardized' whether such meetings are held or not." He accused the writers of undermining UNC's willingness to create a place for liberalism in an otherwise conservative region, and he asked whether "you young gentlemen believe you are doing the University a good turn by writing such stuff as this for the consumption of timid legislators and mill owners." UNC's progressive reputation, he concluded, "was not won, not can it be defended by truckling. . . . Chapel Hill is thought of all over the south as the last stronghold of the liberal tradition. It ought to be worth a better defense than it is getting."[49]

At the workers' event, two of the convicted workers, John "Slim" Anderson and J. P. Hoggard, addressed the crowd, estimated at ninety people. The workers "calmly and self-possessedly proclaimed their innocence." J. H. Wisherd of the English Department, Paul Green, E. E. Ericson, and William T. Couch all spoke of the difficult plight facing the convicted workers as they waited out their appeal. The speakers urged people to donate to the workers' defense fund to defray the expenses of their appeal, despite the slim odds of their convictions being overturned by the North Carolina judicial system. Following the convicted workers' appearance at Gerrard Hall on February 21, the paper reported on the "whole-hearted support" that their backers on campus gave them.[50] The workers' appeal was indeed eventually rejected.

The Burlington case evoked emotions on campus, both in sympathy with and opposition to the more aggressive style of labor activism. In April 1935 the university's Human Relations Institute invited George Soule, editor of the *New Republic*, as the annual Weil Lecturer. The institute's lecture committee also planned to hold a forum on the state of capitalism. The invited participants were Norman Thomas of the American Socialist Party; Chester Wright of the United Textile Workers; Donald Comer, a textile mill president; and Hamilton Fish

Jr., a fiercely anticommunist Republican congressman from New York. During the first week of April 1935, the Human Relations Institute panels convened and instantly produced controversy.[51] During textile union leader Chester Wright's question-and-answer period, a student member of the audience stood and asked "if the speaker had ever been to Russia." The questioner was "vigorously booed by the audience," but the *Daily Tar Heel* could not help but notice the large number who seemed to be in "whole-hearted student agreement with Hamilton Fish's red-baiting republicanism." It was, they believed, "manifest that conservatism is the keynote of most of the student undergraduate body."[52]

The next day, the paper reported that the campus conservatives remained motivated, and when "campus reds and parlor pinks, gunning for Hamilton Fish" tried to dominate two sessions "with discussions of Soviet Russia," they were "enthusiastically booed by a packed Gerrard Hall." (It is not surprising that campus leftists would react strongly to Fish's presence. In 1930, he had chaired the Special Committee to Investigate Communist Activity, a precursor to the House Un-American Activities Committee.) The student paper could not decide whether "the booing of the pink intellectuals was due to their unpopularity as individuals, to the unfairness and maliciousness of their attacks on the speaker, to the conservatism of the audience or to the general feeling that there are matters of more importance and more immediate interest worthy of discussion than Soviet Russia." The author did assert, however, that "these radicals have assumed an importance out of all proportion to their significance as thinkers or organizers."[53] Conservatives and radicals mixing in the audience, nationally famous speakers from the Right and the Left, follow-up seminars, all under the watchful eye of responsible UNC faculty—this was how academic freedom was supposed to function.

By the end of April 1935, the *Daily Tar Heel* noted that "conservatives have found excitement a-plenty" on campus and reported on the formation of a campus chapter of the American Liberty League, an anti–New Deal organization founded in 1934.[54] The paper credited Winthrop Durfee, "platform performer and a man of ideas," with "stirring up some of the conservative thought on campus in order to organize it."[55] At the league chapter's organizational meeting on May 2, twenty-five students joined and elected Durfee as president. Durfee hoped the chapter would "prove to North Carolina and the nation that this University is not a 'hotbed' of radicalism." As one of its first activities, the chapter planned to invite David Clark to speak on campus.[56]

Clark, no doubt delighted by the Liberty League's invitation, accepted, and on May 14, 1935, he hurled the usual accusations and conspiracy theories at UNC, this time in person. While proclaiming that he would not "yield to anyone in my advocacy of legitimate free speech," Clark nonetheless raised again the specter of subversion through academic freedom: "I condemn the cowardly attempt of certain professors to crawl under the cover of freedom of speech while trying to instill subversive doctrines into the minds of boys and girls entrusted into their care." He leveled another warning to UNC that the "politicians of this state have their ears to the ground" and "when they wake up to the fact that the mass of the common people are behind me in condemning radical activities at the University, the University will suffer." The subversive doctrines Clark had in mind were the same ones he had complained about a decade earlier, and he explicitly reached back to the 1920s as the source of UNC's radicalism: "It is my firm conviction that Dr. Chase is responsible for the establishment of teaching atheism, socialism, and communism at the University."[57]

But standing before the packed Gerrard Hall audience, Clark got a taste of the rigors of the scholar's life when audience members got their turn in the question-and-answer session. Dudley DeWitt Carroll, dean of the School of Commerce, asked Clark to define the terms he used to attack the university. As the *Raleigh News & Observer* reported, "At one point when Dean Carroll asked Mr. Clark: 'What is Socialism?' Mr. Clark replied: 'I don't know, and I don't think anybody else does.' The audience fairly howled."[58] Carroll then asked Clark directly: "Do you think the analyzing of the facts of socialism and communism should be permitted in political or economic courses?" Clark ducked, and commented on the question instead, saying he "doubted its sincerity." After persistent attempts to get Clark to answer the question, he managed to reply that "to some extent, yes," socialism and communism could be studied.[59]

Since Clark had singled out them out before as the main purveyors of subversion on the UNC campus, E. E. Ericson and William T. Couch responded with written rebuttals that addressed a different aspect of academic freedom. Ericson could not deny that locally his politics were considered radical. Instead, he insisted that he performed the job UNC had hired him to do and that therefore he was free to hold whatever political views he chose outside the classroom. Ericson's statement first noted that Clark's very presence on campus and the content of his speech were proof that "the University stand is that of providing an 'open forum' for all shades of thought that have representatives and are legal." Refuting Clark's charges, Ericson insisted "with unqualified positiveness that I have never engaged in propaganda in my classroom." Ericson hoisted aloft the banner of university openness by concluding: "Any time Mr. Clark wishes to publish a stenographic report of one of my lectures, he is welcome to do so."[60]

William T. Couch, meanwhile, stressed the importance of expertise and accuracy that UNC's academic freedom encouraged. He first dispensed with Clark's accusations: "I am not an atheist, or a socialist, or a communist." Couch scoffed that because Clark had admitted that he did not even know what socialism was, he was in a poor position to accuse someone of teaching it. But Clark did know enough "to go around parroting and insinuating things he cannot prove, the nature of which he does not understand." Besides, Couch, as director of UNC Press, was "not a member of the University faculty nor am I on the instructional staff. I have never given any courses at the University." Clark "could not possibly have said or done more to shake the faith in his audience Tuesday night in himself and the interests he claims to represent. His refusal to answer and his obvious failure to even understand many of the questions he was asked condemned him and his cause completely." His shabby performance "forced the audience to question his honesty as well as his intelligence."[61] This was a damning criticism coming from a member of the UNC community. David Clark's downfall came not from being a conservative speaking before a liberal audience; it came when he proved himself to be ignorant and ill-informed while speaking before an audience accustomed to testing assertions for accuracy and evidence.

In a busy week for discussing radicalism and reaction, the very next night, May 15, students again packed Gerrard Hall to hear the future of capitalism debated. English Department instructors Arnold Williams and James Wishart used the recent observance of May Day to challenge Winthrop Durfee, the student leader of the new Liberty League chapter, to a debate on capitalism's fate. Both Williams and Wishart were affiliated with the political Left; Williams described himself provocatively as "seventeen miles left of Lenin," while Wishart declared himself a "Jeffersonian communist."[62] Williams made sure to clarify: "We propose the debate as a means of presenting our viewpoint to the students, not in an attempt to spread propaganda or enlist recruits for any radical organization." With the challenge to Durfee issued, E. J. Woodhouse of the Government Department volunteered to join the debate on Durfee's side, claiming that "too many of these radical assumptions go unchallenged."[63] The Carolina Political Union sponsored the main event. The *Daily Tar Heel* predicted a long, wild night: following the allotted seventeen minutes per speaker, "questions will fly from the floor until the assemblage is dispersed by state troopers or the 8:30 [a.m.] class bell."[64]

The debate took place with applause and "shouts" in abundance. It became apparent, however, that Durfee was more interested in bombast than debate. The *Daily Tar Heel* referred to his performance as a "carnival sideshow, a vaudeville act." One writer who called himself "a conservative" expressed dismay at "the loosely rattling tongue of Winthrop Durfee.... His arguments were inane, personal, ridiculous, and at times filthy."[65] Woodhouse took the basic New Deal line that reform could yet save American capitalism. Williams and Wishart, meanwhile, held that "capitalism works to the deterioration of all classes. . . . demands more and more profits . . . can achieve profits only by working men harder and cutting wages lower." Wishart concluded that "The ills . . . can be cured only by a system of production for human use."[66]

The fact that UNC had English instructors claiming, as James Wishart did, that "capitalism is an anachronism and a menace to society" kept critics like David Clark on the warpath.[67] So, too, did E. E. Ericson's public dinner in 1936 with James Ford, the African American vice presidential candidate of the Communist Party, as described in the previous chapter. When critics were not complaining that E. E. Ericson had dined publicly with an African American, they were complaining that UNC permitted a known socialist to hold a position on the faculty.

One Charlotte writer charged that by virtue of his politics, Ericson "was not fit to hold a seat and teach the young men and women who come to the University." This writer also relayed personal experience with what he considered to be the disastrous effects of having someone like Ericson, who was assumed to be an atheist (because he was a Marxist), teach at the university: "We had a boy at the Great University of N.C. He like thousands of others left a Christian home and his church came back with an entire different thought of religion and God. I am a preacher against sending any boy or girl to the Univ. & will be more so if this present question is not settled by firing Ericson & running him from Chapel Hill."[68] D. Sam Cox added that "*somebody* ought to . . . *at once* hand a pink slip to Mr. Ericson. If the President of the University of

North Carolina is not that 'somebody,' please be so good as to tell me in whose hands the power lies."[69]

After receiving one of Frank Graham's stock replies to Ericson's critics about not wanting to upset the South's delicate race relations, M. M. Bosworth, a prominent businessman from Memphis, Tennessee, wrote back to point out that he had "made no reference to the race questions . . . and if you had read my letter carefully you would have understood it accordingly." Therefore Bosworth laid out his concerns once more: "Is Professor Erickson [*sic*] a Communist? If he is not, does he lean to their teachings or approve in any way their government as it is in Russia today? If he is not a Communist, what is his religion and what church does he attend? Do you consider it proper that he should give a negro communist and Vice-Presidential nominee of that party recognition before the world, which necessarily went with that meal in Durham?"[70] Graham replied point by point. Ericson, he insisted, was "not a communist. He is a Christian." Graham did not know if he belonged to any of the Chapel Hill churches, but he noted that Ericson attended the Presbyterian church "quite often" and "also the Methodist Church."[71] (In late October, Ericson spoke to a Baptist student group on "the history of Christian Socialism.")[72] But, having just revealed an eyebrow-raising amount of knowledge about Ericson's personal life, Graham then added the defense most important to sustaining academic freedom when critics raised questions about a faculty member's personal convictions: "I am not a censor of his private conduct, so long as he does his work well, obeys the laws of the state and country, lives a decent life, and is fair to other human beings."[73]

Through the end of 1936 and into 1937, Graham and other university leaders had to continue defending themselves with regard to Ericson's continued presence at the University. Ericson, after all, was still outwardly a socialist, and he spoke publicly on many occasions, even after the public abuse he took following the Ford dinner. Taking full advantage of the Popular Front years, when a commitment to antifascism brought greater credibility to the American Left, Ericson praised the USSR in a Chattanooga address in February 1937. A local paper described Ericson as "an avowed Socialist, emissary of the League for Industrial Democracy" (also known by its acronym LID). He was quoted as saying that "it is high time that we get rid of our inhibitions about Red Russia. The Soviet Union is the most practical experiment yet tried in government."[74] On the heels of Ericson's address, Kate Hinds Steele wrote to Graham: "I wonder if you know just what the LID is—who belong to it [sic]—what funds support it—the nature of its propaganda? I wonder if you approve of the kind of advertisement your college is getting by having one of your faculty thus represent you?" Her conclusion: "Since he likes Russia so well perhaps he could be persuaded to move there."[75]

Not all of the correspondence regarding Ericson was critical, however, and one letter again highlights the extent to which UNC was a focal point for the attention of a wide range of southerners. Ericson's worried yet supportive department chair, George R. Coffman, received one letter of support for Ericson from a struggling textile worker. A Mr. H. Willoughby related that he had had "the pleasure of meeting Mr. Ericson during the worst of Hoover's depression and I had lost my job and me and my family was perishing to death." Willoughby remembered how "the preachers passed us by on one side and the politicians on the other." But Ericson "found us in that condition and like the apostle of old silver and gold he had none but, such as he did have he gave unto us and never one time mentioned communist or anything else to us and that is why we know the textile papers are telling a lie on him. Mr. Ericson is a Great man with a big heart. My family and I don't like to hear anyone criticize him."[76]

Ericson's drama was not the only source of communist-related news in early 1937. In February, C. A. Hathaway, editor of the Communist Party newspaper, *The Daily Worker*, spoke on campus. The *Daily Tar Heel* noted, "For the campus, the coming of a Communist is no novelty." But anticipating the reaction to Hathaway's visit, the article continued: "The people of the State of North Carolina, however are not yet conditioned to the coming of Communists. Some of them will be frightened when they hear that Communist Hathaway is coming, and quite a few will undoubtedly be angry." The article concluded that "when Editor Hathaway comes, we believe that the campus will turn out and listen to what he has to say. Most of the campus may not agree with him. But the campus and/or the people of North Carolina might think of their own reputations before dedicating themselves to narrow-minded intolerance."[77]

A year later, in February 1938, student leader Alexander Heard and the Carolina Political Union hosted the Soviet ambassador to the United States, Alexander Troyanovsky. More than 1,300 students, faculty, and townspeople assembled in Memorial Hall to listen to the "little man with the big smile." While many Americans already were worried about the prospect of another international war, the ambassador cut through the uncertainty by proclaiming: "A great world war has already begun!" Citing the Spanish Civil War and the Japanese invasion of China, Troyanovsky predicted accurately that the "other world powers" would eventually be drawn into a world war. The *Daily Tar Heel* reported that in an afternoon interview, Troyanovsky asserted that "a union between the United States, Great Britain, and the Soviet Union is the only thing that will stop the wartime tactics of aggressor nations like Japan."[78]

Troyanovsky's speech provoked little outcry, but one correspondent put UNC on notice once again that the openness invited by academic freedom was not an unquestioned value. Signing as "Christian Patriot," the writer explained that he was for free speech—except for those instances when he was against it. He complained that "free speech is wonderful, but what about the decided trend toward this sort of thing. It must be stopped." "Christian Patriot" continued: "Such irony, permitting a business destroyer to suggest an alliance of our free country with his RED homeland. A Christian country allied with Christian haters. . . . Other folks have freedom, too. Please respect it. America must make no alliances whatsoever, and especially not with England, France and Russia, *all RED countries*."[79]

The next month, American communist leader Earl Browder's visit to UNC drew an estimated 1,100 people to Memorial Hall. (The figures for Browder's and Troyanovsky's visits are significant when one considers that the enrollment of UNC at this time was still less than four thousand.) Touting both his communism and his patriotism, Browder attacked fascism, asserting that American communists wanted "to do everything in our power" to defeat it. The Soviet Union, he assured the crowd, was "peace loving, and the other known democratic nations of the world need its cooperation (if they can get it and I think they can), in order to preserve peace." But, Browder added, "It is impossible to picture a world democratic front without seeing America at the lead in the movement. We of the Communist movement will do our best to help realize this promise."[80]

Browder's address prompted one writer for the *Daily Tar Heel* to note that the speaker wisely "made no proposals to overthrow the present capitalistic regime, nor did he wear a crop of tousled hair to fit him for the top of a soap-box." Rather, this writer applauded Browder for being intelligent, open about his views, and willing to enter into debate with the audience. The editorial summed up Browder's visit on a positive note: "When an intelligent champion of Marxism mounts the platform to air his cause, any illusion that the communist movement as a slinking snake, always growing larger, plotting to plunge the world into revolutionary chaos fades into its rightful background. Browder was on the platform facing a scrutinous audience which demanded sane, practical ideas. He met their demand."[81]

The *Daily Tar Heel*'s reaction to Browder's speech again highlights the competing meanings of academic freedom during this time. To critics like David Clark and "Christian Patriot," the sheer act of having Browder speak at UNC under the premise of academic freedom invited radicalism to enter into the minds of the students. Ahead of Browder's appearance, Hiram Evans, a leader of the Ku Klux Klan, spoke before a UNC audience estimated at 1,000 and said: "If there was a Klan at Chapel Hill Browder probably would not be heard here."[82] UNC's position, however, was that it was better to have communists (whom they could not wish away) come to campus, get up on the stage, tell the public what they hoped to achieve, and then be prepared to defend their views against an educated, inquiring audience of students and faculty. Shut off that openness, UNC leaders believed, and the communists would have no choice but to operate underground.

The world war that erupted in September 1939 did nothing to calm anyone's fears that the world was a frightening, explosive place. Nineteen thirty-nine also found UNC and Frank Graham fending off accusations of communist sympathies from yet another source: the U.S. Congress, and specifically the House Un-American Activities Committee (HUAC).

Frank Graham's attendance at the inaugural session of the Southern Conference for Human Welfare (SCHW) in November 1938 in Birmingham, Alabama, must have seemed like the most natural thing in the world to him. On the conference's first day, Graham delivered before his fellow southern liberals a rousing call for democracy and human rights, decrying repression as "the way of frightened power."[83] UNC was well represented at the meeting. In addition to Graham, William T. Couch and alumni George C. Stoney and C. Vann Woodward attended.[84] Elected as president of the conference against his expressed wish and in his absence (he left after the first day), Graham's association with the SCHW put him in a difficult spot almost immediately when conservative critics began depicting the conference as a communist-led effort.[85] Even before the conference had ended, Congressman

Martin Dies, chair of the newly formed HUAC, had expressed reservations about the group, hinting that communists were behind the agenda and organization.[86]

It soon became clear that a handful of communist SCHW members had indeed gained positions on various committees, including the civil rights committee, and a kind of self-fulfilling prophecy began to take shape. As liberals recoiled at the news that a handful of communists had burrowed their way into positions of leadership, some left, creating new opportunities for more communist operatives to infiltrate the SCHW. William T. Couch spent 1939 backing away from the SCHW in protest against communist influence and their secretive methods of operation. Graham, while not wild about the discovery of secret communists in the SCHW, remained as president. As he would have done at UNC, he encouraged all members to be open about their political allegiances for the good of the conference.[87] In December 1939, as the attacks continued, Graham wrote: "I do not object to members of any political party, Democrats, Republicans, Socialists, Communists, or what-not coming into an open democratic meeting so long as it is open and above board. Nor do I think that we should run when we find out that a handful of Communists joined the Conference or would like to manipulate it or claim it as their own." Echoing his approach to life on campus, Graham urged openness as a means to fight "against the devious methods of both Communists and Fascists."[88]

Meanwhile, Congressman Dies's interest in the SCHW followed Frank Graham back to Chapel Hill. Dies let it be known that as chairman of HUAC he was contemplating an investigation of the university for communist activity among its faculty members. William T. Couch wrote to Congressman Carl Durham of Chapel Hill to try to forestall any investigation. "No good purpose is served" by such an investigation, he complained; it would undermine the state's trust in UNC. But if an investigation were deemed necessary, he added a bit naively, "the sensible and decent thing to do would seem to be to make the investigation without making public announcements which give the impression that an effort is being made to smear the good name of the University of North Carolina."[89] Couch granted that in his opinion there was "a considerable amount of Communistic influence among the student bodies in most colleges and universities in the United States."[90] The problem, however, was not communist faculty members. "Faculty members have been subjected to so many unwarranted attacks," he explained, "that they have tended to have very little to do with radical student organizations." Instead, radical student groups elsewhere had been allowed to go "to extremes" precisely because they lacked faculty influence, or as Couch put it, "intelligent guidance."[91] This was not the case at UNC, Couch implied, where, he argued, academic freedom in the hands of responsible, trusted UNC faculty and leadership remained a moderating influence that checked thoughtless radicalism among students.

Couch suspected that the impending HUAC investigation was in fact just a smear campaign at the behest of David Clark.[92] Sure enough, in August 1940, Clark was back on the scene with a widely published speech he delivered before the Charlotte Lions Club, attacking Graham, the university, and its academic freedom, in detail and at length. Reviving the same themes he'd been hammering home since the mid-1920s, Clark charged: "There has been at the University a small group of radicals whom I regard as a cancer upon the institution." University faculty "at a state-supported institution, should not be allowed to use their class rooms for propaganda purposes and my charges are that it has been done at the University of North Carolina and that while so doing they have been sure of the protection, if not the encouragement, of the head of the University." It was no comfort to Clark that most universities had some radicals among their faculty, because "the University of North Carolina is the only Southern institution at which there appears to have been a drive for converts or definite contacts with the red movement in the United States."[93]

Next, Clark took dead aim at the issue of trust that featured so critically in UNC's experience of academic freedom. To Clark, the fact that there were a few radicals at UNC was part of the conspiracy that academic freedom facilitated: "Radical professors shout about freedom but what they really desire is license to use a soap box in their classroom and a right to present their atheist, socialist and communist allies to groups of students. They wish to draw their salaries from funds provided by citizens of North Carolina while seeking to tear down our standards of loyalty and morality."[94]

David Clark's speech again brought out his supporters. Mrs. A. H. Crowell, mother of two UNC graduates, agreed with Clark's estimation of the university under Graham. Writing to Josephus Daniels—a UNC trustee, the U.S. ambassador to Mexico, and owner of the *Raleigh News & Observer*—Crowell shared her view that "our University is the rankest center of communism in the United States." The youth of North Carolina were "taught that there is no God, that the churches must be exterminated, that lies are always permissible if they suit your purpose better than the truth, that there is nothing wrong in stealing if you can avoid the toils of the law, that sexual impulses are to be satisfied with no more compunction of conscience than one would drink a glass of water."[95]

How did Mrs. Crowell know all this? She explained: "My information comes from letters, books and pamphlets found in my daughters [sic] trunk." Her son had graduated with his bachelor's degree and completed the two-year medical program, and he was also Phi Beta Kappa; therefore, "the communists would not have dared approach him." Her daughter had also completed both a bachelor's and master's degree at UNC, but somehow she had come away "filled with communistic ideas that it will take me the rest of my life to get out of her, if I ever can." Therefore, she concluded, "the University has done all the harm to me that it can ever do, if I had a thousand children to educate, and money unlimited, I would never send another one to UNC."[96]

Crowell then offered specific suggestions for cleaning up UNC. "The first and most necessary thing to do," she began, "is to fire Erickson [sic]. He . . . should be tarred and feathered, and exiled to Russia." Crowell added that "if Dr. Graham can't get his eyes opened sufficiently to see that more decency, and less liberalism is needed there, he should be ousted too. I think he is probably a good man, conscientious etc., but BLIND." Crowell, flush with the spirit of conspiracy, urged that time was of the essence, because she feared that "the communist students in the various schools plan a revolution when the time is ripe for it."[97]

In another testament to the loyalty of Graham's and UNC's supporters, Josephus Daniels not only took the time from his day job as ambassador to Mexico to respond to Crowell's rather frantic observations; he replied with a four-and-a-half page single-spaced letter. Speaking of Mrs. Crowell's daughter, Daniels politely suggested that "you may have confused her being social-minded with Socialism, which is often mistaken for Communism." But, Daniels assured her, "I doubt if there is a real native-born Communist in North Carolina, and I dare to believe your daughter is not a Communist but a young woman who is looking for a better way and has not found herself. . . . Sound teaching at Chapel Hill," he added, "will displace any half-baked theories which you seem to believe have caused her to drift away from her moorings."[98]

Daniels dismissed the possibility that there were communists on the UNC staff as unlikely. But, as a trustee, Daniels promised to remain vigilant for abuses of academic freedom by radicals who would bring it into the classroom, because that was not what they were hired to do. "My dear Mrs. Crowell," he wrote, "there are too many serious evils in the world for us to draw our weapons upon the few Communists—if there are any—at Chapel Hill." But if Crowell had any real evidence that a university professor was "seeking to teach Communism or Fascism or Nazism at Chapel Hill, I would like for you to furnish it to me." Communism was "a subversive doctrine and cannot live in a free atmosphere such as exists at Chapel Hill. . . . The air at Chapel Hill is so pure and so charged with liberal democracy that none of these poison gasses can exist." Daniels wanted to stay informed because "as a trustee I would give my best efforts to clearing out exotic *isms* that might slip in."[99]

Letters between Graham, William D. "Billy" Carmichael (the comptroller of the university), and Robert B. House (dean of Administration) reveal that the administration took seriously any charges of communists in the faculty and in town generally, even if they were not sure what to do about it. Having endured another round of attacks from David Clark, Graham in 1940 evidently asked House specifically about the possibility of communists on the UNC faculty. House replied, copying the letter to Carmichael: "I cannot answer the question officially," because UNC "has never inquired as to the political affiliations of its employees." Unofficially, however, House could say, "I do not know of anyone on our staff who is a Communist." Ericson evidently lied to House when he "stated to me that he was not a Communist. I know of no others who are even alluded to as Communists."[100]

As the 1930s ended and the 1940s began, Frank Graham continued to encounter accusations that radicalism had come to UNC under the cover of academic freedom. Responding to a student-led demonstration against the new world war, Thomas E. Street sent a letter in May 1940 that was laced with elements of conspiracy theory against which Graham could have no effective rebuttal. Street first assured Graham that "I love and respect you for the great and good man I know you to be." But he worried that "you are sadly mistaken when it comes to questions of dangerous radicalism masquerading as 'liberalism.'" Street then quoted his mother, who had asked simply: "Is there anything which may not be done in the name of 'liberalism'?"[101]

Having read recent ex-communist "confessions" in magazines such as *Reader's Digest*, *Liberty Magazine*, and *Cosmopolitan*, Street had now taken the full measure of communist tactics and feared the worst for

Amid accusations of communism at UNC, students host an antiwar rally as World War II erupts in Europe, ca. late 1930s.

the university. He accepted without question the "warnings which have been given us by people who know about the diabolical and insidious methods used by the Commu-Nazis to destroy us from within." Street implored Graham to wise up: "Is it not plain enough by now that the work of Communists is usually anything but the outright 'teaching of Communism'? If they did that anybody could be on to them." Here was the logic of a conspiracy believer: it was "plain" to Street that the communists could not be seen in their secret and deadly ways. Street admitted that he did not know E. E. Ericson, but "from what I hear, his actions seem suspicious enough to be alarming." This kind of radicalism, he lectured Graham, "is not often something you can walk up and put your finger on, arrest certain persons for; often those who 'smell a rat' cannot find it." Pointing to UNC's influence, Street added: "We, of the obscure, common people can do little except raise our feeble voices in protest, with the hope that some of our intellectuals and leaders will hear us, take action, and have influence where we cannot." He begged Graham to "do more than merely apologize for our dangerous radicals."[102]

Street therefore criticized HUAC chairman Martin Dies for announcing his intention to investigate the university, not for the investigation itself. The announcement, according to Street, "gave the 'radicals' every chance to be on their guard."[103] Street did not expect Dies to turn up actual communists in the UNC faculty, but he reminded Graham how "we have been told repeatedly by those who should know that the Commu-Stalinists are nothing less than the subversive agents of Moscow, who will do *anything*, mostly with 'Trojan horses,' to destroy us from within." He continued:[104]

> No, they don't "teach Communism" very often, at least as such. They merely go about stirring up prejudice, reviving old antagonisms, instigating internal dissension, playing upon people's desire to keep out of war, decrying armaments, in the name of virtue, spreading dangerous, lopsided half-truths—anything and everything to make confusion, disorganization, disunity of the nation—all to make us weak so that we can do nothing effective against them, and finally be easy prey to their fiendish machinations. These are not just my personal views; they are facts as stated by the insiders who know.[105]

In the same vein, the week after Street's letter, T. A. Wilkins of Gastonia sent a telegram charging that Graham was guilty of "perverting 'extra liberalism' might add communism and athenism [atheism]. To my best reasons of belief, you are a free lance, pro-German Communist, and the reakiest [*sic*] atheist. Change, or I will start a signed subscription of voters to eliminate you before any more monies is appropriated to U.N.C. I think our young men are going down under your presidency."[106] Critics like Thomas Street had a point: if radicals like E. E. Ericson chose to operate covertly, there was little UNC could do about it. What UNC could do was to threaten to punish faculty members for being dishonest, not for being communist. UNC leaders struggled to address this wide range of accusations: some just wanted to lump any activism in with radicalism, whereas others had somehow had arrived at the accurate conclusion that, in the case of E. E. Ericson, covert communism had come to UNC.

Having asserted in his 1931 inaugural address that the modern university was "so intimately a part of the context of every real problem of the modern world," Frank Graham may be forgiven if, at times during this tumultuous decade, he wondered what he had gotten himself into. The economic crisis continued to devastate lives, labor violence surrounded Chapel Hill, race-based hostilities simmered constantly, university budgets remained tight, and to end the decade, a new world war had begun. In response to these crises, UNC researchers and students investigated, inquired, wrote, and agitated. And many interested southerners, in turn, watched, read, listened, and reacted to what was coming from UNC. UNC leaders therefore labored mightily during these dramatic times to maintain the balance between the openness needed to develop expertise and the guarantee of one's individual rights, while maintaining the state's trust—all of which were essential parts of the university's academic freedom. While the controversies surely caused Frank Graham and others sleepless nights, they were also the fruits of academic freedom's promise.

Epilogue

"The University Must Go on Being a University"

Frank Graham and the World War II Era

The entrance of the United States into World War II in December 1941 presented Frank Graham and UNC with a dizzying array of new challenges. Graham had already begun in 1940 to anticipate the changes that war mobilization would bring to UNC. He was in the forefront of local preparedness efforts, pledging the university's assistance to and cooperation with the federal government. At Franklin Roosevelt's request, Graham threw himself into wartime service; he spent weeks in Washington, DC, serving on the War Labor Board. At the same time, Graham hoped the university would still adhere to its central mission, as he explained in a letter to UNC parents and students. "The University must go on being a University," Graham said, "ever alert to the needs of its people." War challenged UNC to "meet the double responsibility of carrying out the regular functions and freedom of a historic and progressive state University, and of cooperating to the limit of our capacity with our country in a total war against the axis powers to save the freedom and all things for which America and our University stand." The war was bound to alter life at the University and, as Graham noted, bring "many new things to the peaceful, freedom-loving village of Chapel Hill." These new things included "Naval R.O.T.C., the student flight-training program, the Carolina Volunteer Training Corps, courses in military science, the 'speed-up' of college years from four to three, admission by examination, military and naval research projects, and civilian morale organizations."[1]

Not everything changed at UNC during the war or throughout the 1940s, however. Controversies involving race relations, labor/leftist activity, and academic freedom continued to stir deep emotions at the university and throughout the South. Even though he was gone from campus much of the time, Frank Graham remained at the center of these controversies. While a more complete study of academic freedom and liberalism at UNC during the 1940s will have to wait for further research, a focus on Frank Graham will give a quick view of the challenges presented by the new context of world war and the early Cold War.

The war gave Graham the weapon of patriotism to sharpen his attacks on the South's racists and to resist the nearly pathological fear of organized labor and leftist politics. In his wartime speeches, Graham placed his support of unions and more racial justice at the core of U.S. efforts in the war, and his reputation as one of the South's most renowned liberals grew. But Graham's heart never left the university; he routinely cited academic freedom and the importance of the university to a democratic society as central to the American war effort.

World War II gave African Americans new momentum in their long struggle for civil rights. As many historians have noted by now, the war—and, more specifically, the murderously racist policies of the Nazi state—gave African Americans and white liberals new ammunition in their struggle against segregation.[2] In Raleigh, for example, an African American judge and longtime NAACP leader, Hubert T. Delany, said in 1944 that "white Christians are nothing but plain, ordinary, psalm-singing hypocrites." Delany charged that white southerners paid "lip service and nothing more to Christianity. . . . The White Christians drape themselves with the Cross of Christ at every opportunity but they present the perfect example of hatred. They teach the poor whites and the poor blacks to hate one another; they uphold, tolerate, and condone segregation, disfranchisement, and every other institution that prevents Christianity from being a reality. . . . We have to face the truth in this country. Hitler has no monopoly on fascism. We started it right here; we taught fascism to Hitler; we have been practicing it for years."[3]

Life in Chapel Hill remained fraught with hardship and uncertainty for the local black community. John K. Chapman points out that "as late as 1944 parts of the black community of Chapel Hill had no electricity." But Chapman also relates the story of Edna Lyde, who moved to

Chapel Hill from South Carolina in 1944. Her first job was as a house-keeper at the Carolina Inn. After her supervisor, a white man named Moses, yelled at her for not putting bedsheets in the right place, Lyde quit. Chapman explains that Moses later confronted Lyde on Cameron Avenue, near the Inn: "He told her, 'I'll knock your head against these pillars, knock your brains out,'" to which Lyde replied, "'No you won't. Both of us brains a be settin' up on the pillar.'" The UNC Janitors' Association shared Edna Lyde's willingness to stand up to white authorities in Chapel Hill. In 1942, the Janitors' Association joined local 403 of the State, County, and Municipal Workers of America, and in 1943 they joined the Congress of Industrial Organizations (CIO). The janitors' willingness to organize caused a rift among university administrators. Frank Graham was willing to support their organizing efforts and wrote to Governor Joseph M. Broughton to argue that if the state was not able or willing to pay more, then the janitors should be allowed to bargain collectively. Meanwhile, Chapman reports that in Graham's absence, William D. Carmichael, UNC's controller, and the Board of Trustees continued to try to undermine the union's efforts.[4] Outside of Chapel Hill, some white North Carolinians prepared to answer the wartime momentum for civil rights among black southerners with violence. UNC alumnus Frank Daniels wrote to his brother Jonathan of his concern that the more violent segregationists would deal with black activism in the South "Hitler style."[5]

More firmly than he had ever done before, during World War II Graham chastised those in the South who clung to their views of white supremacy. Graham stressed the connection between racial injustice at home and the Nazi enemy abroad. Shortly after the German invasion of Poland in September 1939, Graham spoke at the inauguration of President Francis Hutchins at Berea College, a school well-known for its racially liberal policies; Berea was integrated from the late 1800s until Kentucky state law forbade the continuation of this policy. Graham established a grim global context before urging the necessity of honest reflection on race relations that a good education could encourage and facilitate: "In a world of dictatorships and wars, the college men and women in America need to use their time and opportunity of peace to make more real our ideals of religious tolerance, inter-racial good will, human freedom and social justice. . . . In our democratic self-examination we should begin at home. We should recognize that the Negro is a human being and an American citizen."[6]

In a nationally broadcast radio address on the "American Forum of the Air" in New York City in January 1944, Graham addressed many of the same themes, invoking the potential of education to yield progressive (if incremental) improvements in race relations: "By education we come to understand the profound origins of racial, religious and social prejudice and through that understanding gradually overcome personal prejudice and group animosities." He continued, "modern science and education reveal that the differences in achievement and civilization are based mainly on differences in environment and opportunity, rather than on differences in race, color, or shape of the head. The difference is more in opportunity than in the capacity to achieve."[7] Graham thus argued that "race prejudice" was not hopelessly rooted in "human nature." The presence and depth of racial prejudice was a result of "its exploitation by the group then dominant in the course of history." But, he continued, "master racialism . . . is not the basis of a superior civilization," words that must have made thousands of segregationists lean a little closer to their radios; preservation of "civilization" was constantly invoked to justify the South's racial apartheid. One can also well imagine the segregationists' response when Graham added for good measure that "master racialism" was "the instrument of Nazi imperialism in total war for global dominion."[8]

As he would do elsewhere during the war years, Graham depicted the United States' effort in World War II as a struggle against this "master racialism." "In opposition to master racialism," he said, "is the American dream now revived in the convictions and aspirations of American youth giving their lives on all fronts of freedom from Salerno to Tarawa. Through this revival of the American dream of human liberty and the equal chance for all people, we can be moved in time to overcome the powers of racial . . . and economic differences, prejudices and discriminations."[9] On WOL radio in Washington, DC, in February 1944, Graham spoke poignantly about the contributions made to the war effort by African Americans. Graham said that "there is no more loyal group of our fellow citizens than the American Negroes, north and south," citing the well-known example of Dorie Miller, the African American cook aboard the USS *West Virginia* who rushed to man an abandoned antiaircraft gun during the attack on Pearl Harbor. What Graham described as a "minimum program" for the future would "abolish the poll tax, provide equal public facilities, equal pay for equal work, equal opportunity to develop, to work, and to fight for our common country."[10]

Frank Graham speaks at a memorial service for Franklin Roosevelt, 1945. Notice the group of African American sailors seated on the right of the photograph.

At other times, Graham's attempts to connect the causes for justice at home with justice abroad did not come off quite as coherently
and showed the limits of his liberalism. Graham spoke at the "Founders' Day" event at Tuskegee Institute in 1944, where first he made explicit the connection between Nazism and the South's racism. "Economic
and political discrimination on account of race or creed is in line with
the Nazi program," Graham proclaimed. The United States, he continued, "must not, in the days of its power, become the stronghold of bigots." But, he then added, "the American answer to differences in color
and creed is not a concentration camp but cooperation. The answer to
error is not terror but light and liberty [the UNC motto] under the moral law."[11] Here, despite putting segregationists in a difficult position by
comparing their racial views to the Nazis, Graham let them off the hook
by calling vaguely for "cooperation." The United States had long given
up hope that the Nazis would somehow begin to cooperate with those of

different "color and creed"; in fact, by 1944 the United States was knee-deep in a bloody war to achieve their unconditional surrender. Graham's misplaced faith that somehow cooperation would prevail was borne out by the freedom struggles of the 1950s and 1960s, when southern segregationists offered fierce resistance to court rulings and federal law. The American answer to "differences in color" was seldom "cooperation."

Even Graham, a leading southern liberal, was still not able or willing to call publicly for state or federal governments to push for the unconditional surrender on the part of segregationists. He did, however, call for an end to the poll tax, and he supported the end of the white primary. He was an enthusiastic supporter of the anti–poll tax campaign and was a member of the Southern Electoral Reform League. In 1944 he pledged his support for "any movement for abolition of poll tax" and "equality in voting."[12] The poll tax, he argued, did not just inflict injustice on potential black voters; it injured the entire South. "The political structure" of the South, he said, "with its poll tax discriminations, is a set-back to a great region."[13] When the U.S. Supreme Court ruled in *Smith v. Allwright* in 1944 that white primaries were unconstitutional, Graham wrote to Frederick Douglass Patterson, president of Tuskegee Institute, calling the decision "a fine thing."[14]

Graham received a number of supportive letters from soldiers in response to his Tuskegee address, the gist of which was summarized briefly by *Time* magazine.[15] Alton Lawrence, mentioned in chapter 5 as a member of the state socialist party who was arrested for his role in organizing Burlington textile workers, wrote now as "Private Alton Lawrence" and said, "Congratulations on that speech. It is well that at least some people realize that one of our chief objectives in this war is to erase racial and national prejudices from the fact [face] of the earth."[16] Mississippi native Corporal Romeo Garrett, who later went on to become the first African American professor at Bradley University, wrote simply to Graham: "You are indeed a powerful light in this world of darkness."[17] First Lieutenant Russell B. Babcock, at the Army School for Special Services, asked Graham for a copy of his Tuskegee address. Babcock noted that he was "specifically interested in material which will make sense to Negro Troops who ask, 'What has American democracy given me which warrants my sacrifice in this war effort?'" It is revealing that Babcock evidently was having difficulty answering this question himself.[18]

Graham's public call for the end of the poll tax, his defense of the patriotism of African American soldiers, and the boldly explicit linkage he established between the cause of racial justice in the South and the aims of the United States in World War II predictably unleashed hostile and often unhinged responses from racist critics. These critics also had very different ideas on what function education served and what lessons the past taught. L. C. Albright of Birmingham, Alabama, felt the need to provide Graham with a history lesson: "My information is that Ethiopia was a Monarchy two thousand years B.C. and they have made practically no progress; in fact they have retrograded, and they have ruled themselves all of this time, except what time Italy ruled, and this was short; and Liberia and Haiti are similar."[19] William J. Woody of Savannah, Georgia, worried that modern education was making the current state of race relations worse. He complained that Graham was "ignorant fond of Negroes and get pay for it [sic]." If, he added, "you are educated you know that by mixing Negro with White blood you lower the standard of the White Race. You don't bring him up to you you go down to him, witness France, Italy, Spain, So Am, Cuba, etc." He continued, "Before the war Hitler said in his newspapers that he could lick the French . . . because they were Negro blooded. You see by the war that his words came true." Mr. Woody had grave doubts about the utility of education. On educating African Americans, he insisted: "You can educate him but he is still a Negro, Education does not improve them except to be better able to skin another Negro." The thought of integrated schools was out of the question because "when you see white and black children in school together they grow up without knowing the differences, they marry, and produce Mongrels." Concluding this rambling discourse on education, Woody cast doubt on the entire enterprise: "Education does not give you a good Character, Colleges learn you how to become a bad man."[20]

Another critic, writing on the potential future of the black vote, revealed the long-held antidemocratic core of southern conservatism by explaining to Graham, "I think it would be a grand thing if the Southern people would rise up and say, 'To hell with democracy if that is what you mean by democracy,' and clamp down on the Negro so tight that he would have to leave. WHY is democracy so perfect anyhow? A little less talk about democracy and a little more talk about decency, a little less blubbering over the garbage man's child and a little more plain respect for the child on the boulevard, please."[21] R. R. Harper also seemed flabbergasted by Graham's views on a biracial democracy, pointing out worriedly that "if they get to vote they will also want to hold office."[22]

J. N. Buie of Red Springs, North Carolina, rejected the premise that Graham could be both a liberal and a trustworthy university president. Buie lashed out at Graham's support for a repeal of the poll tax: "I would judge from your remarks that you are in favor of the niggers voting in N.C. I want to ask you the direct question and will be so kind as to answer me personally, and thru the press if you wish, ARE YOU IN FAVOR OF THE NIGGERS VOTING IN NORTH CAROLINA?" Buie continued his rant by linking Graham's transgression to the health of UNC. "If you are then I think you should resign as President of the University of North Carolina and get you a job at some nigger University, as you would have the opportunity to be with them all the time, in fact, you could eat, sleep and live with them to your hearts content."[23]

The end of World War II removed the clarity Graham could draw upon in making the case for racial justice at home as being in accordance with the United States' purpose in fighting fascism. President Harry Truman appointed Graham to the Committee on Civil Rights in 1946. Graham supported the committee's work to compile the hard facts about racial discrimination and privately became more convinced than ever that segregation needed to end. But when the Truman Commission's report called too loudly for strong federal action in eliminating segregation, Graham dissented and recommended that southerners continue to be educated up to the point where decency and enlightenment would make discrimination vanish.[24] Here was one more invocation of education and expertise to slow down those pushing to change the South's racial hierarchy.

Graham kept abreast of a series of disturbing challenges to academic freedom in the 1940s. He worked behind the scenes to help defend embattled Georgia professors against the attempts of the state's rabid governor, Eugene Talmadge, to drive out professors deemed too liberal on race issues in 1941. Graham lobbied other leaders of Southern universities to defend academic freedom in Georgia.[25] He played a more public role in his defense of University of Texas (UT) president Homer P. Rainey in the mid-1940s. In 1944, the Texas Board of Regents also decided that Rainey was too liberal on issues of race and labor, and they began maneuvering to remove him. Graham considered the episode an outrage. He received confidential copies of a long memorandum from AAUP officials explaining the Rainey controversy at length, and he used this confidential information to update other university presidents on the situation as they sought to orchestrate a defense of Rainey.[26] He sent telegrams to fourteen other southern university presidents, urging them to issue their own statements of support. Graham also sent an impassioned telegram to North Carolinian William J. Battle, a longtime UT professor, to protest Rainey's ouster. Of the Texas Regents, Graham wrote, "God forbid they can get away with such a crime against the university they are supposed to protect and against a state they are supposed to serve."[27]

Rainey's defenders heard Graham's telegram read aloud over the radio at an Austin rally to support the president, much to the delight of his many friends and supporters. Erich Zimmermann, who had taught economics at UNC before moving to UT, described how, while listening to the speeches given at the rally, "suddenly your name was wafted to us over the waves and like a clarion call from a brighter world your brave words gave new hope to our sore hearts. . . . I should have known that you would not fail us in our hour of trial." It was, Zimmermann concluded, "just like you."[28] Ralph Himstead, the general secretary of the AAUP at the time, wrote to express his "deep appreciation to you for your interest and cooperation with reference to the University of Texas situation."[29] Rainey also appreciated Graham's efforts, although they failed to return him to the presidency. He thanked Graham for his "magnificent telegram." Rainey acknowledged Graham as the leader of academic freedom in the South: "All of us greatly admire your fearless and courageous leadership, in fact, it is a genuine inspiration to me."[30]

World War II only deepened Frank Graham's conviction that academic freedom would lead to greater possibilities for democracy and, therefore, for justice. "Against the fascist struggle for the possession of the mind and soul of youth," he told his Tuskegee audience, "the colleges must be outposts of the freedom of the mind and the autonomy of the human spirit."[31] Graham's speech at Berea College came just a little more than two months after the German invasion of Poland. With this new world war clearly on his mind, Graham again connected academic freedom with democracy in his vision of progress overcoming the darkness of the hour. "We should realize," he said, "that our strongest defense in the long run is not a huge army but more equal educational opportunity for all children in all the states, and that our American democracy will be more truly tested in what we do about glaring inequalities than what we merely protest on the Fourth of July." He continued: "In this college air of freedom, traditions of honor become robust with obligations upon college men and women to help make the world freer and fairer

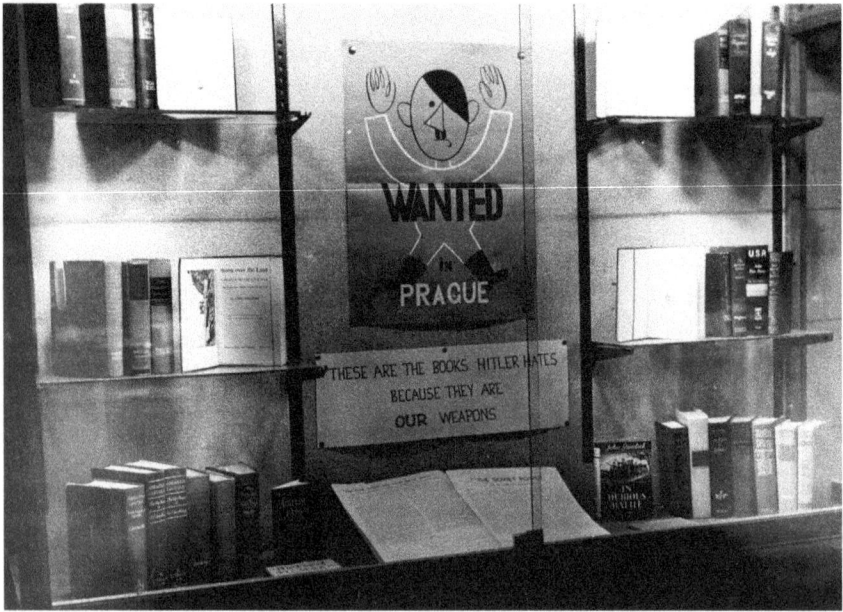

A UNC library book display linking academic freedom with the fight against fascism, 1942.

to all men. . . . It is the personal and social responsibility of college men and women to give all sides a fair hearing; to interpret and champion the freedom and rights of despised minorities, regardless of race, color, class, or creed; to offset vested power with social justice."[32]

In "Democracy and the Second World War," an eloquent statement that, in part, reflects on the importance of academic freedom in a time of war, Graham drew a sharp distinction between totalitarian regimes and democracies. "The dictators," he charged, "have made clear to all the world the primary essentials of freedom by striking down those institutions and ideas which stood across the way of their ruthless march to totalitarian power. Mark up as our democratic necessities the democratic institutions which the dictators struck down: the decent freedom of the Church, legislative assembly, labor union, business enterprise, press, radio, school, and university." He continued, zeroing in next on academic freedom: "As part of this struggle for freedom we propose to maintain, as not the least basic of all, the freedom of the Universities. We would preserve them as places, even in the most critical of times, of peace where men may talk for peace without being tagged as members of the Fifth Column, and where men may talk for aid to the Allies without being stigmatized as war-mongers; in short, where men may study, inquire, report, and talk for or about any decent thing under the American Bill of Rights and the laws and Constitution of the United States." He concluded dramatically: "We must not let Hitler Hitlerize America."[33]

Graham's perceived tolerance for communists still stirred controversy during the war. When Communist Party leader Earl Browder was arrested for a passport violation in 1942, Graham signed a petition protesting Browder's imprisonment. Many on the American Left considered the arrest to be on flimsy grounds and that Browder's main "crime" was being a communist. The *Daily Tar Heel* criticized Graham for representing the university in a poor light by signing the petition. UNC history professor Howard Beale defended Graham in the paper by recounting an exchange he had had recently in one of his classes. "The before-class 'bull-session' opened with a question from a student as to whether I did not think Mr. Graham had been extremely unwise about the . . . petition," Beale explained. "Another student replied that such acts on the part of the President of the University injured the University by creating the impression that the University faculty was full of Communists." Beale disagreed: "I argued that now that we are fighting a war to 'preserve the democratic way of life' it is more important than ever for leaders like Mr. Graham to take stands against violations of democratic liberties at home." As to whether Graham's signature hurt UNC's reputation, Beale connected emphatically the school's fame with its academic freedom and its liberalism: "On the contrary, I thought the University was a great university BECAUSE President Graham and his predecessor and present and past members of the faculty have had the courage to promote progressive principles. . . . This University has a great reputation," he added, "because, above other Southern institutions and more than most American universities of whatever section, it has led in spreading progressive ideas and in teaching of true democracy and had maintained the freedom to do so even at times when democratic ideals are under attack. Democracy desperately needs more and more Frank Grahams."[34]

In the early years of the Cold War, the Taft-Hartley Act of 1947 raised the specter once again of communists having infiltrated the American labor movement. Graham's continued defense of workers' rights brought him in for some of the sharpest attacks he received. John

M. Culp of High Point wrote to criticize Graham as president of UNC, and not just as a liberal, for openly supporting the CIO. Suggesting that Graham was giving aid and comfort to a communist enemy, he urged Graham to "wake up before it is too late. . . . Quit using our tax money to incite and teach disorder. Resign your job. Go 100% CIOPAC if you wish, or run our school as a good North Carolina institution."[35] Graham replied that he was "somewhat astounded by your referring to my 'communistic activities.' I have engaged in no communistic activities. In fact, my democratic faith and activities in behalf of American freedom and democracy are a buttress against communism. I respectfully stand in the democratic tradition of Thomas Jefferson, Andrew Jackson, Woodrow Wilson, and Franklin D. Roosevelt. I realize that to some people that is communism but to the great majority of the people that is Americanism."[36]

Culp mocked the notion that, as an academic, Graham really understood what the "great majority" of Americans thought. Culp described himself as "a common man who has learned by the school of hard knocks and the sweat of my brow and 23 months keeping safe this country and this Americanism you speak of. I have worked on the line with, by the side of every nationality of worker in American industry. I have been asked several times to join the Communist Party as they intended to take the riches away from the rich and divide it among the poor. This was their exact statement. . . . You don't know, actually know the working man—I do—I have spent my life beside him." He continued, "I am a Jeffersonian, a Wilson worshiper, but not a Roosevelt new dealer. I voted for him with gusto at the first election. But I saw his trend and never voted for him again—he was not a Democrat. I firmly believe that had god in his infinite wisdom intended the negro to be my equal and marry my daughter he would have made him my equal in all ways and color." Then, his bigotry unleashed, Culp added, "A Jew is to me a termite. Born a Jew, raised a Jew, lives a Jew, marries a Jew and at death is buried in a Jew cemetery. You can't make anything else out of him." Finally Culp returned to Graham's flaws: "I would class you liberal, hypnotized by Roosevelt's smart line that lulled so many good men to sleep. I say again, when you nurse the CIOPAC and use state owned property to help communist controlled groups plan and figure out how to further disrupt our production . . . you overstepped your bounds. Either be a NC college proffesor [sic] or resign and be a communist organizer in your true collar [sic]."[37]

Austin Hancock of San Antonio, Texas, struck similar themes as John W. Culp. Hancock confessed that he was "grieved and shocked at what is widely said about your un-American-Communistic race equality and un-American teaching and principles in our once great North Carolina University." He suggested that "you should change your American name and become one among the multiplied aliases roving our country like termites—like wolves in the night—or come out and deny your widely reported un-Americanism. I am mailing you 1 booklet unfolding 'that Fair Employment Plot' and other booklet 'The International Jew' both of which have received nationwide circulation. I beg of you to read both."[38]

Herman Davis wrote in February 1947, sounding every bit like David Clark: "I have personally felt sure, without being able to prove it, that there has been considerable infiltration in our institutions of higher learning here in North Carolina. I have also gathered the impression that you have considered the Communist party somewhat lightly, referring to it as 'just another political party.' How do you feel about it now?"[39] Graham responded that he was a "life-long democrat and stand on the American Bill of Rights. I am therefore opposed to communism, which in Russia does not provide the guarantees of the Bill of Rights and would not provide those guarantees if it should triumph in America. . . . I think that our American democracy in its struggles toward fulfillment is prevailing and will prevail over fascism, communism, and other undemocratic philosophies and movements." As to the situation on campus, Graham said what he had been maintaining for years: "I know of no communists in the faculty or on the staff of the University of North Carolina. If there were any in our student body we would guarantee them the rights of American citizens and hope that the freedom and democracy of America would win them with a superior faith and program. . . . By being true to American democracy we provide the strongest bulwark for freedom and democracy in the modern world."[40]

Despite his detractors' claims, Graham did not always take the side of leftist causes and activities. In 1949, Robert B. House, then chancellor of UNC, denied John Gates, secretary of the Communist Party and editor of *The Daily Worker,* use of campus facilities for a speech; Graham upheld the decision. The issue for House was that Gates was under federal indictment for violating the 1940 Smith Act, which outlawed advocacy for the overthrow of the U.S. government. Graham surprised some of his supporters by standing by House's decision, but he responded, as usual, by invoking the need for both trustworthiness and academic freedom. Graham tried to point out that he had no problem with Gates being a communist, since that alone was not illegal. Still, Gates stood charged with "being involved in a conspiracy to overthrow the government by force." In other words, UNC had to show respect for this law. At the same time, Graham reiterated his support for those UNC faculty members who had stated their support for Gates's invitation and their right to "declare against the indictment." As he had done so many times before, Graham insisted: "Our faculty with all their intellectual freedom are conservative or liberal in the highest American tradition and will be protected in their freedom as honorable University teachers and lawful and decent American citizens."[41]

Frank Graham's life took an unexpected turn in 1949 when he was appointed to serve out the remainder of U.S. Senator J. Melville Broughton's term after Broughton died in March of that year. When Governor Kerr Scott offered the position to Graham, he immediately demurred, expressing his desire to remain as UNC president. But after a few more days of recruiting, Graham accepted and resigned from the UNC presidency in March 1949. When election time rolled around in 1950, Graham decided to run for the full term. He lost to Willis Smith in a runoff after a bruising campaign in which his opponents—to no one's surprise, given the history of his critics—depicted Graham as soft on communism and segregation.[42]

Far more often than not, Frank Graham fought the good fight when it came to academic freedom. His leadership helped legitimize the questioning—by white southerners, no less—of the South's investment in racial discrimination and its stifling, cheap labor traditions. Through their defense of academic freedom, Graham and UNC's scholars helped reshape the debate, slowly and at times begrudgingly, over how much freedom all southerners would have and how inclusive a modernizing South would truly be. But while Graham's dedication to the principle of academic freedom remained steadfast, his liberalism was always going to be limited by his context, a legacy that is most apparent in his unwillingness to try to lead a campaign to end a system of segregation that he knew was both unjust and immoral.

Among progressive southerners, however, there was no doubt who the key figure in their regional circle was. In 1947, after Graham had come in for another round of attacks—this time as a possible security risk as a member of the Atomic Energy Commission—John Langston, a Goldsboro attorney, wrote to congressman John H. Folger, who had studied law at UNC, to thank Folger for having recently defended Graham on the floor of the House.[43] Langston wrote: "The intelligent and patriotic people of America are getting sick and tired of the lynching methods of the [notorious Mississippi segregationist John E.] Rankin types in this Country, who aping the tactics of Stalin and Hitler seek to purge every free citizen whose views do not follow the channels of their own vicious thinking." Despite Graham's liberalism and possible naiveté, Langston felt that Graham's most important legacy was maintaining the trust in the educator's role within modern American democracy: "I think Frank Graham is one of the finest, bravest men American Democracy has ever produced. . . . Maybe he *is* sometimes fooled by petitions and organizations which put out initially a good program clothed in beautiful language, but having in the background some ulterior purpose. Who hasn't sometimes been misled by such, except those wary cautious souls who are afraid to do even one good deed for fear sometimes their motives may be questioned?" In his conclusion, Langston went the full measure in his support for the embattled UNC president: "But when they attack Frank Graham, that raises my ire. I don't always agree with him, but the spirit of democracy in this State is elevated because he has lived and moved in our midst. And this comes from a Duke Alumnus, believe it or not."[44]

Acknowledgments

I have been very fortunate to have had the assistance of a number of talented St. Mary's College of Maryland students over the years. Thanks go to Jonathan Robins, Jeremy Young, Carly Swaim, Lisa Beth Carey, and Brianne Coons Carter for their patient reading of microfilm and their lasting interest in this project. Thanks to Facebook, I still get "How's it coming?" inquiries and encouragement from my former students. Our college librarian, Dr. Celia Rabinowitz, and trustee John McAllister both provided me with precious office space during my sabbatical. I was also fortunate to be designated by the college as an Aldom-Plansoen Honor College professor. This award provided me with three years of extra research funds that were greatly appreciated as this book took shape. My work was also helped by an Archie K. Davis Fellowship from the North Caroliniana Society, as well as a Franklin Research Grant from the American Philosophical Society.

Many friends have given me their support over the years. I want especially to thank Jim Giesen, Bryan Grove, Tracy Adams, Pete and Beth Carmichael, Melissa Kean, Sam Chambers, and Rebecca Brown. The idea for this book came from a conversation I had with Bill Link while standing outside Tate Street Coffee in Greensboro, North Carolina, on a blistering summer morning. Bill's steady encouragement and his deep knowledge of North Carolina and of the history of academia have helped keep this project moving forward. William C. Friday and George Stoney both graciously gave their time for interviews with me. Thanks also go to Keith Longiotti of the UNC Photo Archives Division for his invaluable help, as well as copy editor Brent Winter for his keen eye for clarity. It has also been a pleasure to work with Anne Dean Watkins at the University Press of Kentucky.

I am very fortunate to have kind and generous colleagues at St. Mary's College of Maryland, and I wish to express my gratitude especially to

Aileen Bailey, Jennifer and Andrew Cognard-Black, Alan Dillingham, Liisa Franzen, and my fellow members of the history department, especially Tom Barrett, Gail Savage, Adriana Brodsky, and Chris Adams. Because her office is across the hall from mine, Chris especially has had to endure seemingly endless reports on my progress and my frustrations over the years, and I have, I fear, incurred a debt to her I cannot repay. Given the topic of this book, I must also acknowledge Tom Barrett and the St. Mary's College of Maryland faculty for their defense of academic freedom during a dark time for our institution.

I cannot adequately convey how much I value the love and support I receive from my family. Even though I still live a long way from my family's Iowa home, they make the distance seem much shorter than it is. Thanks always to Rosemary and David Hoyt, Michael and Susan Holden, Mary Jo and Roger Kluesner, Ann and Gary Kendell, my wonderful nieces and nephews, my uncles Bill and Richard Brunner, and to the entire Bob and Rosemary Burke family. Finally, I will never get over my good fortune in having Edward and Mary Ann Holden as my parents. We lost my father in 2004, and I still miss him very much. My mother, meanwhile, remains a source of strength and great wit for my entire family. For everything, I thank Mom and Dad once again.

Notes

Introduction

1. "Tapes Show a Besieged Nixon Saw Enemies All Over," *USA Today*, December 3, 2008, http://www.usatoday.com/news/washington/2008-12-03-nixon-disclosures_N.htm.

2. "Protest Bedeviled by a Political Side Show," *New York Times*, September 22, 2008; see also "Between Free Speech and a Hard Place," *New York Times*, September 30, 2007.

3. See, for instance, Stanley Fish, *Save the World on Your Own Time* (Oxford, UK: Oxford University Press, 2008), and Matthew W. Finkin and Robert C. Post, *For the Common Good: Principles of American Academic Freedom* (New Haven, CT: Yale University Press, 2009).

4. See Thomas L. Haskell, ed., *The Authority of Experts: Studies in History and Theory* (Bloomington: Indiana University Press, 1984), ix.

5. "Memorandum on the University News Bureau," folder 1526, box 42, University Papers, University Archives, University of North Carolina at Chapel Hill Library (hereafter cited as University Papers).

6. "Students Hear Head of University Hit at Anti-Darwinism Bill," *Greensboro Daily News*, February 14, 1925.

7. "General Report of the Committee on Academic Freedom and Academic Tenure (1915)," appendix A in *Freedom and Tenure in the Academy*, ed. William W. Van Alstyne (Durham, NC, and London: Duke University Press, 1993), 393.

8. See, for example, William W. Van Alstyne, "Academic Freedom and the First Amendment in the Supreme Court of the United States: An Unhurried Historical Review," and David Rabban, "A Functional Analysis of 'Individual' and 'Institutional' Academic Freedom under the First Amendment," in *Freedom and Tenure in the Academy*. See also G. Edward White, "Justice Holmes and the Modernization of Free Speech Jurisprudence," *California Law Review* 80 (March 1992): 391, and R. George Wright, "The Emergence of First Amendment Academic Freedom," *Nebraska Law Review* 85 (2007): 793.

9. Wright, "The Emergence of First Amendment Academic Freedom," 794.

10. Dahlia Lithwick and Richard Schragger, "*Jefferson v. Cuccinelli*: Does

the Constitution Really Protect a Right to 'Academic Freedom?'" *Slate*, June 1, 2010, http://www.slate.com/id/2253938.

11. Van Alstyne, "Academic Freedom and the First Amendment," 82. Van Alstyne notes that it was not until the 1952 *Adler v. Board of Education* case that a member of the Supreme Court explicitly described academic freedom as a matter of free speech protected by the First Amendment (105). David M. Rabban adds that it was not until the 1967 *Keyishian v. Board of Regents* case that academic freedom was cited explicitly as a "special concern of the First Amendment." Rabban, "A Functional Analysis," 230.

12. Van Alstyne, "Academic Freedom and the First Amendment," 82.

13. Quoted in Van Alstyne, "Academic Freedom and the First Amendment," 84. Van Alstyne notes that Holmes's famous post–World War I shift to his "marketplace of ideas" theory of freedom of speech was still, in the end, a minority view. In the 1925 *Gitlow* case, for instance, Holmes said: "If in the long run the beliefs expressed in proletarian dictatorship are destined to be accepted by the dominant forces of the community, the only meaning of free speech is that they should be given their chance and have their way" (98). A provocative statement, but also a dissenting opinion from the majority of the court.

14. Chase was not a voice in the wilderness, however. Important reconsideration of free speech and the first amendment was being undertaken by no less than Louis Brandeis and Oliver Wendell Holmes Jr. G. Edward White argues that by the 1920s, "the locus of philosophical energy animating solicitude for free speech was shifted from the individual as an autonomous being to the individual as a participant in a democratic society. The sources of protection for free speech became identified not with the interest of the individual whose liberty government existed to further, but with the social interest in furthering democratic principles by encouraging independent public discussion and debate. Holmes was to emerge as one of the founders of modern First Amendment theory at the same moment in time when this second stage in the reorientation of the premises of free speech jurisprudence was taking place." From G. Edward White, "Justice Holmes," 406–7.

15. Van Alstyne, "Academic Freedom and the First Amendment," 86.

16. David M. Rabban, "A Functional Analysis," 237. See also Frederick Rudolph, *The American College and University: A History* (Athens and London: University of Georgia Press, 1990); Lawrence R. Veysey, *The Emergence of the American University* (Chicago and London: University of Chicago Press, 1965); John R. Thelin, *A History of American Higher Education* (Baltimore and London: Johns Hopkins University Press, 2004).

17. "Men, Let Us Think," *Tar Heel*, May 26, 1922.

18. "First in Our Hearts Today," *Daily Tar Heel*, November 11, 1931.

19. Bruce Clayton's *The Savage Ideal: Intolerance and Intellectual Leadership in the South, 1890–1914* (Baltimore: Johns Hopkins University Press, 1972)

highlights the well-publicized southern cases of John Spencer Bassett at Trinity College (now Duke University) in 1903 and Andrew Sledd at Emory College in 1902.

20. Merle Curti and Vernon Carstensen, *The University of Wisconsin: A History, 1848–1925* (Madison: University of Wisconsin Press, 1949), 1:525. Thank you to Professor David Brown of Elizabethtown College for pointing me in the direction of this quote.

21. John Dewey, "Academic Freedom," in *John Dewey: The Middle Works, 1899–1924*, ed. Jo Ann Boydston (Carbondale and Edwardsville: Southern Illinois University Press, 1976), 2:55.

22. Ibid.

23. Ibid., 2:57.

24. Ibid., 2:59.

25. Thomas Haskell, "Justifying the Rights of Academic Freedom," in *The Future of Academic Freedom*, ed. Louis Menand (Chicago: University of Chicago Press, 1998), 45–46.

26. Dewey, "Academic Freedom," 66, 65.

27. Daniel Joseph Singal, "Toward a Definition of American Modernism," *American Quarterly* 39, no. 1 (Spring 1987): 11.

28. Van Alstyne, "Academic Freedom and the First Amendment," 98.

29. Walter P. Metzger, "The 1940 Statement," in *Freedom and Tenure in the Academy*, 13–14.

30. Interview with William C. Friday, July 20, 2006. In possession of author.

31. Howard Odum to Beardsley Ruml, March 3, 1926, #3167, folder 90, Howard Washington Odum Papers, Southern Historical Collection (SHC), University of North Carolina at Chapel Hill Library (hereafter cited as Odum Papers).

32. "Memorandum on the University News Bureau," University Papers.

33. Jonathan Daniels, *A Southerner Discovers the South* (New York: Macmillan, 1938), 140.

34. Clayton, *The Savage Ideal*. On the later attacks on southern academic freedom, see Patrick Novotny, *This Georgia Rising: Education, Civil Rights, and the Politics of Change in Georgia in the 1940s* (Macon, GA: Mercer University Press, 2007); Wayne Hamilton Wiley, "Academic Freedom at the University of Virginia: The First Hundred Years from Jefferson through Alderman" (PhD diss., University of Virginia, 1973); Alice Carol Cox, "The Rainey Affair: A History of the Academic Controversy at the University of Texas, 1938–1946" (PhD diss., University of Denver, 1970); Paul Conkin, *Gone with the Ivy: A Biography of Vanderbilt University* (Knoxville: University of Tennessee Press, 1985).

35. "Smashing Attack Made by Bryan on Evolution," *Raleigh News & Observer*, April 28, 1923; "Evangelist Ham Raps Evolution," *Raleigh News & Observer*, November 6, 1923; "Ham Declares Evolution Is as Much Fact as Santa Claus," *Raleigh News & Observer*, February 20, 1924.

36. "Evangelist Ham Finds His Audience Fundamentalists," *Raleigh News & Observer*, February 29, 1924.

37. Quoted in Willard B. Gatewood Jr., *Preachers, Pedagogues, and Politicians: The Evolution Controversy in North Carolina, 1922–1927* (Chapel Hill: University of North Carolina Press, 1966), 125. Gatewood's book on this episode in North Carolina history remains the best and most thorough analysis to date.

38. Ibid., 10.

39. Ibid., 128.

40. Ibid., 129.

41. Ibid., 132.

42. Harry Chase's willingness to testify at the hearings, with university appropriation decisions still looming, stands in stark contrast to the inactivity of University of Tennessee president Harcourt Morgan, who, in Edward Larson's words, "held his tongue" while his state mulled over both the Butler Bill against evolution and a plan to expand the university. See Edward Larson's *Summer for the Gods: The Scopes Trial and America's Continuing Debate over Science and Religion* (Cambridge, MA, and London, UK: Harvard University Press, 1997), 57.

43. Quoted in Louis Round Wilson, *The University of North Carolina, 1900–1930: The Making of a Modern University* (Chapel Hill: University of North Carolina Press, 1957), 512–13.

44. Gatewood Jr., *Preachers, Pedagogues, and Politicians*, 133.

45. "Students Hear Head of University Hit at Anti-Darwinism Bill," *Greensboro Daily News*, February 14, 1925.

46. Ibid.

47. "Chase's Talk against Poole Bill Pleasing," *Greensboro Daily News*, February 15, 1925.

48. Harry W. Chase to Bertram W. Wells, February 13, 1925, folder 1558, University Papers.

49. Harry W. Chase to Walter Murphy, February 14, 1925, folder 1558, University Papers.

50. Edgar Knight, "Mud or Monkey in North Carolina," *Independent*, May 14, 1927.

51. Harry W. Chase to Edgar Pharr, February 16, 1925, folder 1558, University Papers.

52. Ibid.

53. "Freedom of Speech," *Presbyterian Standard*, February 18, 1925.

54. Quoted in Gatewood Jr., *Preachers, Pedagogues, and Politicians*, 143.

55. Quoted in Gatewood Jr., *Preachers, Pedagogues, and Politicians*, 144–45.

56. William C. Dowd Jr. to Frank P. Graham, May 13, 1940, folder "Communism: Dies Committee, 1940," box 1, Frank Porter Graham Papers, 1932–1949, GA/CU: President's Office Records, University Archives (hereafter cited as Graham Papers).

57. "Putting Any Kind of Ideas in Their Heads," *Daily Tar Heel*, February 28, 1928.

58. David Cohn, "Chapel Hill," *Atlantic Monthly*, March 1941, 323.

59. Frederick Rudolph describes the "Wisconsin Idea" as a "program of university service" that "rested on the conviction that informed intelligence when applied to the problems of modern society could make democracy work more efficiently." See Frederick Rudolph, *The American College and University: A History* (New York: Vintage Books, 1962), 363.

60. Rob Christensen, *The Paradox of Tar Heel Politics: The Personalities, Elections, and Events That Shaped Modern North Carolina* (Chapel Hill: University of North Carolina Press, 2008), 69.

61. David Carlton, "The Revolution from Above: The National Market and the Beginnings of Industrialization in North Carolina," *Journal of American History* 77, no. 2 (September 1990): 457–62. See also Douglas Carl Abrams, *Conservative Constraints: North Carolina and the New Deal* (Jackson: University Press of Mississippi, 1992); Anthony J. Badger, *Prosperity Road: The New Deal, Tobacco, and North Carolina* (Chapel Hill: University of North Carolina Press, 1980); William A. Link, *The Paradox of Southern Progressivism, 1880–1930* (Chapel Hill: University of North Carolina Press, 1992); Joseph L. Morrison, *Governor O. Max Gardner: A Power in North Carolina and New Deal Washington* (Chapel Hill: University of North Carolina Press, 1971); George B. Tindall, *The Emergence of the New South, 1913–1945* (Baton Rouge: Louisiana State University Press, 1968); and Philip J. Wood, *Southern Capitalism: The Political Economy of North Carolina, 1880–1980* (Durham, NC: Duke University Press, 1986).

62. Jacquelyn Dowd Hall, James Leloudis, Robert Korstad, Mary Murphy, Lu Ann Jones, and Christopher B. Daly, *Like a Family: The Making of a Southern Cotton Mill World* (Chapel Hill: University of North Carolina Press, 1987), 36.

63. Tindall, *Emergence of the New South*, 225.

64. Link, *Paradox of Southern Progressivism*, 203.

65. George Brown Tindall, *Springtime for Chapel Hill: A Southern Renaissance* (Chapel Hill: Center for the Study of the American South, 1993), 2; Louis Round Wilson, *The University of North Carolina, 1900–1930* (Chapel Hill: University of North Carolina Press, 1957), especially books 2 and 3; William D. Snider, *Light on the Hill: A History of the University of North Carolina at Chapel Hill* (Chapel Hill and London: University of North Carolina Press, 1992), 137–237.

66. "Mrs. Bingham's Gift," *Asheville Times*, August 13, 1917.

67. Interview with William C. Friday, July 20, 2006. In possession of author.

68. Gerald W. Johnson, "Chase of North Carolina," *American Mercury*, June 1929, 185.

69. Tindall, *Springtime for Chapel Hill*, 3–4. See also "Chase Inaugurated

President of State University as Huge and Notable Throng Applauds," *Charlotte Observer*, April 29, 1920.

70. Tindall, *Emergence of the New South*, 226; Christensen, *Paradox of Tar Heel Politics*, 48–56.

71. Tindall, *Springtime for Chapel Hill*, 5; Wilson, *The University of North Carolina*, especially chapters 29 and 30.

72. "Growth of University in Last Ten Years Has Been Astounding," *Daily Tar Heel*, November 11, 1931.

73. Edwin Mims, *The Advancing South* (New York: Doubleday, Page & Co., 1926), 117.

74. "Growth of University in Last Ten Years Has Been Astounding," *Daily Tar Heel*, November 11, 1931.

75. "Big Changes Have Taken Place in Ten Years," *Greensboro Daily News*, August 15, 1926.

76. "University Is Leader in Research Movement," *Daily Tar Heel*, December 11, 1928.

77. George Streator, "The Colored South Speaks for Itself," *The Crisis*, December 1933, 274.

78. Mims, *The Advancing South*, 114–15.

79. Melissa Kean, review of *Tulane: The Emergence of a Modern University, 1945–1980*, by Clarence L. Mohr and Joseph E. Gordon, *Journal of Southern History* (November 2002): 999–1000. In addition to Mohr and Gordon's history of Tulane and her own forthcoming history of Rice University, Kean also cites as early examples Thomas G. Dyer's *The University of Georgia: A Bicentennial History, 1785–1985* (Athens: University of Georgia Press, 1985) and Conkin's *Gone with the Ivy*. James Axtell's *The Making of Princeton University* (Princeton, NJ, and Oxford: Princeton University Press, 2006) also places its subject within a well-developed historical context.

80. See, for example, Van Alstyne, "Academic Freedom and the First Amendment"; Rabban, "A Functional Analysis"; White, "Justice Holmes and the Modernization of Free Speech Jurisprudence"; and Haskell, "Justifying the Rights of Academic Freedom."

81. See Glenda Gilmore, *Defying Dixie: The Radical Roots of Civil Rights, 1919–1950* (New York and London: W. W. Norton, 2008); Patricia Sullivan, *Days of Hope: Race and Democracy in the New Deal Era* (Chapel Hill: University of North Carolina Press, 1996); John Egerton, *Speak Now against the Day: The Generation before the Civil Rights Movement* (New York: Knopf, 1995); Morton Sosna, *In Search of the Silent South: Southern Liberals and the Race Issue* (New York: Columbia University Press, 1977); John T. Kneebone, *Southern Liberal Journalists and the Issue of Race, 1920–1944* (Chapel Hill: University of North Carolina Press, 1985); Charles W. Eagles, *Jonathan Daniels and Race Relations: The Evolution of a Southern Liberal* (Knoxville: University of Tennessee

Press, 1982); and Tony Badger, "Fatalism, Not Gradualism: The Crisis of Southern Liberalism, 1945–1960," in *The Making of Martin Luther King and the Civil Rights Movement*, ed. Brian Ward and Tony Badger (New York: New York University Press, 1996), 78. A more recent entry into the topic area comes with Jonathan W. Bell's solid essay on liberalism in Florida, "Conceptualising Southern Liberalism: Ideology and the Pepper-Smathers 1950 Primary in Florida," *Journal of American Studies* (April 2003): 17–45.

82. Battles over academic freedom continue to surface at UNC. In the summer of 2002, a Christian fundamentalist group, the Family Policy Network, sued UNC for assigning incoming students to read *Approaching the Qur'an: The Early Revelations* by Michael Sells. The suit claimed that the assignment violated state law separating church and state. Speaking on the Fox News Channel's *Hannity and Colmes* program, James Yacovelli of the Family Policy Network charged that UNC's assignment of the book amounted to "veiled coercion . . . to get students to accept Islam from a distorted point of view." He worried that UNC students who read the book would not see that Islam, in its "true culture," amounted to little more than the desire to "kill the infidels and drive planes into us, and blow us up." Eventually UNC allowed students to opt out of reading the book if they wrote a short essay of explanation. Such challenges would have looked familiar to UNC administrators and professors during the interwar years. See Andrew Chase Baker, "Reading the Koran in Chapel Hill," *Religion in the News*, Fall 2002, www.trincoll.edu/depts/csrpl/rinvol5no3/koran%20unc.htm; and "Evolution on the Front Line," American Association for the Advancement of Science, www.aaas.org/news/press_room/evolution. The next summer saw another round of criticism of the assignment of Barbara Ehrenreich's *Nickel and Dimed: On (Not) Getting By in America*. Critics complained that the book was too anti-business and that the assignment offered no reading to counter Ehrenreich's conclusion. See Jane Stancil, "Group Says 'Nickel and Dimed,' the Assigned Reading for Freshmen, Has a Liberal Bias," Common Dreams, http://www.commondreams.org/headlines03/0708-07.htm.

83. See Robert Putnam, "Bowling Alone: America's Declining Social Capital," *Journal of Democracy* 6, no. 1 (1995): 67, and James S. Coleman, "Social Capital in the Creation of Human Capital," *American Journal of Sociology* 94 (1988): 98.

84. Gerald M. Mara, "Thucydides and Plato on Democracy and Trust," *Journal of Politics* 63, no. 3 (August 2001): 820–45.

85. See Charles J. Holden, "Patriotism Is Not Stupidity: Student Antiwar Activism at UNC in the 1930s," *North Carolina Historical Review* (January 2008): 29–56.

86. Christensen, *Paradox of Tar Heel Politics*, 110.

87. Cohn, "Chapel Hill," 328.

1. "Race Was a Delicate Matter"

1. "Clan Representative Comes to University to Organize Klu Klux," *Tar Heel*, January 28, 1921.

2. "Unmask the Klan Is Verdict of Phi," *Tar Heel*, February 6, 1923.

3. Ibid.

4. "Di Society in Favor of Recent Anti-Mask Bill," *Tar Heel*, February 13, 1923.

5. John Herbert Roper interview with Guy and Guion Johnson, #4235, folder 5, box 1, John Herbert Roper Papers, SHC (hereafter cited as Roper Papers).

6. Daniel J. Singal, *The War Within: From Victorian to Modernist Thought in the South, 1919–1945* (Chapel Hill: University of North Carolina Press, 1981), 296.

7. Ibid., 316.

8. John K. Chapman, "Black Freedom and the University of North Carolina, 1793–1960" (PhD diss., University of North Carolina at Chapel Hill, 2006), 191–92.

9. *The Crisis*, May 1919, 13.

10. Arthur Waskow, *From Race Riot to Sit-In: A Study in the Connections between Conflict and Violence* (New York: Doubleday, 1967).

11. Raymond Gavins, "The NAACP in North Carolina during the Age of Segregation," in *New Directions in Civil Rights Studies*, ed. Armstead L. Robinson and Patricia Sullivan (Charlottesville: University of Virginia Press, 1991), 105.

12. Charles Kirk Pilkington, "The Trials of Brotherhood: The Founding of the Commission on Interracial Cooperation," *Georgia Historical Quarterly* 69, no. 1 (Spring 1985): 62.

13. Their white associates sometimes uncovered that lie as well. In 1925, J. A. Dickey, a researcher from Cornell University, wrote UNC sociologist Eugene C. Branson to describe what he had witnessed on a field trip through Arkansas and Texas. While visiting a cotton plantation, Dickey reported, "I saw a hard boiled manager on one of these farms take a 16 year old negro boy from a mule and spank him into insensibility while the boy's old father looked on. When through with the little negro he swiftly fetched him astride the mule but the negro fell off on the other side and had to be assisted astride the mule. Peasantry in its worst form exists on these plantations." Dickey also pointed to a fundamental problem that researchers like himself and those at UNC encountered: "No one has ever been able to get the good will of these owners or rather their managers sufficiently and get away with the facts. I am going to try it for a month or more. The Census taker simply gets to the manager's office and has to take his word for the facts." J. A. Dickey to E. C. Branson, April 11, 1925, folder 301, box 6, E. C. Branson Papers, SHC (hereafter cited as Branson Papers).

14. Link, *Paradox of Southern Progressivism*, 265.

15. Ibid., 252.

16. Louis Mazzari's biography of Arthur Raper reveals Raper's comparative aggressiveness in studying race issues compared to other white CIC members. See Louis Mazzari, *Southern Modernist: Arthur Raper from the New Deal to the Cold War* (Baton Rouge: Louisiana State University Press, 2006), 51–76.

17. Singal, *The War Within*, 151.

18. Warren Ashby, *Frank Porter Graham: A Southern Liberal* (Winston-Salem, NC: John F. Blair, 1980), 36–37.

19. Charles Maddry Freeman, "Growth and Plan of a Community: A Study of Negro Life in Chapel Hill and Carrboro, North Carolina" (MA thesis, University of North Carolina at Chapel Hill, 1944), 46.

20. Ibid.

21. "University Students in Settlement Work," *Charlotte Observer*, March 1, 1914, quoted in Freeman's "Growth and Plan for a Community," 61. John K. Chapman refers to UNC's outreach efforts during these years—the same years when segregation was hardening in Chapel Hill—as "a way of giving back with one hand a small part of what they had taken with the other" (227).

22. Freeman, "Growth and Plan for a Community," 62.

23. Ibid., 63–64.

24. "Negro Night School Promising," *Tar Heel*, October 6, 1917.

25. Ibid.

26. "Negro Problems in Theme of Illustrated Lecture," *Tar Heel*, February 9, 1918.

27. Ibid.

28. On white southern paternalism before the 1920s, see Bruce Clayton, *The Savage Ideal*, 198–201.

29. "Dr. Branson Launches Negro Study Course," *Tar Heel*, February 16, 1918.

30. "Dr. Mangum Lectures on Negro Housing Question," *Tar Heel*, March 9, 1918.

31. Ibid.

32. "University Aids Negro School," *Tar Heel*, February 14, 1920.

33. "Dr. Raper Discusses the Education of the Negro," *Tar Heel*, March 16, 1918.

34. "House and Church in Negro Section Razed in Sunday Night Fire," *Tar Heel*, January 28, 1921.

35. "Janitors of Dormitories Organize and Walk Out," *Tar Heel*, May 4, 1918.

36. Guy Benton Johnson and Guion Griffis Johnson, *Research in Service to Society: The First Fifty Years of the Institute for Research in Social Science at the University of North Carolina* (Chapel Hill: University of North Carolina Press, 1980), 134.

37. "'White Likker' and City Negroes Mix," *Tar Heel*, February 25, 1921. John K. Chapman's dissertation points out that the "institutional culture of Jim Crow at the university taught students to see black workers not as human, but as stereotypical 'faithful servants.' This led to paternalistic relationships between students and black university workers, and it often led to ridicule of these workers and a misunderstanding of their lives." See Chapman, "Black Freedom," 215.

38. "Dr. Nathan Vaccinates All Campus Janitors," *Tar Heel*, February 21, 1922.

39. "'Dean' Andy Is to Ride on High," *Tar Heel*, December 1, 1927.

40. "Repudiates Dean Andy Article," *Tar Heel*, December 3, 1927.

41. "Dean Andy the Victim of Reporter's Fancy," *Tar Heel*, December 3, 1927.

42. UNC invited several African American leaders to campus throughout the 1920s. With these invitations, UNC moved toward the CIC's interracialist plan to appeal to white southern youth and to establish contacts among the white and black elites. For instance, in 1921 UNC welcomed R. R. Moton, head of Tuskegee Institute, to campus. According to the article in the *Tar Heel*, Moton (misidentified as "Morton") gave what amounted to a ringing endorsement of white paternalism. The paper described Moton as "the leader of the element of his race who believes that the greatest progress will come to the colored race through a system of education given them by the white race that will enable them to stride forward industrially and intellectually." Moton no doubt delivered a very conservative speech, but his mere presence on campus reflected the newer interracialist approach emerging in the 1920s. Just having Moton speak before UNC students was bold. UNC would grow even more daring with its invitations as the 1920s went on. "Head of Tuskegee Speaks in Gerrard Hall on Race Question," *Tar Heel*, March 18, 1921.

43. "Democracy and the Ku-Klux Klan," *Journal of Social Forces* 1, no. 2 (January 1923): 178–79.

44. Guy B. Johnson, "A Sociological Interpretation of the New Ku Klux Movement," *Journal of Social Forces* 1, no. 4 (May 1923): 440–42.

45. Ibid.

46. In the growing body of literature on this subject, see especially Gilmore, *Defying Dixie*; Sullivan, *Days of Hope*; Egerton, *Speak Now against the Day*; Nan E. Woodruff, *American Congo: The African American Freedom Struggle in the Delta* (Cambridge, MA: Harvard University Press, 2003); Greta de Jong, *A Different Day: African American Struggles for Justice in Rural Louisiana, 1900–1970* (Chapel Hill: University of North Carolina Press, 2002); and Peter F. Lau, *Democracy Rising: South Carolina and the Fight for Black Equality since 1865* (Lexington: University Press of Kentucky, 2006).

47. Johnson, "A Sociological Interpretation of the New Ku Klux Movement," 440–42.

48. Guy B. Johnson, "The Race Philosophy of the Ku Klux Klan," *Opportunity*, September 1923, 268.

49. Ibid., 270.

50. Guy B. Johnson, "The Negro Migration and Its Consequences," *Journal of Social Forces* 2, no. 3 (March 1924): 406.

51. "Negro Scientist Speaks Monday," *Tar Heel*, January 17, 1925.

52. "Ku Klux Klan Question to Be Aired Out Here," *Tar Heel*, January 21, 1925.

53. J. W. Bailey to E. C. Branson, February 12, 1925, folder 297, box 6, Branson Papers.

54. Michael O'Brien, *The Idea of the Modern South, 1920–1941* (Baltimore and London: Johns Hopkins University Press, 1979); Singal, *The War Within*; Michael James Milligan, "The Contradictions of Public Service: A Study of Howard Odum's Intellectual Odyssey" (PhD diss., University of Virginia, 1994); Wayne Brazil, "Howard W. Odum: The Building Years, 1884–1930" (PhD diss., Harvard University, 1975); Fred Hobson, *Tell About the South: The Southern Rage to Explain* (Baton Rouge: Louisiana State University, 1983).

55. Guy Johnson later pointed out that his and Odum's collaborations, despite their contributions, were also unlikely to offend. As he told interviewer John Herbert Roper, "This sort of writing—in 1925 and 1926—was fairly safe, because even conservative people like spirituals and songs." John Herbert Roper interview with Guy and Guion Johnson, Roper Papers.

56. Daniel Singal, for example, credits William Terry Couch with transforming the magazine into a "prime topic of conversation not only on campus but out in the state as well." Singal, *The War Within*, 270.

57. R. K. Fowler, "Slaves," *Carolina Magazine*, October 1926.

58. "Outline of the Position Held by the Carolina Magazine Board," October 25, 1926, folder 1616, University Papers.

59. Committee report to President Harry W. Chase, October 26, 1926, folder 1616, University Papers.

60. Gerald W. Johnson, "Mentioning the Unmentionable," reprinted in *Carolina Magazine*, January 1927, 23.

61. Ibid., 23–24. Virginia had in fact moved toward using eugenics as a basis of codifying racial definitions with the Racial Integrity Act of 1924, and the University of Virginia was steeped in the eugenics teaching of Professor Ivey Foreman Lewis. See Gregory Michael Dorr, "Assuring America's Place in the Sun: Ivey Foreman Lewis and the Teaching of Eugenics at the University of Virginia, 1915–1953," *Journal of Southern History* 66, no. 2 (May 2000): 257–96.

62. Johnson, "Mentioning the Unmentionable," 23–24.

63. Ibid., 24.

64. Lewis Alexander, "Book Review. *Fine Clothes to the Jew*," *Carolina Magazine*, May 1927, 41–42.

65. Ibid.

66. Ibid., 42–43.

67. "The Pasture," *Carolina Magazine*, May 1928, 46.

68. Ibid.

69. Ibid.

70. John Herbert Roper interview with Guy and Guion Johnson, Roper Papers.

71. Link, *Paradox of Southern Progressivism*, 257–58.

72. "Johnson Praises American Negro," *Tar Heel*, March 26, 1927, 4.

73. John Herbert Roper interview with Guy and Guion Johnson, folder 5, box 1, Roper Papers.

74. Howard W. Odum to Gerald Johnson, March 25, 1927, Odum Papers.

75. Howard W. Odum to Gerald W. Johnson, March 25, 1927, folder 130, box 2, Odum Papers. Shortly after James Weldon Johnson's visit to UNC, Odum received an invitation to speak at the NAACP annual conference, sharing a stage with W. E. B. DuBois and Hamilton Fish Jr. Odum declined, citing a busy schedule. Walter White to Howard W. Odum, May 10, 1927, folder 135, Odum Papers; Howard W. Odum to Walter White, May 17, 1927, folder 136, Odum Papers. Guy Johnson remembered that when Odum was introducing James Weldon Johnson that evening, he referred to the invitee as "Mr. Johnson." "At that point," Guy Johnson recalled, Hamilton "got up and stalked out." The next day Hamilton then lit into Guion Johnson, asking if she could "*account* for such conduct on the part of Odum." Guion Johnson shot back, "I'm not here to account for Odum." She was there to take Hamilton's class—a perfect response in light of the general thrust of this book. See John Herbert Roper interview with Guy and Guion Johnson, #4235, folder 5, box 1, Roper Papers.

76. J. G. de Roulhac Hamilton to Harry W. Chase, March 28, 1927, folder 1630, University Papers.

77. Ibid. Connor's letter covered largely the same ground, to such an extent that one can surmise they discussed it beforehand. In Connor's judgment, "it was exceedingly unwise to permit a regularly scheduled class in the University to be conducted by a negro; nor do I think it ought to be permitted." Whether he or Chase liked it or not, "narrow race prejudice" was "widespread and deep-rooted in North Carolina." However, Connor in fact did like it: "Personally, I think it is a prejudice which, under prevailing conditions, is well-founded and justifiable, and which we certainly cannot afford to ignore." See R. D. W. Connor to Harry W. Chase, March 23, 1927, R. D. W. Connor Papers, SHC. Handwritten across the top: "never written."

78. "The Sun Rises," *Tar Heel*, April 12, 1927.

79. Ibid.

2. "Go Ahead and Do Harm"

1. Memorandum, "The Institute for Research in Social Science," folder "Annual Reports, 1924–1925," box 1, collection #40075, series 1: General,

subgroup 1: Administrative Files, Academic Affairs: Institute for Research in Social Science Records, University Archives. Despite the careful references to "cooperation," IRSS stalwarts Guy and Guion Johnson recalled several decades later that "Odum was convinced that basic research was needed to prove to mill owners that their paternalistic approach to mill labor was a denial of democracy and at the same time unproductive." See Johnson and Johnson, *Research in Service to Society*, 201.

2. Quoted in Brazil, "Howard W. Odum," 481.

3. Harry Woodburn Chase, "The Social Responsibility of the State University," *Journal of Social Forces* 1, no. 5 (September 1923): 520.

4. Allen Tullos, *Habits of Industry: White Culture and the Transformation of the Carolina Piedmont* (Chapel Hill and London: University of North Carolina Press, 1989), 289.

5. Wood, *Southern Capitalism*, 122–33.

6. Interview with Guy and Guion Johnson, folder 5, box 1, Roper Papers.

7. E. C. Branson to L. L. Arnold, February 16, 1916, folder 50, box 2, Branson Papers.

8. "Gripping Novel of Modern Labor Conditions Being Written by Local Authors," *Tar Heel*, May 23, 1919.

9. On post–World War I labor activities in the South, see Hall et al., *Like a Family*, 186–95.

10. "Nichols Speaks on Views of Laborites," *Tar Heel*, May 29, 1920.

11. "Troops Ordered Out in Concord Strike," *New York Times*, August 15, 1921.

12. "James Barrett Speaks on the Labor Question," *Tar Heel*, November 11, 1921.

13. "A Great Chapel Hill Privilege," *Tar Heel*, November 4, 1921.

14. Tindall, *Emergence of the New South*, 334.

15. Owen Lovejoy, "A Three Year Cycle for Social Work Conferences," *Journal of Social Forces* (January 1923): 129–30.

16. Wood, *Southern Capitalism*, 76.

17. "Dangerous Tendencies," *Southern Textile Bulletin*, December 20, 1923, 22. Tannenbaum was arrested in 1914 for taking part in a march of unemployed workers that turned violent when the police arrived. He served a one-year prison term.

18. Frank Tannenbaum, *Darker Phases of the South* (New York: Negro Universities Press, reprint 1969), v.

19. "Dangerous Tendencies," *Southern Textile Bulletin*, December 20, 1923, 22. Besides the *Journal of Social Forces*, there was other evidence of UNC's interest in industrial-labor relations that Clark would have noticed, because it is apparent that he became an avid reader of the *Tar Heel*. In February 1923, students in the North Carolina Club presented papers on labor-capital relations

and corporate taxation for discussion. An industrial management class offered an annual field trip to visit Liggett and Myers Tobacco Company and the Erwin Cotton Mills, both in Durham. See "Papers Read by James and Somers at North Carolina Club Meeting," *Tar Heel*, February 16, 1923; "Industrial Management Class Is to Take Trip," *Tar Heel*, February 23, 1923.

20. "Child Labor Menaces Society Says Lovejoy," *Tar Heel*, November 24, 1922, 1.

21. John J. Parker to Howard W. Odum, January 4, 1924, folder 28, box 1, Odum Papers.

22. Gerald W. Johnson to Howard W. Odum, April 27, 1927, folder 134, box 2, Odum Papers.

23. Howard W. Odum to Harry W. Chase, January 7, 1924, folder 28, box 1, Odum Papers.

24. Howard W. Odum to John J. Parker, January 18, 1924, folder 1520, box 42, University Papers.

25. Harry W. Chase to John J. Parker, January 9, 1924, folder 1519, box 42, University Papers. My emphasis.

26. John J. Parker to Harry W. Chase, January 28, 1924, folder 1521, box 42, University Papers.

27. Harry W. Chase to A. W. McLean, December 21, 1925, folder 1592, box 44, University Papers.

28. "Breeding Radicals," *Southern Textile Bulletin*, September 24, 1925. In a later issue, Clark used the same quote from the college paper, changing "ills" to "evils," accuracy never being his strong suit. See "College Bred Agitators," November 26, 1925. The North Carolina Club was a creation of Branson's. He organized interested UNC students into county clubs charged with studying conditions in their home counties. All the county clubs then met regularly as the North Carolina Club.

29. "Breeding Radicals," *Southern Textile Bulletin*, September 24, 1925. Carl Emmett Rankin, on the other hand, pointed out in his 1935 study of UNC that given the basic requirements for matriculation, it required some effort on behalf of students to take classes in the social sciences, because very few such classes were required. Rankin observed that "there are no required courses in which contact is made with the problems and issues of present-day American life." Carl Emmett Rankin, "The University of North Carolina and the Problems of the Cotton Mill Employee" (PhD diss., Columbia University, 1934), 126–27.

30. "Mill Owners Slam Door in Face of the University's Researchers," *Greensboro Daily Times*, December 20, 1925.

31. "Memoranda Concerning the Proposed Investigation of the Economic and Social Aspects of the Southern Textile Industry by the Institute for Research in Social Science at the University of North Carolina," folder 1595, box 44, University Papers.

32. Ibid.

33. Brazil, "Howard W. Odum," 468–87.

34. "College Bred Agitators," 22.

35. "The Pinehurst Meeting," *Southern Textile Bulletin*, December 3, 1925, 22.

36. Johnson and Johnson, *Research in Service to Society*, 203.

37. "Industry Declines to Be Studied," *Greensboro Daily News*, December 21, 1925.

38. "Orders and Orders," *Carolina Magazine*, March 1926, 2.

39. "University Heads Are Silent over Rejection," *Charlotte Observer*, December 22, 1925.

40. Willard B. Gatewood Jr., *Preachers, Pedagogues, and Politicians*.

41. Odum to W. C. Jackson, February 12, 1926, folder 88, Odum Papers.

42. "The Voice of an Ally," *Southern Textile Bulletin*, January 14, 1926, 22.

43. Quoted in Nell Battle Lewis, "The University of North Carolina Gets Its Orders," *The Nation*, February 3, 1926, 114.

44. Ibid.

45. Ibid. Guy Benton Johnson and Guion Griffis Johnson concluded decades later that the IRSS's research on the textile industry was, on the whole, "somewhat favorable to the cotton manufacturers." See *Research in Service to Society*, 209.

46. "Orders and Orders," *Carolina Magazine*, March 1926, 2.

47. Tullos, *Habits of Industry*, 293–94.

48. "Research Institute," *Greensboro Daily News*, March 28, 1926.

49. Ibid.

50. Harry W. Chase to J. A. Gray, April 26, 1927, folder 1633, box 45, University Papers. See also Randall L. Hall and Ken Badgett, "Robinson Newcomb and the Limits of Liberalism at UNC: Two Case Studies of Black Businessmen in the 1920s South," *North Carolina Historical Review* 4 (October 2009): 373–403.

51. Oral history interview with Dr. Robinson Newcomb, Harry S. Truman Library and Museum, http://www.trumanlibrary.org/oralhist/newcomb.htm.

52. Ibid.

53. Harry W. Chase to James A. Gray, May 3, 1927, folder 1634, box 45, University Papers.

54. "Dr. Chase Enters Formal Denial," *Raleigh News & Observer*, July 18, 1928, 4.

55. Both Brazil, "Howard W. Odum," 507, and Milligan, "The Contradictions of Public Service," make reference to this incident. Guion Griffis Johnson recalled later how "once a student [employee of the IRSS] named Newcombe [*sic*] went to a tobacco factory in Winston-Salem. Newcombe was called in by President Chase and asked to turn over all of his memoranda and records from

the factory. Chase had them burned and Newcombe was fired [from the IRSS]. Now I can't document that, but it happened." Interview with Guy and Guion Johnson, folder 5, box 1, Roper Papers.

56. Howard W. Odum to T. J. Woofter, January 31, 1928, folder 161a, Odum Papers.

57. "Our Enemies," *Southern Textile Bulletin*, April 21, 1927, 22.

58. "The Greensboro Conference," *Southern Textile Bulletin*, December 15, 1927, 22.

59. Howard W. Odum to Paul Blanshard, April 22, 1927, folder 133, box 10, Odum Papers; Howard W. Odum to Paul Blanshard, April 25, 1927, folder 134, box 10, Odum Papers.

60. Paul Blanshard, "Servants of the Spindle I," *New Republic*, September 21, 1927, 114–16; Paul Blanshard, "Servants of the Spindle II," *New Republic*, September 28, 1927, 143–45.

61. "Program to Reduce Working Hours in Southern Industry to 54 a Week Is Begun Here," *Greensboro Daily News*, December 12, 1927.

62. "Our Greatest Menace," *Southern Textile Bulletin*, January 5, 1928, 22, 27.

63. Ibid.

64. "Organizing," *Southern Textile Bulletin*, February 2, 1928, 20.

65. "Advocating Russian Vulgarity," *Southern Textile Bulletin*, February 23, 1928, 28.

66. "If Dr. Chase Leaves," *Greensboro Daily News*, February 8, 1926, p. 143 of the Clipping File, through 1975, vol. 7, North Carolina Collection (NCC), UNC Library. Chase's frustration did not appear suddenly. In 1926, Chase wrote privately: "It looks to me sometimes that as though for the last twelve months every interest that is hostile to the University has been emboldened to come out of hiding and to try to do it damage while the going is good. Sometimes I get very much depressed over the situation, and wonder if somebody else could not guide the University through this period better than I can; and then again I wonder if it is a good time for the University to change leadership. So you can see my perplexed state of mind about it all." Harry W. Chase to Haywood Parker, February 1, 1926, folder 1596, box 44, University Papers.

67. Harry W. Chase to D. D. Carroll, H. W. Odum, and Frank Graham, March 6, 1928, folder 1653, box 46, University Papers.

68. Ibid.

69. Ibid.

70. "Chase Inaugurated President of State University as Huge and Notable Throng Applauds," *Charlotte Observer*, April 29, 1920.

71. Chase to Carroll, Odum, and Graham, March 6, 1928, folder 1653, box 46, University Papers.

72. Johnson and Johnson, *Research in Service to Society*, 213.

73. "Dr. Chase Enters Formal Denial," *Raleigh News & Observer*, July 18,

1928, 4. Malcolm Young, a journalist and UNC graduate, had accused UNC of forcing Cassidy out for political reasons. Young believed that the National Association of Manufacturers had pressured UNC to get rid of Cassidy, Holland, Schwenning, and Robinson Newcomb because of their interest in labor reform. Cassidy allegedly met with D. D. Carroll to plead his case and was told that "the friendship and 'respect' of the National Association of Manufacturers had to be retained." Carroll and Chase denied the accusation. See "Claims Cassidy Was Forced Out," *Raleigh News & Observer*, July 20, 1928, 7. See also Johnson and Johnson, *Research in Service to Society*, 210–14.

74. Quoted in Van Alstyne, "Academic Freedom and the First Amendment," 87.

75. Chase to Carroll, Odum, and Graham, March 6, 1928.

76. Harry W. Chase to Haywood Parker, March 8, 1928, folder 1654, box 46, University Papers.

77. Ibid.

78. Ibid.

79. John A. Salmond, *Gastonia, 1929: The Story of the Loray Mill Strike* (Chapel Hill and London: University of North Carolina Press, 1995), 1–22; Hall et al., *Like a Family*; Tullos, *Habits of Industry*.

80. Wood, *Southern Capitalism*, 127.

81. Tindall, *Emergence of the New South*, 339–45.

82. Ibid.

83. Salmond, *Gastonia, 1929*, 60–61.

84. "The Only Hope for Mill Workers," *Daily Tar Heel*, April 20, 1929.

85. Luther Hodges to Harriet L. Herring, August 14, 1929, folder 14, box 1, Harriet L. Herring Papers, SHC.

86. Tindall, *The Emergence of the New South*, 345–47; Salmond, *Gastonia, 1929*, 122–37, 155.

87. Hall et al., *Like a Family*, 216.

88. Wood, *Southern Capitalism*, 87.

89. Benjamin Stolberg, "Madness in Marion," *The Nation*, October 23, 1929, 462.

90. Hall et al., *Like a Family*, 216–17.

91. Stolberg, "Madness in Marion," 463.

92. "Communism Takes a Back Seat in the Textile Warfare," *Daily Tar Heel*, October 5, 1929.

93. "A Few Discrepancies in Mr. Gossett's Textile Situation Views," *Daily Tar Heel*, December 14, 1929.

94. "Baby Radicals," *Southern Textile Bulletin*, December 26, 1929.

95. "Sinister Shadows," *Southern Textile Bulletin*, January 9, 1930.

96. "'Crack-Brained Professors' and 'Baby Radicals,'" *Daily Tar Heel*, January 12, 1930.

3. "A Complex and Baffling Age"

1. "Another Revolt in North Carolina," *Washington Post*, June 20, 1930. Graham's and the university's liberal reputation cut both ways, of course. History professor Howard Beale reported to Graham that he "ran into in the South in place after place . . . a feeling toward the University of North Carolina, particularly in mill towns, which made it difficult or impossible for University of North Carolina graduates to get teaching positions there." Beale worried that "there seems to be a feeling that the University of North Carolina implants in its graduates dangerous views on certain subjects." See Howard Beale to Frank Graham, August 2, 1934, MS 99–097, folder 10, box 10, Howard Beale Papers, State Historical Society of Wisconsin Archives (hereafter cited as Beale Papers).

2. Quoted in "Frank Graham's Primary Education," *The Nation*, April 22, 1950, 368.

3. Charles Kuralt, "Introduction," in John Ehle, *Dr. Frank: Life with Frank Porter Graham* (Chapel Hill: Franklin Street Books, 1993), xv, xviii.

4. Interview with Phil Hammer, conducted by Bruce Kalk, June 7, 1991, L-55, Southern Oral History Program, Center for the Study of the American South, UNC (hereafter cited as Southern Oral History Program).

5. Interview with C. Vann Woodward, conducted by John Egerton, January 12, 1991, A-341, Southern Oral History Program. Graham and his wife Marian hosted weekly dinners for students, an important means of maintaining personal contact with the student body.

6. Interview with William C. Friday, July 20, 2006. In possession of author.

7. Ibid.

8. Ibid.

9. Quoted in Snider, *Light on the Hill*, 203.

10. "New President Well Known for Humanizing Qualities," *Daily Tar Heel*, November 11, 1931.

11. "First in Our Hearts Today," *Daily Tar Heel*, November 11, 1931.

12. David Cohn, "Chapel Hill," *Atlantic Monthly*, March 1941, 323.

13. "Gardner Calls Graham to High Office in State," *Daily Tar Heel*, November 12, 1931.

14. Ashby, *Frank Porter Graham*, 5–13, 14–43.

15. Ibid.

16. Ibid.

17. Ibid.

18. Ibid., 58.

19. Graham's letter was then republished as "Evolution, the University and the People," in the *Alumni Review* 13 (1924–25): 205–7.

20. Ibid.

21. Ibid.

22. E. C. Branson to Frank P. Graham, March 30, 1925, folder 300, box 6, Branson Papers.

23. Numan V. Bartley, *The New South, 1945–1980* (Baton Rouge: Louisiana State University Press, 1995), 51.

24. Christensen, *Paradox of Tar Heel Politics*, 71.

25. "Compensation Law in North Carolina," *New York Times*, March 24, 1929, 54.

26. "Incidentally," *Raleigh News & Observer*, September 29, 1929.

27. Ibid.

28. Ibid. In February 1930, Frank Graham reemerged on the public stage as the author of a "few simple working principles born of our democratic experiment and experience." In his "industrial bill of rights," Graham hoped to help shape a more progressive industrial era for the South, which would indirectly point to the need for research institutions such as UNC. As the region was gripped by labor unrest, Graham asserted that "the constitutional and legal rights of person and property and free speech and assembly be guaranteed equally to all persons in this commonwealth without regard to birth-place, race, ownership or labor status, unionism or non-unionism, religion, politics, or economic views." The principles of free speech and free assembly were, to Graham, "essential Americanism" that could withstand "the fallacies, fanaticism, and violence of communism, fascism, and anarchism." Preserving this founding principle would, he maintained, allow the nation's cherished democracy to "prevail over class hatreds and dictatorships, economic unreason, and social injustice." See "Over 400 Prominent North Carolina Citizens Sign Mr. Graham's Statement," *Daily Tar Heel*, February 16, 1930.

29. Abrams, *Conservative Constraints*, 8–14.

30. Ashby, *Frank Porter Graham*, 87–91.

31. Quoted in Ashby, *Frank Porter Graham*, 84.

32. In 1932 the state organized the campus at Chapel Hill, North Carolina State University, and the North Carolina College for Women (now UNC–Greensboro) into the Consolidated University of North Carolina. Graham, as president of the consolidated university, kept his office in Chapel Hill and remained UNC–Chapel Hill's president and chief administrator as well.

33. Ashby, *Frank Porter Graham*, 87.

34. Ibid.

35. Ibid.

36. Quoted in Ashby, *Frank Porter Graham*, 92.

37. "New President Sees University as Outpost of Light and Liberty," *Daily Tar Heel*, November 12, 1931.

38. Ibid.

39. Ibid.

40. Ibid.

41. Ibid.
42. Ibid.

4. "A New Negro Is About to Come on the Scene"

1. Chapman, "Black Freedom," 244.

2. Paul Green diary, 1928–1939 volume, p. 190, NCC. In all likelihood, the student was quoting a young African American character named Tommy, from Green's 1934 play *The Honeycomb*, performed by the Carolina Playmakers in 1934, or the character Tom Sterling from Green's 1931 play *In Potter's Field*, republished as *Roll Sweet Chariot* in 1934. Green won a Pulitzer Prize in 1927 for *In Abraham's Bosom*, a play noted for its radically honest depiction of southern race relations.

3. Paul Green diary, 1928–1939 volume, p. 146, NCC.

4. *Daily Tar Heel*, December 8, 1931.

5. Patricia Sullivan describes Clark Foreman's grim mood as being representative of white southern liberals at the beginning of the decade. "Liberal and humane sympathies were isolated and repressed in the South. An unspoken code of self-censorship seemed to prevail at private or public colleges; it was clearly understood that any questioning of the racial status quo would probably bring dismissal." See Sullivan, *Days of Hope*, 37.

6. Paul Green diary, 1928–1939 volume, p. 211, NCC.

7. "Negro Lawyers Fired On," *New York Times*, October 6, 1933.

8. Augustus M. Burns, "North Carolina and the Negro Dilemma, 1930–1950" (Ph.D. diss., University of North Carolina at Chapel Hill, 1969), 1.

9. William J. Maxwell, *New Negro, Old Left: African-American Writing and Communism between the Wars* (New York: Columbia University Press, 1999), 16.

10. Sullivan, *Days of Hope*; Egerton, *Speak Now against the Day*; Woodruff, *American Congo*; de Jong, *A Different Day*; and Lau, *Democracy Rising*.

11. "Negro Election Officials Urged," *Raleigh News & Observer*, April 21, 1933.

12. "Asks Equality in Negro Education," *Raleigh News & Observer*, May 23, 1933.

13. Badger, "Fatalism, Not Gradualism," 78.

14. "Lynchings, Fears, and Folkways," *The Nation*, December 30, 1931, 719.

15. Ibid.

16. Quoted in Burns, "North Carolina and the Negro Dilemma," 16.

17. R. W. B., "Sam Barber, Colored," *Daily Tar Heel*, May 27, 1931.

18. Ibid.

19. Clipping from *Southern Textile Bulletin* editorial, probably dated between December 8 and December 11, 1931, folder "Race Relations: Langston

Hughes *Contempo* Controversy, 1931–1932," box 1, series 1: Subject Files, Graham Papers.

20. Langston Hughes to A. J. Buttitta, June 6, 1932, *Contempo* Collection, Harry Ransom Center, University of Texas at Austin. Clark would have been even more furious to learn of the friendly relations between UNC faculty and allies and the editors of *Contempo*, Milton Abernethy and Buttitta. A week after Hughes's visit, Jonathan Daniels needled Abernethy: "Are you a racket or a revolution?" See Jonathan Daniels to Milton Abernethy, November 25, 1931, *Contempo* Collection.

21. R. B. House to Carolina Coach Company, May 9, 1932, #3581, folder 7, box 1, subseries 1, R. B. House Papers, SHC (hereafter cited as House Papers).

22. H. H. Hearn to R. B. House, May 10, 1932, House Papers.

23. R. B. House to H. H. Hearn, May 11, 1932, House Papers.

24. According to Paul Crouch, Ericson joined the Communist Party during the mid-1930s as an "undercover member" operating under the alias "Spartacus." See Paul Crouch, "Brief History of the Communist Movement in North and South Carolina," p. 4, NCC. Communist Party USA records from the mid-1930s do make reference to a UNC faculty member taking out a secret membership and operating under the name of "Spartacus." "Jim Weaver" (an alias for Communist Party organizer Don West, who was wanted for arrest in Atlanta) wrote Communist Party headquarters on March 14, 1935, saying that Ericson was "very anxious to have an interview with you, Comrade [Earl] Browder, and I urge that every effort be made to have a personal interview with Ericson." In the same report Weaver indicated that Ericson was going to China the next year as an "exchange professor." On July 13, 1935, Crouch reported on a "comrade in our District, who is in a rather strategic position and has been doing very good work for us (though only recently a new member) is going to another country for us. . . . The Party name of this comrade is 'Spartacus.' He joined in April of this year." See reel 298, delo 3882, CPUSA Papers, Library of Congress, Washington, DC. On campus, Ericson was admired and respected by both students and faculty. Early in Ericson's tenure at UNC, his department chair, George Coffman, wrote: "By all reports he is one of our ablest and most popular teachers. And on the basis of my knowledge, I affirm that he is one of the best men in linguistics in the country." George Coffman to R. B. House, June 11, 1931, folder "English, 1930–1932," box 1, Graham Papers.

25. Ericson met Ford in Baltimore while teaching at Johns Hopkins in the summer of 1932. A number of progressive/leftist campus groups had gathered into a "United Peace Movement." Therefore, Ericson explained, it was "natural that when Ford came to Baltimore he should meet a number of us." They all dined "quietly and without any attendant publicity." As for dining with Ford in Durham, Ericson defended himself further: "In my own case I wish to say that I have never selfishly and indiscreetly flouted the accepted folkways of my

Southern friends in this respect. I had twice, before the Ford incident, turned down invitations to dine publicly with a Negro literary celebrity because of my fear of the repercussions. In the Ford case I was under the pressure of seeming to make light of a hospitality extended me by my Negro friends . . . and of slighting a former acquaintance in the person of Ford. Furthermore, I felt fortified by the fact that there were twenty other white people present, including a half-dozen Southerners." E. E. Ericson to R. B. House, May 20, 1940, folder "Communism Dies Committee, 1940," box 1, Graham Papers.

26. See Novotny, *This Georgia Rising*, and Cox, "The Rainey Affair."

27. "Says Carolina Professor Dined with Negro Reds," *New York Times*, October 31, 1936, clipping in folder "Race and Ethnic Relations: Negroes: Ericson Controversy, 1936," box 13, Graham Papers.

28. Frank P. Graham to Kemp P. Lewis, November 25, 1936, folder "Race and Ethnic Relations: Negroes: Ericson Controversy, 1936," box 13, Graham Papers.

29. Ibid.

30. This account is drawn from W. T. Sloan to "Honorable Mayor & Board of Alderman," August 26, 1937, folder "Chapel Hill, Town of, Police Department (Riot) 1937–38," box 30, subgroup 3: Outside Organizations (Part 1), Graham Papers.

31. The manager of the university's physical plant, P. L. Burch, prepared a report to UNC officials that told the story similarly. One difference is that Burch reported that the crowd of African Americans had stopped traffic coming and going between the two towns. P. L. Burch to L. B. Rogerson, August 25, 1937, folder "Chapel Hill, Town of, Police Department (Riot) 1937–1938," Graham Papers.

32. W. T. Sloan to "Honorable Mayor & Board of Alderman," August 26, 1937, Graham Papers.

33. Guy B. Johnson to Frank P. Graham, September 30, 1937, folder 1536 "Chapel Hill Race Riot, 1937," Guy B. Johnson Papers, SHC (hereafter cited as Johnson Papers).

34. Freeman, "Growth and Planning in a Community," 21–22.

35. The black population of Chapel Hill was 891 out of a total of 2,699 in 1930. By 1940 it had risen to 1,124 out of a total of 3,654. In Carrboro, the black population in 1930 was 256 out of a total of 1,242; in 1940 it was 437 out of 1,455. Lee Coleman, "Chapel Hill Negroes Look at Their Community," 5, Johnson Papers.

36. Freeman, "Growth and Planning in a Community," 24.

37. Ibid., 34. The King's Daughters is a Christian-based service organization that was founded in the late 1800s and grew to have chapters all over the world.

38. Coleman, "Chapel Hill Negroes," 9, 10, 36–37, Johnson Papers.

39. Ibid., 11, 21.

40. Ibid., 8.

41. Ibid., 53. Abrams has argued that New Deal farm programs such as the Agricultural Adjustment Act had an adverse effect on black farmers in North Carolina by displacing thousands of tenant farmers, many of whom would have relocated to urban areas in hopes of finding work. See Abrams, *Conservative Constraints*, 161–89.

42. Ibid., 13.

43. "Chapel Hill Negroes Lazy; Durham Men to Take Work," *Durham Morning Herald*, August 31, 1937, 16.

44. "Better Police Protection Is Essential Step toward Remedy of a Bad Situation," *Chapel Hill Weekly*, August 27, 1937, 1.

45. Coleman, "Chapel Hill Negroes," 34–35, Johnson Papers.

46. W. T. Sloan to "Honorable Mayor & Board of Aldermen," August 26, 1937, Graham Papers. Carrboro chief of police Mills did not charge James Horne and indicated he would not press the matter any further unless Tom Atwater decided he would press charges against Horne. Mills also said he hoped the incident would be forgotten as quickly as possible.

47. "Negro Quarter Needs Police Protection," *Chapel Hill Weekly*, August 27, 1937.

48. Chapman, "Black Freedom," 191.

49. Coleman, "Chapel Hill Negroes," 10, Johnson Papers.

50. Ibid., 14.

51. Ibid., 15, 20–21, 37.

52. "Letters to the Editor," *Daily Tar Heel*, December 8, 1938.

53. "Black Justice," *Daily Tar Heel*, February 2, 1939.

54. Richard Lowry Hughes, "The Southern Committee for People's Rights, 1933–1938" (MA thesis, Wake Forest University, 1995).

55. Olive Stone, "The Present Position of the Negro Farm Population: The Bottom Rung of the Farm Ladder," *Journal of Negro Education* 5, no. 1 (January 1936): 20–31. Stone soon worked her way into the heart of the civil rights movement in the 1930s. When UNC history professor Howard Beale wrote to Roger Baldwin, director of the American Civil Liberties Union, for information on lynching, the ACLU secretary referred him back to Olive Stone, who "had just then compiled a summary of the status of civil rights in the South for use in an article being prepared by Jonathan Daniels of the *Raleigh News and Observer*." See Lucille B. Milner to Howard K. Beale, April 9, 1936, folder 24, box 1, Beale Papers.

56. Ibid.

57. Ibid. Stone's interpretation of southern history could have come from Beale, who gave W. E. B. DuBois feedback on *Black Reconstruction*. See W. E. B. DuBois to Howard K. Beale, January 14, 1936, MS99–097, folder 36, box 7, Beale Papers.

58. "Citizens Plan Negro Center for Chapel Hill," *Daily Tar Heel*, October 18, 1939; "Unique Community Housing Plan to Provide 66 Modern New Homes for Negro Employees," *Daily Tar Heel*, April 27, 1940.

59. N. C. Newbold's actual title was Director of the Division of Negro Education in the State Department of Public Instruction of North Carolina.

60. W. W. Brierley to William P. Few, April 17, 1935, folder "Race and Ethnic Relations: Division of Cooperation in Education and Race Relations," box 13, Graham Papers.

61. "Division of Cooperation in Education and Race Relations: A Brief Account of Activities, May 1, 1935–May 10, 1938," p. 3, folder "Ethnic and Race Relations: Division of Cooperation in Education and Race Relations, 1938: May–June," box 13, Graham Papers.

62. Ibid., 3–4.

63. Ibid., 5.

64. Unsigned to N. C. Newbold, n.d. [has "enclosed 1-11-37" written on top], folder "Race and Ethnic Relations, Division of Cooperation in Education and Race Relations, 1937," box 13, Graham Papers.

65. Katharine Lackey to N. C. Newbold, January 13, 1937, folder "Race and Ethnic Relations, Division of Cooperation in Education and Race Relations, 1937," box 13, Graham Papers.

66. W. J. Trent Jr. to Guy B. Johnson, n.d., folder 1308, Johnson Papers. The rest of the material in the folder suggests the letter is dated in the mid-1930s.

67. "Negroes Boycott Durham Store with White Help," *Daily Tar Heel*, February 20, 1936.

68. "Smart Theatre Owners," *Carolina Times*, December 18, 1937.

69. "1,000 College Students Fight Insults of White Theater Corporation," *Carolina Times*, January 15, 1938.

70. "The Voice of Youth," *Carolina Times*, January 15, 1938.

71. "What About It Students?" *Carolina Times*, February 12, 1938.

72. Telephone interview with author, January 23, 2006.

73. Interview with Junius Scales, October 6, 1976, New York, New York, by Mark Pinsky, transcribed by Joe Jaros, pp. 22–23, interview B-52, Southern Oral History Program.

74. Paul Green diary, 1928–1939 volume, pp. 180–81, NCC.

75. Janet Seville, "Let's Drop the Labels," *Carolina Magazine*, November 1938, 6–8.

76. "Letters to The Editor," *Daily Tar Heel*, December 8, 1938.

77. "Report on Findings Made to the Division of Cooperation in Education and Race Relations, University of North Carolina and Duke University, Thursday, December 10th," folder "Race and Ethnic Relations: Division of Cooperation in Education and Race Relations, 1936: July–December," box 13, Graham Papers.

78. "Minutes, Third Annual Conference, May 9–10, 1938," p. 190, folder "Ethnic and Race Relations: Division of Cooperation in Education and Race Relations, 1938: May–June," box 13, Graham Papers.

79. Quoted in Neal Cheek, "An Historical Study of the Administrative Actions in the Racial Desegregation of the University of North Carolina, 1930–1955" (PhD diss., University of North Carolina at Chapel Hill, 1973), 37. See also Gilbert Ware, "Hocutt: Genesis of Brown," *Journal of Negro Education* 52, no. 3 (Summer 1983): 227–33.

80. Ibid.

81. C. Durham Grandy to Frank P. Graham, August 31, 1938, folder "Race and Ethnic Relations: Negroes: Higher Education in N. C. 1938," box 13, Graham Papers.

82. W. W. Pierson to Edwina Thomas, April 27, 1938, folder "Race and Ethnic Relations: Negroes: Admissions, 1937–41, 1947–48," box 13, Graham Papers.

83. Edwina Thomas to Frank P. Graham, May 17, 1938, folder "Race and Ethnic Relations: Negroes: Admissions, 1937–41, 1947–48," box 13, Graham Papers.

84. Frank P. Graham to Edwina Thomas, May 25, 1938, folder "Race and Ethnic Relations: Negroes: Admissions, 1937–41, 1947–48," box 13, Graham Papers.

85. Frank P. Graham to Edwina Thomas, August 15, 1938, folder "Race and Ethnic Relations: Negroes: Admissions, 1937–41, 1947–48," box 13, Graham Papers.

86. Hubert U. Barbour to Frank P. Graham, February 6, 1939, folder "Race and Ethnic Relations: Negroes: Admissions, 1937–41, 1947–48," box 13, Graham Papers.

87. Frank P. Graham to Hubert U. Barbour, February 13, 1939, folder "Race and Ethnic Relations: Negroes: Admissions, 1937–41, 1947–48," box 13, Graham Papers.

88. Pauli Murray, *Pauli Murray: The Autobiography of a Black Activist, Feminist, Lawyer, Priest, and Poet* (Knoxville: University of Tennessee Press, 1989), 126.

89. Pauli Murray to Frank P. Graham, January 17, 1939, folder "Race and Ethnic Relations: Negroes: Admissions, 1937–41, 1947–48," box 13, Graham Papers.

90. Frank P. Graham to Pauli Murray, February 3, 1939, folder "Race and Ethnic Relations: Negroes: Admissions, 1937–41, 1947–48," box 13, Graham Papers.

91. Ibid. It is difficult to know what Graham thought would happen regarding changes in educational opportunities for African Americans. Years later, Graham pointed out repeatedly that he had to follow the law. He explained

how "those who thought that they could disregard the Supreme Court decisions with regard to the Southern bi-racial structure, were disregarding the Supreme Court of the United States" and its decision in *Plessy*. "And I thought, just
as we now follow the Supreme Court [after *Brown*], we were then bound by the
Supreme Court and we couldn't jump over the Supreme Court." He reiterated,
"We couldn't just imagine that the court decisions were not there and do as we
pleased according to our conscience. We were bound by the law of the land.
Now, admittedly, the law of the land often wasn't equitably administered, but
it was there and it was there until the Supreme Court overruled it." Frank Porter Graham interview, pp. 13–14, #B-0004–1, Southern Oral History Program.

92. Pauli Murray to Frank P. Graham, February 6, 1939, folder "Race and
Ethnic Relations: Negroes: Admissions: 1937–41, 1947–48," box 13, Graham
Papers.

93. "Officials Faced by Negro Entrance Application," *Daily Tar Heel*, January 5, 1939. In contrast, Graham received a letter after the publication of
the Murray-Graham exchange that hinted at greater changes to come. Walter
White, executive secretary of the NAACP, wrote to congratulate Graham for his
"straightforward facing of the problem of professional and graduate training for
Negroes." Then (teasingly for the historian), White added, without elaboration:
"Its spirit is magnificent not only in what it actually says but in what, knowing
you as I do, I can read between its lines." What was White reading between its
lines? If he thought he saw a quick end to segregation, he was engaged in wishful thinking. Walter White to Frank P. Graham, February 11, 1939, folder "Race
and Ethnic Relations: Negroes: Admissions, 1937–1941, 1947–48," box 13, Graham Papers.

94. Murray, *Pauli Murray*, 126–27.

95. Ibid., 121.

96. "We Leave It to You," *Carolina Magazine*, February 1939, 1.

97. Glenn Hutchinson, "They Call It Equal Opportunity," *Carolina Magazine*, February 1939, 9–12.

98. "Letters to the Editor: Grad Students on Negro," *Daily Tar Heel*, January 12, 1939.

99. Glenn Hutchinson, "Jim Crow Challenged in Southern Universities,"
The Crisis, April 1939, 103–5.

100. Ibid.

101. Ibid.

102. Howard K. Beale to the *Tar Heel* editor, January 8, 1939, folder 20, box
18, Beale Papers.

103. Paul Green diary, 1928–1939 volume, pp. 290–91, NCC.

104. "Inter-Racial Discussion Group Adopts Resolution to Admit Negro
Graduates Immediately," *Daily Tar Heel*, February 16, 1939.

105. Ibid.

106. Harry F. Comer to Frank P. Graham, January 30, 1939, folder "Race and Ethnic Relations: Negroes: Higher Education in North Carolina, 1939: January–April," box 13, Graham Papers.

107. W. T. Couch, "Negroes and the University," *Carolina Magazine*, February 1939, 8–9.

108. "Majority of Psychologists against Negro Admittance," *Daily Tar Heel*, January 15, 1939. In September 1939, North Carolina College of Negroes tried to initiate a law program for black students with the help of faculty from the UNC School of Law, but it did not survive.

109. "The South in the Nation," March 30, 1939, folder 858, Graham Papers.

110. Iola Pryce to Frank Porter Graham, March 30, 1939, folder 858, Graham Papers.

111. Hildrus A. Poindexter to Frank Porter Graham, March 31, 1939, folder 858, Graham Papers.

112. Josiah Bailey to Frank Porter Graham, April 12, 1939, folder 859, Graham Papers.

113. Daphne Athas, *Chapel Hill in Plain Sight* (Hillsborough, NC: Eno Publishers, 2010), 38.

114. Janet Green, "A Daughter's Biography of Paul Green: Talk by Dr. Janet Green to Phi Theta Kappa, Purchase, NY, July 1981," http://www.ibiblio.org/paulgreen/daughter.html. Wright did know about the threats, however. Daphne Athas recalls a conversation she had with Wright in England years later. She reminded him of the summer of 1940, to which Wright replied, "'Oh Carrboro, Carrboro, how could I forget it?' 'Do you hate it?' I asked. 'Well, it was very embarrassing,' he said. 'And I was scared. They threatened my life. . . . But no I don't hate it. You must understand that that was just my experience there, that's all. When I think of Carrboro, that's what I think of.'" Daphne Athas, *Chapel Hill in Plain Sight*, 40.

115. J. D. Blake to W. D. Carmichael, August 9, 1940, folder "Race and Ethnic Relations: Negroes: Campus/Community Relations, 1940–41; 1947," box 13, Graham Papers.

116. R. B. House to Mary L. Cobb, February 19, 1940, folder "Race and Ethnic Relations: Negroes: Higher Education in N. C., 1940," box 13, Graham Papers.

5. "The Rankest Center of Communism"

1. *Daily Tar Heel*, May 6, 1931.

2. "Local Socialist Club Conducts Initial Meeting," *Daily Tar Heel*, September 29, 1931.

3. "New Chapter of John Reed Club Organizes Here," *Daily Tar Heel*, October 27, 1931. Guion Griffis Johnson recalled years later that she and her husband, Guy B. Johnson, attended "some meetings" of the John Reed Club. Interview with Guion Griffis Johnson, folder 5, box 1, Roper Papers.

4. "Voting in Presidential Polls," *Daily Tar Heel*, October 28, 1932.

5. "Communism at Chapel Hill," *Southern Textile Bulletin*, November 19, 1931. The quotes from the Burlington *Daily News* and *Daily Tar Heel* are included in this article.

6. E. C. Branson to "My dear Boy," November 10, 1931, folder 399, box 6, Branson Papers.

7. Paul Green, *The Enchanted Maze* (New York, Toronto, Los Angeles: Samuel French, 1939), 74.

8. As Robert Cohen has argued about schools outside the South, critics viewed academic leftist activism as propaganda only and denied that it could be the result of honest inquiry. Those on the Left could not convince them otherwise. Ellen Schrecker, meanwhile, has pointed out that at universities outside the South, leftist activity on campus was tolerated in the mid-1930s, if not especially welcome. See Robert Cohen, *When the Old Left Was Young: Student Radicals and America's First Mass Student Movement, 1929–1941* (Oxford: Oxford University Press, 1992), and Ellen Schrecker, *No Ivory Tower: McCarthyism and the Universities* (Oxford: Oxford University Press, 1988).

9. "Negro Lecturer Gives Humorous History of Life," *Daily Tar Heel*, November 21, 1931.

10. "Land of the Free," *Daily Tar Heel*, November 24, 1931.

11. "Southern Gentlemen, White Prostitutes, Mill-Owners, and Negroes," excerpted in *Southern Textile Bulletin*, clipping in folder "Race Relations: Langston Hughes *Contempo* Controversy, 1931–1932," box 1, series 1: Subject Files, Graham Papers.

12. Clipping from *Southern Textile Bulletin* editorial, probably dated between December 8 and December 11, 1931, in folder "Race Relations: Langston Hughes *Contempo* Controversy, 1931–1932," box 1, series 1: Subject Files, Graham Papers.

13. Thomas P. Graham to Frank P. Graham, December 18, 1931, folder "Race Relations: Langston Hughes *Contempo* Controversy, 1931–1932," box 1, series 1: Subject Files, Graham Papers.

14. Ibid. One aspect of the Langston Hughes incident showed Frank Graham's magnanimous side. When Graham supporter and textile merchant George Thomas of Charlotte wrote of his intention to pull his ads from the *Southern Textile Bulletin* in protest of David Clark's attack, Graham urged Thomas "not to do that." Graham explained why: "If the *Textile Bulletin* is having as hard a time financially as practically all enterprises, institutions, and business corporations are having, then every bit of advertising means right much in these stringent times." See Frank P. Graham to George Thomas, January 4, 1932, folder "Race Relations: Langston Hughes *Contempo* Controversy, 1931–1932," box 1, series 1: Subject Files, Graham Papers.

15. Clare Colquitt notes that the founding editors "worked out of a college

dorm room to put together the first issue of *Contempo* in May, 1931." See Clare Colquitt, "'Contempo' Magazine: Asylum for Aggrieved Authors," *Library Chronicle of the University of Texas at Austin* 27 (1984): 19–45.

16. R. B. House to C. W. Tillett, Jr., December 12, 1931, folder "Race Relations: Langston Hughes *Contempo* Controversy, 1931–1932," box 1, series 1: Subject Files, Graham Papers.

17. R. B. House to E. O. Lewis, August 10, 1932, folder "Race and Ethnic Relations: Negroes: Tatum Petition Controversy, 1932: July–Sept," box 13, subseries 1: Office of the Chancellor (Part 3), series 2: UNC-CH, subgroup 2: UNC Campus Files, Graham Papers.

18. "David and Goliath," *Daily Tar Heel*, December 2, 1931.

19. *Alumni Review*, January 1932, 134.

20. "Events in Mill Struggle Basis of 'Strike Song,'" *Daily Tar Heel*, December 8, 1931.

21. "Their Latest Effort," *Southern Textile Bulletin*, January 7, 1932, 18.

22. Ibid. For a slightly different version, credited to Wiggins, see Shelly Romalis, *Pistol Packin' Mama: Aunt Molly Jackson and the Politics of Folksong* (Urbana and Chicago: University of Illinois, 1999), 179.

23. "Michael Gold Declares Future of Theatre Depends on Mass Drama," *Daily Tar Heel*, April 21, 1932. For an excellent analysis of Gold's significance, see Alan M. Wald, *Exiles from a Future Time: The Forging of the Mid-Twentieth-Century Literary Left* (Chapel Hill and London: University of North Carolina Press, 2002), 39–70.

24. "Right to Think and Investigate," *Winston-Salem Journal*, September 10, 1932.

25. S. F. Teague to Frank Graham, September 1932, folder "Race and Ethnic Relations: Negroes: Tatum Petition Controversy, 1932: July–Sept," box 13, subseries 1: Office of the Chancellor (Part 3), series 2: UNC-CH, subgroup 2: UNC Campus Files, Graham Papers.

26. W. H. Ruffin to Francis Bradshaw, November 12, 1932, folder "Race and Ethnic Relations: Negroes: Tatum Petition Controversy, 1932: Oct–December," box 13, subseries 1: Office of the Chancellor (Part 3), series 2: UNC-CH, subgroup 2: UNC Campus Files, Graham Papers.

27. Ralph F. Bellamy to C. C. Weaver, September 13, 1932, folder "Race and Ethnic Relations: Negroes: Tatum Petition Controversy, 1932: July–Sept," box 13, subseries 1: Office of the Chancellor (Part 3), series 2: UNC-CH, subgroup 2: UNC Campus Files, Graham Papers.

28. Ibid.

29. Albea Godbold to Frank P. Graham, September 9, 1932, folder "Race and Ethnic Relations: Negroes: Tatum Petition Controversy, 1932: July–Sept," box 13, subseries 1: Office of the Chancellor (Part 3), series 2: UNC-CH, subgroup 2: UNC Campus Files, Graham Papers.

30. Jonathan Daniels to Frank P. Graham, September 9, 1932, folder "Race and Ethnic Relations: Negroes: Tatum Petition Controversy, 1932: July–Sept," box 13, subseries 1: Office of the Chancellor (Part 3), series 2: UNC-CH, subgroup 2: UNC Campus Files, Graham Papers.

31. "Ruinin' Our Boys," *Raleigh News & Observer*, September 18, 1932.

32. J. L. Hamme to Frank P. Graham, September 9, 1932, folder "Race and Ethnic Relations: Negroes: Tatum Petition Controversy, 1932: July–Sept," box 13, subseries 1: Office of the Chancellor (Part 3), series 2: UNC-CH, subgroup 2: UNC Campus Files, Graham Papers.

33. Morrison, *Governor O. Max Gardner*, 117.

34. Frank P. Graham to J. Edward Dowd, September 24, 1932, folder "Race and Ethnic Relations: Negroes: Tatum Petition Controversy, 1932: July–Sept," box 13, subseries 1: Office of the Chancellor (Part 3), series 2: UNC-CH, subgroup 2: UNC Campus Files, Graham Papers.

35. "Made Liberal by Comparison," *Daily Tar Heel*, October 29, 1932.

36. "Alton Lawrence Freed under Bond," *Raleigh News & Observer*, September 10, 1934.

37. "Police Refuse Bond by Graham," *Raleigh News & Observer*, September 9, 1934.

38. "Alton Lawrence Freed under Bond," *Raleigh News & Observer*, September 10, 1934.

39. "President Graham Offers Bail," *Southern Textile Bulletin*, September 13, 1934.

40. "A Man Stands Up," *Raleigh News & Observer*, September 10, 1934. When Alton Lawrence's case was dismissed for lack of evidence, the *Southern Socialist*, published in High Point and edited for a time by Lawrence himself, celebrated a bittersweet victory. As Lawrence was quoted: "This doesn't alter the fact that I was the guest of the High Point police jail for five days . . . or that the mill owners were quite successful in their main purpose, that of keeping several of us in jail by hook or by crook during the most crucial period of the strike." See "Case of Lawrence Dismissed for Lack of Evidence," *Southern Socialist*, February 8, 1935. Paul Crouch asserted that Alton Lawrence later joined the Communist Party. Paul Crouch, "Brief History of the Communist Party in North and South Carolina," NCC, p. 4.

41. John A. Salmond, "'The Burlington Dynamite Plot': The 1934 Textile Strike and Its Aftermath in Burlington, North Carolina," *North Carolina Historical Review* (October 1998): 398–434; Tullos, *Habits of Industry*, 86–133.

42. Ibid.

43. W. T. Couch and J. O. Bailey, "Dynamite in Burlington," *Carolina Magazine*, April 1935, 18–21; "Dynamite in Burlington," *The Nation*, April 24, 1935, 483–84.

44. C. Vann Woodward to Glenn Rainey, September 24, 1934, item 3, box

7, Glenn Rainey Papers, Special Collections, Robert W. Woodruff Library, Emory University (hereafter cited as Rainey Papers). See also Anthony Dunbar, *Against the Grain: Southern Radicals and Prophets, 1929–1959* (Charlottesville: University of Virginia Press, 1981), and James J. Lorence, *A Hard Journey: The Life of Don West* (Urbana and Chicago: University of Illinois Press, 2007).

45. C. Vann Woodward to Glenn Rainey, September 24, 1934, item 3, box 7, Rainey Papers.

46. "Burlington Minister to Lead Discussion on Dynamiting Case," *Daily Tar Heel*, February 17, 1935.

47. "Alleged Mill-Bombers to Plead Own Defense at Mass Meeting Here," *Daily Tar Heel*, February 20, 1935. To Glenn Rainey, Woodward described his own involvement: "The Burlington workers . . . were framed in a charge of dynamiting a mill thirty miles from here. Pretty raw sort of thing, with not even a half-hearted regard for the formalities of legal decorum. I helped organize a mass meeting to raise funds, appeal, propaganda, etc. Paul Green, Couch et al. on the committee." C. Vann Woodward to Glenn Rainey, March 3, 1935, item 4, box 7, Rainey Papers.

48. "Our Help to the Strikers," *Daily Tar Heel*, February 21, 1935.

49. "'Defending' Liberalism," *Daily Tar Heel*, February 26, 1935. Having sent the articles to Glenn Rainey, Woodward characterized them as "the prevailing undergraduate opinion. Strange situation here—or is it true elsewhere? The radical and advanced liberal opinion is mainly among the faculty (a *very few*, two socialists among them), and the graduate students in the English department. You know perfectly well that in our undergraduate days it was in the student body, if anywhere, that the radical opinion lay. So soon are we superannuated?" Woodward to Rainey, March 3, 1935, item 4, box 7, Rainey Papers.

50. "Burlington Prisoners Given Whole-Hearted Support by Group Here," *Daily Tar Heel*, February 22, 1935. The faculty and graduate students committed to the workers' appeal began to meet as the Chapel Hill Defense Committee for the Burlington Workers. UNC members of the committee included Paul Green, E. E. Ericson, William T. Couch, C. Vann Woodward, and J. H. Wisherd of the English Department. Ultimately the committee was forced to rely on communist-backed International Labor Defense lawyers to carry on the appeal at all. The Chapel Hill activists' reliance on the ILD lawyers ultimately had serious consequences when the state Supreme Court finally heard the workers' case in the fall of 1935. The ILD sent David Levinson to join the local attorneys defending the workers' case. Rather than arguing the specifics of the case—and there were plenty of specifics to debate—Levinson instead attacked the entire North Carolina justice system. To no great surprise, the court angrily dismissed Levinson's statements and upheld the convictions, even though most of the workers were paroled within a year. See Salmond, "The 'Burlington Dynamite Plot,'" 429–34.

51. "Institute Lecturers to Speak on Industrial Relations Today," *Daily Tar Heel*, April 3, 1935.

52. "Student Reaction," *Daily Tar Heel*, April 4, 1935.

53. "The Honorable Fish," *Daily Tar Heel*, April 5, 1935.

54. "American Liberty," *Daily Tar Heel*, April 25, 1935. For more on the American Liberty League, see George Wolfskill, *The Revolt of the Conservatives: A History of the American Liberty League, 1934–1940* (Westport, CT: Greenwood Publishing Group, 1974).

55. "American Liberty," *Daily Tar Heel*, April 25, 1935.

56. "Liberty League Organizes Here," *Daily Tar Heel*, May 3, 1935.

57. "Clark Hits Carolina Radicals," *Daily Tar Heel*, May 15, 1935.

58. "Clark Attacks University Group," *Raleigh News & Observer*, May 15, 1935.

59. "Clark Hits Carolina Radicals," *Daily Tar Heel*, May 15, 1935.

60. "Attacked Professors Ericson, Couch Reply to Clark Charges," *Daily Tar Heel*, May 16, 1935. That same month two graduate students, L. H. McCain and W. F. McNeir, dismissed allegations that Ericson propagandized in the classroom as "sheer ignorance, and of a vicious sort." While Ericson did discuss politics in class, "so does every teacher of the sophomore survey course in English literature. Even a lackwit must know, or be capable of understanding, that to teach Wordsworth, Coleridge, Byron . . . without referring to their social views would be impossible." Moreover, when Ericson "mentions political topics in his classes, he never does so with the intention of proselytizing his students. No one in any of his classes can say fairly that Dr. Ericson ever uses his class time inculcating Ericson politics." When the "mental cripples" who attacked Ericson grew up, the authors feared that they would likely "become members of state legislatures" and "pass anti-evolution laws." "More About Ericson," *Daily Tar Heel*, May 10, 1935.

61. "Attacked Professors Ericson, Couch Reply to Clark Charges." The next month, Josephus Daniels gave a rousing defense of UNC at an alumni luncheon. Daniels recalled that as "far back as I can remember the University of North Carolina has always been under attack from the thoughtless, the uniformed and those who would make this university . . . devoted not to the search for truth but rather to a propagation of faith in a social and economic order in which they were entrenched and in which they wished no change or truth to threaten their entrenchment. . . . No, my fellow alumni," he continued, "I am not afraid of radicalism in the American colleges. I am afraid of a more widespread, deeper danger, I am afraid of dry-rot . . . if our colleges did not put into our youth something of the explosive quality of the idea." We should remain mindful, however, that the "explosive quality of the idea" Daniels cherished did not extend to the idea of ending racial segregation, a system he had helped create in North Carolina at the turn of the century. "A Free University Is North Carolina's Fairest Hope," *Raleigh News & Observer*, June 16, 1935.

62. "Capitalism on Judgment Docket as Williams, Woodhouse Meet," *Daily Tar Heel*, May 15, 1935.

63. "Woodhouse Rallies to Aid Durfee in Debate against Left-Wingers," *Daily Tar Heel*, May 2, 1935. Woodhouse was no reactionary. The next year he invited Alton Lawrence to speak to his classes on the socialist prospects for the 1936 election. See "Woodhouse Classes Hear Former Secretary of N.C. Socialist Party," *Daily Tar Heel*, October 20, 1936.

64. "Capitalism on Judgment Docket as Williams, Woodhouse Meet," *Daily Tar Heel*, May 15, 1935.

65. "Now You're Talking," *Daily Tar Heel*, May 17, 1935.

66. "Audience Shouts, Applauds as Capitalists and Radicals Debate over Social Order," *Daily Tar Heel*, May 16, 1935. American Liberty League chapter cofounder Dupont Snowden wrote to the paper on May 19 distancing himself somewhat from Durfee. Durfee's "efforts" to popularize the chapter, he believed, had "led to a general misconception of what the American Liberty League is." Snowden referred readers to the League's national charter, which stated explicitly that it was "a nonpartisan organization." See "Speaking from the Right," *Daily Tar Heel*, May 19, 1935. The April momentum accumulated by the UNC chapter of the American Liberty League petered out by the end of May. The *Daily Tar Heel* reported that at its final meeting of the school year, Winthrop Durfee, "perpetrator of the league on this campus, was the only member present." See "The Last Round-Up," *Daily Tar Heel*, May 23, 1935.

67. "Woodhouse Rallies to Aid Durfee in Debate against Left-Wingers," *Daily Tar Heel*, May 2, 1935.

68. [Illegible] to Frank P. Graham, October 28, 1936, folder "Race and Ethnic Relations: Negroes: Ericson Controversy, 1936," box 13, Graham Papers.

69. D. Sam Cox to Frank P. Graham, October 27, 1936, folder "Race and Ethnic Relations: Negroes: Ericson Controversy, 1936," box 13, Graham Papers.

70. M. M. Bosworth to Frank P. Graham, December 1, 1936, folder "Race and Ethnic Relations: Negroes: Ericson Controversy, 1936," box 13, Graham Papers.

71. Frank P. Graham to M. M. Bosworth, December 9, 1936, folder "Race and Ethnic Relations: Negroes: Ericson Controversy, 1936," box 13, Graham Papers.

72. "Ericson to Speak," *Daily Tar Heel*, October 31, 1936.

73. Frank P. Graham to M. M. Bosworth, December 9, 1936, folder "Race and Ethnic Relations: Negroes: Ericson Controversy, 1936," box 13, Graham Papers.

74. Clipping from Chattanooga newspaper, folder "Race and Ethnic Relations: Negroes: Ericson Controversy, 1937–1938," box 13, Graham Papers.

75. Kate Hinds Steele to Frank P. Graham, February 11, 1937, folder "Race and Ethnic Relations: Negroes: Ericson Controversy, 1937–1938," box 13,

Graham Papers. Ericson claimed he did not relish all the attention and felt badly for the trouble he had caused Graham, Coffman, and the university. As he wrote to Graham in July 1937: "I have wished a thousand times that my views were more orthodox, so that you would not have to carry me as a cross. But believe me, as I know myself, I am not an exhibitionist . . . but only a man trying to preserve his integrity and intellectual honesty. I feel quite sure I have your sympathy in this." Indeed he did. Graham replied, "This little note is simply to ask you not to worry about any load that I am carrying. I want you and the other members of our staff to preserve their integrity and intellectual honesty. Such matters should always come first." See Frank P. Graham to E. E. Ericson, July 24, 1937, folder "Race and Ethnic Relations: Negroes: Ericson Controversy, 1937–1938," box 13, Graham Papers.

76. H. Willoughby to George R. Coffman, June 3, 1937, folder "Race and Ethnic Relations: Negroes: Ericson Controversy, 1937–1938," box 13, Graham Papers.

77. "Communist Editor Institute Speaker," *Daily Tar Heel*, February 19, 1937; "Communist," *Daily Tar Heel*, February 20, 1937. There is nothing in the subsequent editions of the *Daily Tar Heel* that suggests Hathaway's visit caused any controversy.

78. "World Situation Stated in Talk by Troyanovsky," *Daily Tar Heel*, February 9, 1938.

79. "Christian Patriot" to "Board of Regents," n.d. [1938 written on top], box 1, "Communism General 1938–41," Graham Papers.

80. "Program of Peace Endorsed, Fascism Damned, Isolationism Condemned by Earl Browder," *Daily Tar Heel*, March 4, 1938.

81. "Browder and a New Communism," *Daily Tar Heel*, March 5, 1938.

82. *Chapel Hill Weekly*, November 19, 1937. See also Charles J. Holden, "A Various Course and a Wide Meaning," *North Carolina Historical Review* (July 1999): 300.

83. Egerton, *Speak Now against the Day*, 188. See also Thomas A. Krueger, *And Promises to Keep: The Southern Conference for Human Welfare, 1938–1948* (Nashville: Vanderbilt University Press, 1967), 20–39.

84. Egerton, *Speak Now against the Day*, 186–91.

85. Dunbar, *Against the Grain*, 191.

86. Ibid., 190.

87. Singal, *The War Within*, 292–93.

88. Quoted in Dunbar, *Against the Grain*, 194.

89. W. T. Couch to Carl Durham, April 19, 1940, folder "Communism Dies Committee, 1940," box 1, Graham Papers.

90. Ibid. See also Singal, *The War Within*, 265–301.

91. W. T. Couch to Carl Durham, April 19, 1940, Graham Papers.

92. Ibid.

93. "Communism and Socialism at Chapel Hill," copy of address delivered by David Clark to Charlotte Lions Club, August 12, 1940, folder "Communism General, 1938–41," box 1, Graham Papers.

94. Ibid.

95. Mrs. A. H. Crowell to Josephus Daniels, March 27, 1941, folder "Communism General, 1938–41," box 1, Graham Papers. In all likelihood, the daughter was Ruth Crowell, who graduated from UNC in 1940 and had some connection with liberal activists such as those in the American Student Union.

96. Ibid.

97. Ibid.

98. Josephus Daniels to Mrs. A. H. Crowell, April 4, 1941, folder "Communism General, 1938–41," box 1, Graham Papers.

99. Ibid.

100. R. B. House to Frank P. Graham, August 6, 1940, folder "Communism General, 1938–41," box 1, Graham Papers.

101. Thomas E. Street to Frank P. Graham, May 28, 1940, folder "Communism Dies Committee, 1940," box 1, Graham Papers.

102. Ibid.

103. Ibid.

104. Ibid.

105. Ibid.

106. T. A. Wilkins to Frank Graham, June 7, 1940, folder "Communism Dies Committee, 1940," box 1, Graham Papers.

Epilogue

1. "Dear Parents and Students," copy of letter in MS-99-097, folder 10, box 10, Beale Papers.

2. See, for instance, Sullivan, *Days of Hope*; Neil R. McMillen, ed., *Remaking Dixie: The Impact of World War II on the American South* (Jackson: University of Mississippi Press, 1997); and, more recently, Gilmore, *Defying Dixie*.

3. "Delany Delivers Attack on 'Enemies of Negroes,'" *Raleigh News & Observer*, April 22, 1944.

4. Chapman, "Black Freedom," 232, 256, 277, 279.

5. Quoted in Timothy Tyson, *Radio Free Dixie* (Chapel Hill: University of North Carolina Press, 1999), 32.

6. "The Opportunities of Peace for More Freedom and Democracy in the South and in the Nation," folder 860, Graham Papers.

7. "Opening Statement of Dr. Frank Graham on American Forum of the Air—Station WOR—New York—January 12, 1944—9:30 p.m.," folder 1745, Graham Papers.

8. Ibid.

9. Ibid.

10. "My People," February 13, 1944, folder 1745, Graham Papers.

11. "Founders' Day Address," April 2, 1944, folder 1745, Graham Papers.

12. Telegram to Mark Etheridge, folder 1681, Graham Papers.

13. "Founders' Day Address," April 2, 1944, folder 1745, Graham Papers.

14. Frank Graham to F. D. Patterson, April 28, 1944, folder 1745, Graham Papers.

15. "Progress Report," *Time*, April 10, 1944. The article refers to Graham as UNC's "famed liberal President."

16. Alton Lawrence to Frank Graham, April 18, 1944, folder 1745, Graham Papers.

17. Romeo Garrett to Frank Graham, April 14, 1944, folder 1745, Graham Papers. On Romeo B. Garrett, see http://www.webjam.com/bsa/romeo_b_garrett.

18. Russell B. Babcock to Frank Graham, April 17, 1944, folder 1745, Graham Papers.

19. L. C. Albright to Frank Porter Graham, April 4, 1944, folder 1745, Graham Papers.

20. William J. Woody to Frank Porter Graham, April 17, 1944, folder 1745, Graham Papers.

21. F. T. to Frank Graham, November 3, 1944, folder 1681, Graham Papers.

22. R. R. Harper to Frank Graham, April 28, 1944, folder 1745, Graham Papers.

23. J. N. Buie to Frank Graham, April 28, 1944, folder 1745, Graham Papers.

24. Ashby, *Frank Porter Graham*, 224–25.

25. See Frank Porter Graham to Frank McAllister, October 16, 1941, and Graham to Robert S. Lynd, December 6, 1941, folder 860, Graham Papers.

26. "Memorandum," November 19, 1943, folder 1758, Graham Papers.

27. Graham telegram reprinted in *Daily Tar Heel*, November 7, 1944.

28. Erich W. Zimmermann to Frank P. Graham, November 4, 1944, folder 1758, Graham Papers.

29. Ralph Himstead to Frank P. Graham, November 25, 1944, folder 1758, Graham Papers.

30. Homer P. Rainey to Frank P. Graham, January 18, 1945, folder 1850, Graham Papers.

31. "Founder's Day Address," April 2, 1944, folder 1745, Graham Papers.

32. "The Opportunities of Peace for More Freedom and Democracy in the South and in the Nation," November 25, 1939, folder 860, Graham Papers.

33. Frank P. Graham, "Democracy and the Second World War," in *Defense for America*, ed. and introd. William Allen White (New York: Macmillan Company, 1940), 105–14.

34. "Complete Facts on Browder Case Cleared Up by Beale," *Daily Tar Heel*, April 24, 1942.

35. John W. Culp to Frank P. Graham, February 22, 1947, folder 1970, Graham Papers.

36. Frank P. Graham to John W. Culp, March 18, 1947, folder 1970, Graham Papers.

37. John W. Culp to Frank P. Graham, March 26, 1947, folder 1970, Graham Papers.

38. Austin Hancock to Frank P. Graham, April 17, 1947, folder 1970, Graham Papers.

39. Herman Davis to Frank P. Graham, February 21, 1947, folder 1970, Graham Papers.

40. Frank P. Graham to Herman Davis, February 27, 1947, folder 1970, Graham Papers.

41. *Alumni Review*, December 1948, quoted in Peter A. Carmichael, "Free versus Kept Education," *Journal of Higher Education* 20, no. 8 (November 1949): 428. See also Ashby, *Frank Porter Graham*, 238–39.

42. See Julian M. Pleasants and Augustus M. Burns III, *Frank Porter Graham and the 1950 Senate Race in North Carolina* (Chapel Hill: University of North Carolina Press, 1990).

43. See "Wallace Backers Quashed in House," *New York Times*, June 17, 1947.

44. John D. Langston to John H. Folger, June 6, 1947, folder 1970, Graham Papers.

Index

Page numbers in *italics* refer to illustrations or their captions.

as president of Consolidated
  University of North Carolina,
  185n32
race relations at UNC and, 95, 103,
  192n93
radio addresses during World War
  II, 152
secretary of UNC's YMCA, 29
segregation at UNC and, 108–9,
  110–12, 117, 191–92n91
service on War Labor Board, 149
Southern Conference for Human
  Welfare and, 140–41
state funding for UNC and, 83
Tatum controversy and, 126–28
George Thomas and, 194n14
Tuskegee Institute speech, 153–54
on UNC's mission, 82
Graham, Katherine, 83
Graham, Thomas P., 124
Grandy, C. Durham, 109
Graves, Louis, 78, 99
Gray, James A., 59, 60
Green, Janet, 117
Green, Paul, 186n2
  Burlington Dynamite Case and,
    131, 132, 197n50
  The Enchanted Mesa, 122
  Langston Hughes's 1931 visit to
    UNC and, 92, 122
  race relations and, 87, 88, 106, 115
  Richard Wright and, 117
Greensboro Daily News, 10, 57, 58, 59
grocery store boycotts, 105

Haberman, Clyde, 1
Hadley, Edwin Marshall, 71
Hall, Jacquelyn, 13
Ham, Mordecai, 8
Hamilton, J. G. de Roulhac, 45–47,
  94, 132
Hamlett, W. A., 39

Hamme, J. L., 128
Hammer, Phil, 76–77
Hancock, Austin, 161
Harper, R. R., 155
Harris, Louis, *78*
Haskell, Thomas L., 1
Hathaway, C. A., 138, 200n77
Heard, Alexander, 138
Hearn, H. H., 92–93
Herring, Harriet, 49, 56, 61, 68
Hibbard, Addison, 41
High Point (NC), 129–30, 196n40
Himstead, Ralph, 157
Hobhouse, Leonard Trelawney, 80
Hocutt, Thomas, 107–8
Hodges, Luther, 68
Hoey, Clyde, 109, 113
Hoffman, Alfred, 68
Hoggard, J. P., 132
Holland, Thomas, 61, 183n73
Holmes, Oliver Wendell, Jr., 4,
    168n13, 168n14
Holt Plaid Mill, 130–31
Horne, James, 95–96, 189n46
House, Robert B., 92–93, 117–18,
    125, 144, 161
House Un-American Activities
    Committee (HUAC), 133,
    140–41
Hughes, Langston, 42–43, 90, 92,
    122–25, *123*, 126–27
Hutchins, Francis, 151
Hutchinson, Glenn, 112–14

Industrial Workers of the World
    (IWW), 34, 51
Institute for Research in Social
    Science (IRSS), 15, 49, 54, 55–56,
    58, 59–60, 181n45
interracial sex, 40, 41, 43

janitors, 34, 151

historical examinations of white
southern liberalism, 20
race relations in the 1930s and,
89–90
Link, William A., 13
Lithwick, Dahlia, 4
Little, John, 30–31
Locke, Alain, 42, 43
Loray Mill, 66–67
Lovejoy, Arthur, 64
Lovejoy, Owen, 52
Lyde, Edna, 150–51
lynching, 88, 90, 92, 189n55

Madry, Robert, 2, 7, 16
Mangum, Charles, 31, 32–33, 35–36
Mara, Gerald M., 21
McAuliffe v. Mayor of New Bedford, 4
McKie, G. M., 31
McKnight, Roy W., 94
McLaurin v. Oklahoma State Regents,
118
McLean, A. W., 55
medical instruction clinics, 103
Mencken, H. L., 16
Metzger, Walter, 7
Miller, Dorie, 152
Mills, R. H., 96, 189n46
Mims, Edwin, 16, 19
Missouri ex rel. Gaines v. Canada, 21–
22, 108, 110, 115, 118
Mitchell, Broadus, 68
Morrison, Cameron, 15, 51, 70, 72,
80
Morse, Wayne, 76
Moss, Rev. W. D., 30
movie theater boycotts, 105–6
"Mulatto" (Hughes), 43
Murphy, Walter, 10, 12
Murray, Pauli, 110–12
Muste, A. J., 68

National Association for the
Advancement of Colored People
(NAACP), 28, 44, 89, 178n75
National Textile Workers Union
(NTWU), 66–67, 68–69
Negro Night School, 30
Newbold, N. C., 103, 104, 190n59
Newcomb, Robinson, 59–60, 181–
82n55, 183n73
New Deal programs, 97–98, 103, 136,
189n41
Nichols, L. E., 50–51
Nixon, Richard, 1
North Carolina A&T, 105, 106
North Carolina Club, 55, 179–80n19,
180n28
North Carolina College for Negroes,
115, 193n108
North Carolina Cotton
Manufacturers Association,
55–56

Odum, Howard, *53*
academic study of labor relations
and, 49, 50, 53–54, 56, 57–58,
59–60, 61, 72
academic study of race relations
and, 29
Carolina Magazine controversy
and, 40
Harry Chase on, 65
David Clark and, 53–54
collection of African American folk
songs, 34, 39, 177n55
contributions to UNC, 15
invitation to speak to NAACP,
178n75
Guy and Guion Johnson on labor
research of, 179n1
James Weldon Johnson's visit to
UNC and, 45
Journal of Social Forces, 36